JERRY BAKER'S

PERFECT PERENNIALS!

www.jerrybaker.com

Other Jerry Baker Books:

JERRY BAKER'S
PERFECT PERENNIALS!

HUNDREDS OF FANTASTIC FLOWER SECRETS FOR YOUR GARDEN

by Jerry Baker,
America's Master Gardener®

Published by American Master Products, Inc.

Published by American Master Products, Inc.
Executive Editor: Kim Adam Gasior
Project Editor: Cheryl Winters Tetreau
Interior Design and Layout: Sandy Freeman
Cover Design: Kitty Pierce Mace
Indexer: Nan Badgett

Publisher's Cataloging-in-Publication

Baker, Jerry
    Jerry Baker's perfect perennials! : hundreds of
fantastic flower secrets for your garden / author,
Jerry Baker ; editor, Kim Adam Gasior. — 1st ed.
        p. cm.
        Includes index.
        ISBN 978-0-922433-93-3

    1. Perennials. I. Baker, Jerry. II. Gasior, Kim Adam
III. Title. IV. Title: Perfect perennials!

SB434.O53 2001   635.9'32

Printed in the United States of America
2 4 6 8 10 9 7 5 3 1   softcover

CONTENTS

INTRODUCTION

C'mon, folks—what would you give for a garden that gets better year after year, with less and less work on your end? No, I'm not pullin' your leg—it's absolutely possible, with my perfect perennials! When you fill your yard with these fun and flower-full plants, you'll not only create a landscape that's the envy of your neighbors; with my help and some great advice from my gardening mentor, my Grandma Putt, you'll also do it for less cash and in less time than you ever imagined.

In this book, I've gathered together hundreds of my best time-tested tips, tricks, and tonics for all aspects of planning, planting, and enjoying the best perennial garden possible! Here's a sneak preview of what you'll find:

Part 1: "Down and Dirty: Getting Started" covers everything you need to know in order to choose the right site, pick the right plants, and get them off to a rip-roaring start. Not artistic? Don't worry! I've included lots of tips for creating a great planting plan, with no special drawing skills required. Hate planning *anything* on paper? I've got you covered, too—learn how to set out a great-looking garden with whatever perennials you already have on hand!

Part 2: "Let's Get Growing!" is the place to turn to for the nitty-gritty on keeping your perennials (and bulbs, too) hearty, healthy, and looking their very best. Once you've seen how terrific your first perennial planting turns out, you'll want to fill your yard with these fabulous flowers. But you don't need to cash in your retirement account to afford more perennials—just follow my simple tips for increasing your collection with the plants that are already growing in your yard.

Part 3: "Perennial Possibilities" explores the pretty and practical ways perennials can light up your landscape—from sprucing up shady spots to attracting beautiful birds and butterflies. You'll also get the lowdown on all the traditional garden favorites, as well as some new and exciting selections for you more adventurous gardeners to try.

Part 4: "Light Up Your Life with Bulbs!" is your source for the basics on growing and enjoying bulbs, corms, rhizomes, tubers, and more. Check out the bulbs for every reason and season, and every spot in your yard. I've included dozens of tips for top-notch tulips, delightful daffodils, and other garden classics, as well as some lesser-known bulbs that add an exciting touch to all kinds of perennial beds and borders.

Throughout this book, look for the special repeating features like "Jerry's Gems" (some of my very best tips), "Making Cents" (money-saving hints), "Mixers & Elixirs" (recipes for homemade pest controls and fertilizers), and "Grandma Putt's Wisdom" (time-tested tips that'll help you avoid time- and money-wasting mistakes). You'll also find illustrated perennials arranged alphabetically (and with handy growing tips) throughout the book, starting on this page.

So there's no more excuses! It's time to bring some old-fashioned charm and beauty to your 21st-century backyard. Read on, my friends, and welcome to the wonderful world of perfect perennials!

Achimenes
Achimenes hybrid

A beautiful bulb perfectly suited for pots and hanging baskets

PART 1

DOWN AND DIRTY:

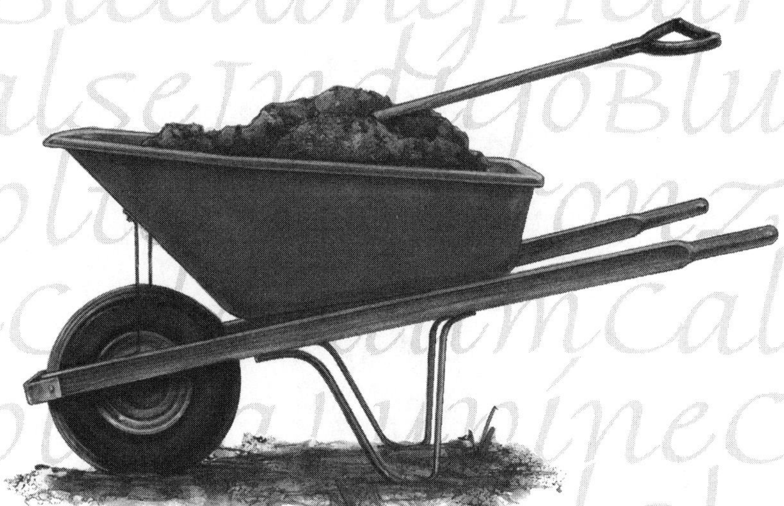

GETTING STARTED

CHAPTER 1

THE BEST-LAID PLANS

Don't pay a pro hundreds of dollars to plan a garden for you! You can get top-notch results on your own by following the same steps as designers do. To get the best match between the garden and the gardener, first, sit back and imagine your dream garden....

What's Your Style?

You know you want a perennial garden—but where on earth do you start? Before you grab your checkbook and head off to the local garden center, gather some ideas and make some plans. Even if you're normally not much for putting your thoughts on paper, jotting down a few priorities now will go a long way toward getting you the most bang for your gardening bucks later!

➤ PUT IT ON PAPER

So, what do you want from your perennial garden, anyway? It may sound like a silly question, but if you can put it down in words, you've already done 90 percent of your planning! Here are a few questions to get you thinking:

ৰ Do you want a garden that looks great from spring to frost? Or do you just want to perk up a spot for a particular season—say, a border around a deck where you do a lot of summer entertaining?

ৰ Are there particular colors you would like, maybe to match the color of your house? Or do you have a favorite flower color or color combination?

ৰ Do you already have a site in mind that you'd like to beautify? Would you like to liven up your front yard, make a walkway more inviting, or add color along your driveway?

ৰ Are you looking for easy-care perennials you can plant and forget, or do you like to putter around in your garden and get things picture-perfect?

ৰ Do you enjoy bringing flowers indoors for bouquets or for drying, pressing, or other crafts?

ৰ Are you hoping to attract birds, butterflies, and/or hummingbirds to your yard?

Don't let me limit you and your imagination with these questions—after all, there are as many reasons to have a

Adam's needle
Yucca filamentosa

Evergreen foliage and white flowers; perfect for hot, sunny sites

flower garden as there are people who plant one! For more ideas of what perennials and bulbs can add to your yard, check out "Perennial Possibilities," starting on page 169, and "Light Up Your Life with Bulbs!" starting on page 269.

CHECK, PLEASE!

Formal gardens have:
- ☑ Straight edges
- ☑ Sharp corners
- ☑ Carefully chosen colors
- ☑ Repetition
- ☑ Symmetry
- ☑ Higher maintenance needs

Informal gardens have:
- ☑ Curved beds
- ☑ Mixed heights and colors
- ☑ One of this and one of that
- ☑ Minimal maintenance needs

DON'T DO IT BY THE BOOK

Looking for more sources of inspiration? I'll let you in on a little secret. You know those glossy gardening books and magazines that are chock-full of photos of gorgeous yards? Well, those are probably the worst place to get ideas for your own garden! You only see the plantings at their absolute best—perfectly manicured, in full bloom, and under ideal conditions. You don't see the garden a day or a week later, after a nighttime storm has flattened the delphiniums, or a horde of slugs has made Swiss cheese out of the hostas.

So where's the *best* place to get great garden ideas? Watch the community calendar in your local paper for announcements of tours of home gardens in your area. You'll get to see what regular folks can create in a setting much like yours, with similar time and budgets, instead of what a high-paid designer, a team of full-time gardeners, and a top-quality photographer can do. The second-best place for idea-gathering? Many garden centers are now installing display gardens to show off their wares. While these gardens may be much too grand to copy on a home scale, at least you'll get to see what the plants look like in the ground instead of sitting in a tiny pot.

THE FORMALITY FACTOR

Your own personality has a big impact on your garden. Are you the kind of person who goes shopping with a list—and buys only what you went for? Do you spend a lot of time color-coordinating your home furnishings? If you answered yes to either of these questions, then you'll probably get the most pleasure from a more formal perennial garden, with geometric beds and borders, carefully planned color scheme, and symmetrical plantings.

Or are you the more easygoing type of person—one who buys things on impulse, gathers a collection of favorite furniture based on comfort rather than looks, and enjoys a riot of colors? If so, then you'll probably be more comfortable with a casual style of garden, with odd-shaped or curving beds, and a mix of all shapes and sizes of perennials.

African lily
Agapanthus africanus

True-blue blooms that look great in pots and in the garden

Select a Site

Do you already know where you want your garden? If so, then it's time to take stock of the conditions that your site has to offer: the sunlight, soil, space, and so on. Or maybe you've come home from the garden center with a carload of impulse buys and now need to find a spot to suit them? Well, then, I'll tell you how to do that, too!

Unless you're growing perennials mainly to bring their flowers indoors, it makes sense to put your new garden where you can easily see and admire it—in the front yard, by a window, or near your porch or patio.

 ## SURFACE VALUE

You can put a perennial garden pretty much anywhere, but some spots take a lot more work than others. If the site you're eyeing has already had flowers in it, or if it's currently part of your lawn, then congratulations! It's passed the first test. Or,

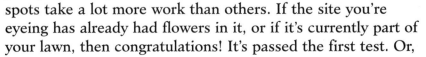

Amaryllis
Hippeastrum
hybrid

Grow outdoors in
the South; pot up
for winter bloom
in the North

are weeds and woody brush there now? If so, it's going to take some time to get that stuff cleared out and the site ready to plant. Rocky sites also take some "sweat" equity to reclaim. Challenging sites can be worth the effort if you're not in a hurry, but if you want results right away, start with a nearly-ready-for-flowers spot.

LET THERE BE LIGHT

The most important thing you can know about your chosen garden site is the amount of sunlight it gets during the day. Fortunately, it's a snap to figure out. All you need to do is check the site every hour or so over the course of a sunny day—ideally in early summer, after all the trees have leafed out—and make a note as to whether it's in sun or shade. At sunset, simply total up the number of hours the site was in the sun.

A **full-sun** site gets at least six hours of sunlight a day, ideally, with at least four of those hours in the afternoon. A site in **partial shade** means it gets between three and six hours of sun a day. A **shady** site gets three hours of sun or less.

DIG IN!

Sure, it's easy to see what's on the surface of a site, but how about what's underneath it? Before you decide you want to plant in a particular spot, grab a shovel and dig a test hole about 1 foot deep, if you can. In the process, you'll find out if your soil has lots of rocks, if it's hard and compacted, or if it's filled with tree roots—all factors that may encourage you to look elsewhere!

NO DRAIN, NO GAIN!

Most perennials and bulbs hate soggy soil, so it's critical to check your site's drainage *before* you plant. Simply dig a hole about 10 inches deep and 4 to 6 inches wide, fill it with water, and let it drain overnight. The next day, fill the hole with water again, then see how long the water sits in the hole. If it's gone within 10 hours, the drainage is good enough to grow a wide variety of perennials.

But if the hole still has water sitting in it after 10 hours, you'll need to either limit yourself to growing perennials that can tolerate "wet feet," or else improve the drainage of the site. The simplest way to do this is to raise the soil level by spreading several inches of topsoil over the site. To keep the soil from washing away, support the sides of the bed with low stone walls, bricks, or landscape timbers.

 LOAM ON THE RANGE

Get a group of gardeners together, and they'll soon be swapping dirty stories—"My soil has so much clay, I can make my own flowerpots!" or "I've got so much sand, the neighborhood kids are having a sand castle contest in my backyard!" Clay (or "heavy") soil holds lots of nutrients, but it also holds a lot of water—often, too much. Sandy (or "light") soil, on the other hand, drains quickly, but the nutrients leach away at the same time. The best soil for perennials and bulbs contains a balance of sand, clay, and silt (medium-sized particles)—what gardeners call loam. It holds a good supply of nutrients and doesn't dry out too fast, but it doesn't stay too soggy, either.

> **Try This!**
>
> When you want to find out what kind of soil you have, use this test: Simply roll a handful of moist soil into a ball, just like a snowball. Squeeze it hard, then open your hand. If the ball breaks apart into a pile of crumbs, count your blessings: You've got loam! If the ball packs more solidly, like a baseball, your soil is mostly clay. And if you can't even form a ball with your soil, it contains a lot of sand.

TAKE A SOIL TEST

Smart gardeners know that good soil is the key to a great-looking garden. So when you're considering a spot for perennials and bulbs, it makes sense to take the time to check the site's fertility level with a soil test. Sure, you can buy products to test your soil's nutrient content right at home, but I don't really recommend them; the results can be undependable, no matter how careful you are. It's worth spending a few bucks to get a soil test kit from your county's Cooperative Extension Service office.

Follow the instructions to collect a good sample of

soil—it takes just a few minutes!—mark on the form that you'll be growing a flower garden, and drop the sample in the mail. Look for the results in a few weeks. Besides telling you what's in your soil now, they'll give you suggestions of what to add if anything's out of balance. What a deal!

Certain trees, such as black walnut, produce a chemical in their roots that is toxic to many plants. But if you can't follow the standard advice of planting at least 60 feet away from these trees, don't despair! A number of perennials, including Siberian irises (*Iris sibirica*), hostas, astilbes, and many ferns, can tolerate or even thrive in these conditions.

GIMME SHELTER!

If your site is sheltered a bit by trees, shrubs, fencing, or some other windbreak, that's good news—you'll be able to grow the widest range of perennials and bulbs. Open sites exposed to strong wind can be tough on plants, causing tall stems to topple over, and drying out the soil in a snap. It's still possible to grow beautiful perennials on exposed sites; just look for low-growing kinds or compact selections of normally tall perennials, or be prepared to spend time putting up stakes. Mulching will also help keep your watering chores to a minimum.

DON'T pHRET OVER pH

Another term you'll hear gardeners toss around is "pH"—in other words, how acidic or alkaline the soil is. The pH scale runs from 0 to 14, with the midpoint of 7.0 being neutral (neither acid nor alkaline). Traditional wisdom says that garden plants grow best when the soil's pH is in the 6.5 to 7.0 range, but I've found that perennials and bulbs are pretty forgiving. Most can adapt to a pH anywhere from 6.0 up to 8.0, which is a good thing, because believe me, it's a real hassle to drastically change your soil's pH!

If you really want to know your pH rating, you can buy a cheap do-it-yourself kit at your local garden center. (Unlike the nutrient test kits, pH test kits are generally pretty reliable.) Or have the soil tested by your local Cooperative Extension Service for a small fee. But if other plants are already growing fine in your yard, chances are the pH is just fine for perennials, too.

 ### TREES A CROWD

Some trees, such as silver and Norway maples, are notorious for their shallow root systems. If you clear out their near-the-surface roots to plant perennials under them, they'll quickly make more feeder roots that'll out-compete your perennials for water and nutrients. So, if possible, avoid planting in these sites; otherwise, be prepared to experiment with the toughest shade plants, such as hostas and Lenten roses (*Helleborus*).

Pick Your Plants

Now for the fun part—deciding which perennials and bulbs would be perfect for your new garden! Here are some pointers I've gathered over the years to help you get a great start.

MADE FOR THE SHADE

I often hear folks complain that they have too much shade for flowers, but that doesn't have to be the case. True, shady sites can be a real challenge, but they can also be beautiful—and nothing beats a stroll through a shady garden on a hot summer afternoon! If you're picking plants for a shady site, look for light-colored blooms—whites, soft yellows, and

Arrow-leaved violet
Viola sagittata

Wildflower with small purplish flowers; for spring bloom in light shade pastel pinks—because deep blues and reds just don't show up in the shade. Perennials with variegated foliage (leaves striped or speckled with yellow or white) also help brighten up the gloom!

FUN IN THE SUN

Sunny sites offer you the most possibilities for fabulous flowers. Here, you can use the richest flower colors. Glowing reds, sunny yellows, awesome oranges, and perky purples will really pop! Full-sun sites aren't the best spot for pastels because soft-colored blooms tend to look faded and tired in strong sun. But white flowers can usually hold their own in a sun-drenched spot.

FLORAL AND HARDY

The greatest thing about growing perennials is that they come back every year—or at least they're supposed to! You can increase the odds that your perennials will make a return appearance by choosing plants that are adapted to your climate. The easiest way to know this is to look at each plant's hardiness rating. Based on a map put out by the USDA, the hardiness rating tells you the areas where a given plant is likely to survive the winter. It's not a foolproof system, but it does help you make an educated guess when buying perennials and bulbs for your garden. Where can you find a plant's hardiness rating? You'll see it listed in many books and catalogs and sometimes on the label of container-

Astilbe
Astilbe hybrid

Plumes of blooms that light up shady areas all summer

Every year, my Grandma Putt had the prettiest flowers in town, and the neighbors were always after her secret. "It's simple," she said, "just give the plants what they want!" If you set shade-lovers out in the sun, they'll get sunburned and look awful. Plant sun-lovers in the shade, and they'll get spindly and not flower. Be realistic about the conditions your yard has to offer, and choose perennials and bulbs that are naturally adapted to them. You'll save yourself a lot of work in the long run!

grown plants. Don't know what hardiness zone you garden in? Check out the map on page 339.

➤ YOU'VE GOT MAIL!

Once you've narrowed down the field based on the growing conditions you can offer, you'll still have a plethora of plants to choose from. Now's the time to get out your wish list and see if you can find the perfect perennials and bulbs for your plans. But how do you know what's available? My favorite resource for garden planning is a stack of mail-order nursery catalogs. They're full of beautiful pictures, and many have helpful lists of perennials and bulbs for particular uses. And best of all, they're usually free!

JERRY'S GEMS

I like to buy perennials and bulbs that are hardy to one zone number colder than where I garden, just in case. For instance, I did a lot of gardening in Zone 5, so I tried to buy plants rated for Zone 4 whenever I could. I don't know if my theory really works, but I felt better knowing that my plants had a better chance of survival in case we got a colder-than-usual winter.

➤ PICK THE RIGHT HEIGHT

Sometimes you'll have a choice between a full-sized and a compact version of the same plant. New England asters (*Aster novae-angliae*), for example, can range from 2-foot 'Purple Dome' to 5-foot 'September Ruby'. If you want tall plants to block an unsightly view, or if you plan to cut the flowers for indoor arrangements, long stems can be a plus—just keep in mind that those plants will likely need staking for support! Compact cultivars can be a good choice if you have limited space, or if you don't want to bother staking.

➤ THE TALL AND SHORT OF IT

Just how tall should your plants be? It mainly depends on your site, so go out and take a look. Will the new flowerbed be along a path or walkway? If so, then it doesn't need tall

Autumn crocus
*Colchicum
autumnale*

Showy rosy pink
flowers look like
spring crocus but
appear in fall

plants: 1 to 2 feet in height will be fine. Or do you want to
hide the view of your neighbor's trash cans? Then your
tallest plants should probably be 4 to 6 feet high. Most gardens look best with plants of varying heights, so choose
some plants that are lower than the maximum, too.

FABULOUS FOLIAGE

When you're choosing new plants for your flower garden,
don't ignore those that have lovely leaves as well! You have
to look at the leaves all season long, whether the flowers are
there or gone, so it just makes sense to choose plants that
have good-looking foliage, too. If you like tulips, for
instance, check out 'Red Riding Hood', with purple-speckled
leaves that are pretty for weeks before the red flowers
appear. Among perennials, hostas are the best for fantastic
foliage, coming in an amazing array of shapes, sizes, textures, and colors. But there are many others, too, including
purple-leaved heucheras (*Heuchera*), silver-leaved lamb's
ears (*Stachys byzantina*), and
golden oregano (*Origanum vulgare* 'Aureum').

WANTED:
THE PERFECT PERENNIAL

Caring gardener seeks good-looking, adaptable perennial for long-term relationship.
I'm willing to dig in and bring the food and
beverage, but my dream perennial needs to
pull its weight, too—flowering for at least
four weeks (ideally, six or more). Greatlooking foliage is a plus! High-maintenance
candidates need not apply.

SPREAD 'EM!

Want to double—or even triple—
your flower display in the same
amount of space? Look for
perennials and bulbs with cultivars that bloom at different
times. Peonies, for instance,
come in "early," "midseason,"
and "late" cultivars; when the
early ones are finishing, the midseason ones are just getting
started, and so on. Planting at least one of each type can
extend the total bloom time from just two weeks up to eight
weeks—or even longer! Irises, astilbes, asters, and daylilies
are just a few plants that offer this season-extending option.

Scents and Sensibility

A colorful garden is great, but a colorful *and* fragrant garden is divine! It's fun to include at least a few perennials and bulbs with scented blooms to perfume your yard and add a special touch to your flower arrangements. Some of the most powerfully scented bulbs and perennials include pinks (*Dianthus*), August lily (*Hosta plantaginea*), lily-of-the-valley (*Convallaria majalis*), true lilies (*Lilium*), and peonies. There are many perennials with fragrant foliage, too: Think of bee balm (*Monarda*), lavenders, sages (*Salvia*), and thymes, just to name a few.

➤ NO FUSS, NO MUSS

Want the best-looking blooms for the least amount of work? Make sure you keep maintenance needs in mind when choosing plants for your new garden. Here are some traits that make for an easy-care perennial:

- Lives longer than four years

- Can go at least three years before needing to be divided

- Doesn't need daily deadheading (gardening jargon for "picking off dead flowers")

- Doesn't need staking

- Not prone to pests or diseases

- Vigorous without being a pest (through either creeping roots or producing many seedlings)

There aren't too many perennials that meet all six of these

Try This!

As you're gathering your plant ideas, make a list of perennials and bulbs that catch your eye, then look up their needs later. If a plant looks promising for your site and needs, put a star next to it; if not, make a note of why. (For instance, if the plant likes steady moisture and you have a dry site, jot down "needs moist soil" behind the name.) That way, you'll remember why it won't be appropriate, and you won't be tempted to buy it later! You can stop once you get about 20 starred plants, since that will give you plenty to choose from for your new garden.

Whether or not a perennial is low maintenance often depends on where you live. Delphiniums, for instance, are a snap to grow in cool, moist climates, but elsewhere, you'll spend a lot of time staking, spraying, and replanting, and the results can still be disappointing. If you want to grow a flower, but never see it thriving in your neighbors' yards, think twice about buying it!

criteria, but I can think of two—'Goldsturm' black-eyed Susans (*Rudbeckia fulgida* 'Goldsturm') and 'Autumn Joy' sedum (*Sedum* 'Autumn Joy'). If minimal maintenance is high on your wish list, look for these plants, or any plants that have at least four of these characteristics.

REACH OUT AND TOUCH ME!

Perennials that have scented leaves are especially nice along a path, where you can brush against them as you walk by. And don't forget to plant a few by your favorite garden bench, too! That way, you can enjoy their fragrance while you relax in your garden.

Design for Non-Designers

You have the perfect site, and you know what you want to grow—now's the time to figure out how to put it all together. Understanding a few basic design ideas will help you create a great-looking garden without having to pay through the nose.

FLOWERBED IN A BOX

Some folks have a gift for planning things on paper, but not me—I need to see the real thing! To get a visual on a new bed or border, I first use my garden hose to outline the edge of it. Once that looks right, I set out buckets and boxes of different sizes to simulate the clumps of perennials. (Trash cans work great as "pretend" shrubs, large perennials, or grasses.) I get a few strange looks from the neighbors, but it's worth it—it's a whole lot easier moving boxes and buckets around than digging up and moving the plants!

Balloon flower
Platycodon grandiflorus

Balloonlike buds open to starry blue blooms all summer long

Picture This!

Photos can make garden planning easier—especially if it's too wet, cold, or snowy to work outdoors. Take some snapshots of your proposed garden spot from the angle you're most likely to look at it. (If you'll see it from two sides, take shots both ways.) Make several photocopies—color ones if you like, though black-and-whites are fine—and sketch out your ideas right on the copies. Don't forget to save the original photos. Then you can make an album of "before" and "after" garden photos to show off to friends and family!

Room with a View

You're putting some work into this new garden, so you should get to enjoy it, too! As part of the planning process, think about how it will look from your house, or from your deck or patio, as well as from the street. Otherwise, your neighbors will have pretty flowers to look at all the time, but you'll only get to see them occasionally when you're either leaving or coming home.

Grandma Putt's WISDOM

*D*on't have a hose long enough to outline your new garden? My Grandma Putt liked to use an old length of clothesline to figure out where a new flowerbed would look good. Or sometimes, she'd sprinkle flour around the area to make an easy-to-see outline. If she wanted to change it, she'd just brush away the flour with her foot and draw a new line. Talk about simple!

Move It Out!

Planning to place your new garden next to your house or garage? Keep in mind that roof overhangs can block rain from reaching the soil below, creating a bone-dry strip where plants won't thrive. Plan on leaving a 2-foot-wide

Bearded iris
Iris Bearded
Hybrid

Big, beautiful
blooms in
practically any
color you can
imagine

unplanted area (covered with mulch, gravel, or stepping stones) *behind* the border. That way, all the plants will get rain, so you'll cut back on your watering chores. They'll get better air circulation, too, meaning there's much less chance of disease taking hold. And best of all, you'll get a handy access path between the wall and the plants, making maintenance on both the house and garden a breeze!

➤ A LITTLE LINGO

Professional designers have a few terms they use to describe different types of flower gardens. **Borders** are gardens sited against a structure (such as a wall or fence) or along a boundary. They can be any width or length, but they're usually longer than they are wide. (An **herbaceous border** typically has mostly perennials, perhaps with some annuals, bulbs, and grasses, while a **mixed border** includes shrubs and even small trees, too.) **Beds** tend to be smaller than borders, and they can be any size and shape. An **island bed** is simply a bed surrounded by grass. While it's handy to understand these terms when you're reading about other gardens, don't get hung up on deciding exactly what kind of garden you have; believe me—your plants couldn't care less!

Try This!

If you want to make your flower garden wider than 4 feet, plan on making some kind of access path through it—such as a few carefully placed stepping stones. That way, you can safely reach all parts of the bed without tromping on your plants.

➤ SMART SIZING

Every time I start a new garden, I'm tempted to make it bigger than I really should. But before I get carried away, I remember Grandma Putt's advice: "Praise large gardens, but plant small ones!" A bed that's 6 to 8 feet long and 3 to 4 feet wide has enough room to hold a good variety of perennials and bulbs: some that bloom early, others in mid-season, and still others that bloom late in the year. Plus, you'll be able to reach in easily from both sides for weeding, staking, and other maintenance. If that new garden works out well, then you can always make it bigger later on.

CHECKERS, ANYONE?

One simple, but often-overlooked, secret to a great-looking garden is to set out your perennials and bulbs in a triangle or checkerboard pattern, rather than a straight line. Rows tend to make a perennial bed look more like a veggie patch than a flower garden!

DRIFTING ALONG

In a small area, you can get away with planting one of this and one of that. But most times, you'll get more color impact if you set out plants in groups (designers call these "drifts"). I like drifts of odd numbers of plants (three, five, seven, and so on), because it creates a more natural look. But hey—if you only have two or four or six of something, you can still plant them together!

THINK LIGHT FOR NIGHT

Are you one of those hardworking people who rarely get to see their garden by daylight—except on weekends? If you do most of your gardening and outdoor entertaining in the evening, be sure to include lots of white and light yellow blooms and silvery foliage in your flower gardens. These colors will reflect any available light, making them easy to spot in the dusk. As a plus, light-colored blooms tend to attract night-flying moths, so you'll have wildlife to enjoy, too!

Color Considerations

There's no need to get bogged down in complicated color theories when you're planning a simple flowerbed or border. It does help, though, to have two or three main colors in mind when you're picking out your plants. You might, for instance, choose a blue and yellow theme, or maybe a red, orange, and yellow combo. (Single-color gardens are a possibility too, but they can get boring without another color to liven them up.) Deciding on a few basic colors will make pinning down your plant choices a snap, and you'll get a classier look rather than a hodgepodge of any and every color.

HOT AND COLD

You'll often hear garden designers talk about "hot" and "cool" colors. Hot colors include bright yellow, orange, and reds: the can't-miss colors that reach and grab you from across the yard. Cool colors include the softer shades of blue, pink, and peach; they look pretty up close, but get lost if you look at them from a distance. Believe it or not, white usually acts like a hot color, because it, too, catches your eye from a distance.

FLOWER FORMS

Flowers come in an amazing array of shapes! Here are some of the most common flower forms you'll run across:

Bowls and trumpets: Daylilies (*Hemerocallis*), true lilies (*Lilium*), poppies (*Papaver*)

Daisies: Asters (*Aster*), black-eyed Susans (*Rudbeckia*), purple coneflowers (*Echinacea*)

Flat-heads: Stonecrops (*Sedum*), yarrows (*Achillea*)

Globes and buttons: Bee balms (*Monarda*), globe thistles (*Echinops*), ornamental onions (*Allium*), phlox, sea hollies (*Eryngium*)

Plumes: Astilbes (*Astilbe*), goldenrods (*Solidago*), many ornamental grasses

Spikes: Delphiniums (*Delphinium*), foxgloves (*Digitalis*), gayfeathers (*Liatris*)

STEP 'EM UP...

In a garden that you'll see from one side only, set the shortest plants (up to 2 feet tall) closest to the front, increasing in height to the tallest plants (3 feet plus) at the back. If you'll see the flowers from all sides, though, set the tallest plants in the middle and work down to the low-growers along the outer edges.

...AND MIX 'EM UP, TOO!

Variety isn't just the spice of life—it packs a punch in the garden, too! So when you're planning your plantings, try to combine perennials and bulbs with different flower forms: some daisies, some spikes, some buttons, some trumpets, and so on. The same goes for the form of the plants themselves: Choose a couple of "carpets," a few mounds, and a handful of grassy, bushy, and/or upright forms. Having an assortment of textures and forms is way more interesting than a large bunch of all daisies, for example, or a mass planting of mounds!

➤ Plants Have Habits, Too!

In garden lingo, "habit" refers to the overall outline of a plant (not to be confused with plant shapes; see "Flower Forms" at left). Here are a few examples of the habits you'll find in perennials:

Bushy: Peonies (*Paeonia*), wild indigos (*Baptisia*)

Carpet: Bugleweed (*Ajuga*), lamb's ears (*Stachys byzantina*), pinks (*Dianthus*)

Grassy: Daylilies (*Hemerocallis*), irises (*Iris*), most ornamental grasses

Mounded: Hardy geraniums (*Geranium*), hostas (*Hosta*), mums (*Chrysanthemum*)

Upright: Foxgloves (*Digitalis*), hollyhocks (*Alcea*), true lilies (*Lilium*)

Bear's breeches
Acanthus mollis

Handsome foliage and prickly spikes of pink and white flowers

And the Show Goes On

Some of the most spectacular perennials—including poppies, peonies, and irises—are also the shortest-blooming ones. So, while I can't imagine a perennial garden without these classics, I also make sure I include plants that bloom in other seasons, too! It's easy to tuck in small bulbs for spring color, then the traditional early-summer perennials, then some later-summer and fall flowers, too (think of asters, mums, dahlias, and ornamental grasses, to give you just a few ideas). That way, while some plants are dying back, others are coming into bloom. There'll be something to see all through the growing season!

 A WINTER WONDERLAND

Want your garden to look good all year round? Well, it's tricky to have flowers in winter in most parts of the country, but there are other ways to add excitement to your "off" season. Here's how:

✔ Include perennials and bulbs with evergreen foliage, such as barrenworts (*Epimedium*), bergenias (*Bergenia*), Italian arum (*Arum italicum*), and Lenten roses (*Helleborus* x *hybridus*).

✔ Add perennials with interesting seedheads that last into the winter—purple coneflowers (*Echinacea purpurea*) and Siberian irises (*Iris sibirica*) are two. (Just remember not to cut them down right after they bloom!)

Grandma Putt's WISDOM

*O*ver the years, Grandma Putt experimented with many different plants in her garden—even those that, at first glance, seemed like they wouldn't grow well in our area. A good example of this was one of her favorites: tuberous begonias. Although these tropical-looking plants originated in Bolivia, it turns out that they also grow well in Michigan, where we lived. When we did a little research, we learned that Bolivia is extremely mountainous, with elevations up to 15,000 feet. Seems the higher up these plants grow, the more cold-hardy they will be!

✔ Toss in a few ornamental grasses, too, for winter height, color, and sound. Some grasses that look great into the colder months include fountain grass (*Pennisetum alopecuroides*), Japanese silver grass (*Miscanthus sinensis*), and switch grass (*Panicum virgatum*).

SUPER SPACE SAVERS

Psssst—want to know the secret to getting twice the flowers in the same amount of space? It's simple: Just choose plants that know how to share! For instance, plant spring bulbs around the base of later-emerging perennials, such as daylilies (*Hemerocallis*), hostas, and ornamental grasses. By the time the bulbs are finished flowering, the perennials are tall enough to cover up the yellowing bulb foliage. You can use the same trick by pairing early-flowering perennials, such as Virginia bluebells (*Mertensia virginica*) and bleeding hearts (*Dicentra*), with later-blooming perennials, like bluebeard (*Caryopteris* x *clandonensis*) and Russian sages (*Perovskia*).

Make a Map

You don't need an art degree to create a functional planting plan for your new perennial garden—just some paper and a pencil. And, on the off chance that you *do* make a mistake or change your mind, a good, solid eraser is a handy tool, too!

What'cha Got?

A good garden plan starts with a rough sketch of your existing yard and its existing features—the house, garage, vegetable garden, fences, trees, shrubs, and so on. This doesn't have to be on graph paper; in fact, I like to use an opened-up brown paper grocery bag if I'm planning a big space!

Your "base" map will work best if you try to sketch it to scale from the beginning, but don't get too bogged down in making it exact, down to the inch. When it looks right to you, make several photocopies, or use tracing paper as an overlay to position your new perennial garden where it belongs.

Reality Check, Please!

When you're sketching out plans on a piece of paper, it's easy to get carried away and make your new garden larger than you originally planned. Don't do it! If the garden's

Bee balm
Monarda didyma

A hummingbird favorite with bright red blooms and fragrant foliage going to be against a wall or fence—somewhere you can only reach from one side—figure on 3 feet as the maximum width. If you can reach the garden from two sides, you can make it 4 or 5 feet across. Or, if you want even bigger beds and have the room, incorporate a garden path into the design to help you get at the weeds without stepping on (and crushing) your flowers.

LIVING ON THE EDGE

Whether you make the edges of your flowerbeds straight or curved is really a matter of individual taste. Straight edges are easy to lay out, and they definitely make mowing easier. While I'm all for low maintenance, though, I think gently curved edges look more decorative. Whichever way you go, here's a tip to reduce trimming chores: Avoid sharp corners on your beds, and make sure that the perennials at the edge of the garden are set back far enough so that your mower can trim the turf edge without shredding your flowers.

Try This!

Once you've pinpointed the ideal site for your new garden, draw it to scale on graph paper. I find it's easy to use this simple scale: 1 inch on paper equals 1 foot of actual garden space. Not enough room on the paper? Use a bigger scale, then—maybe 1 inch to represent every 2 or 3 feet. Just remember to note the scale you've chosen somewhere on your map, for future reference.

DON'T BE A COPYCAT

If you're planning gardens to go on two sides of a door or path, try to make each one a little different. Mirror-image plantings are okay if you want a very formal effect, but they can look really boring in most yards!

LET'S CALL IT A DRAW

Ready to fill in your garden with plants? Using the same scale that you chose for the perimeter of the bed, draw circles, ovals, or free-form blobs to indicate the various groups of plants. Start drawing in the biggest plants first, near the back of the bed (or the middle, if you'll see the bed from all sides). Next, figure out where the shortest plants will go (along the edge of the garden). Lastly, fill in the remaining space with drifts of medium-sized plants. How much easier can it get?

BE A CUTUP

If you need some help fine-tuning your plant choices, an old nursery or seed catalog that shows the various perennials you have in mind can help. Cut out the pictures, and place them on your sketch. Move the pictures around until the placement looks good to you. It will be much easier to move them around now, on paper, than after the real McCoys have been planted, and you decide they'd look better elsewhere!

> ## PERFECT PARTNERS
>
> Still not sure if your plant choices will look good together? Gather a flower or two of each variety from your yard, if you already have the plants growing in other beds, or check out your local florist for similar-looking blooms. Group them in a bouquet, and see if you like the effect. If the flowers combine well in a vase, they'll be great together in your garden!

GARDEN BY THE FOOT

Not sure how much space to allow for each plant? Figure that most perennials will fill about 4 square feet of space. Small bulbs and perennials, however, will need only 1 square foot.

COLOR YOUR WORLD

When it came time to plan my first flower garden, Grandma Putt had me get out my crayons to color in my drawing of the flowerbed. This helped me see if I liked the mix of colors. If the effect on paper wasn't pleasing enough, Grandma had me put aside the sketch and start studying the catalogs again. She was a real taskmaster!

Big blue lilyturf
Liriope muscari

Evergreen clumps ideal for edging paths, beds, and borders

Designing on the Fly

Okay—we all know that it's best to plan your garden *before* you start collecting the plants for it. That way, you'll buy only the plants that you need, and you'll know how big they'll get, when they'll bloom, and what conditions they need. But let's face it—who among us hasn't made a few impulse buys at the garden center? Or perhaps we've come home with some unplanned acquisitions from a gardening friend or relative, and we need to get them in the ground pronto. In this section, I'll share some tips on making a pretty garden if you have the plants—but not a plan.

Mixing perennials and bulbs with a variety of shapes and colors will give your garden a lot of zip, but don't forget to include some repetition, too! Repeating clumps of the same plants, or of similar colors, along the length of the bed can visually tie the whole planting together quite nicely.

SAVE SOME FOR LATER

Going plant shopping without doing your homework first can lead to what I call "garden center syndrome": buying a whole bunch of perennials already in bloom. Sure, an instant garden looks great—for a few weeks, anyway. After that, though, the show is done, and you have to wait a whole year for the next batch of flowers. So the moral of the story is that it's fine to start with a few plants already in bloom, but don't forget to pick up some perennials that will bloom later in the season, too!

FIVE STEPS TO FABULOUS FLOWERBEDS

Ready to get going on your garden? Gather up all your plants, then set them out over the prepared bed, rearranging them until the placement looks pleasing. The same design pointers I gave for planning your garden still apply here:

1. Keep the shorter plants toward the front and the tallest plants at the back (or in the middle, if you'll see the garden from all sides).

2. If you have the room, set out drifts of three or more of the same plant to avoid a spotty look.

3. Repeat clumps of the same plant, or at least the same color, at various spots along the length of the bed. This will help make the garden look planned, rather than just a random collection of plants that were thrown together.

4. Mix up perennials and bulbs with different flower forms (spikes, plumes, trumpets, buttons, and so on) and a variety of plant habits (carpeting, bushy, grassy, etc.) to add visual interest.

5. Include some perennials and bulbs with great-looking foliage to provide a show all season long.

TOOL TIME

The very first thing you should plant in any new garden? Stepping stones! (And yes, I consider them to be tools of the trade, just like spades, forks, and the like, because no garden should be without them!) They'll fill some space and give you something to work around as you set out your perennials, and they'll look nice, too. Plus, they'll give you easy access to all parts of the bed, making it a snap to rearrange the layout of the plants—and to reach all parts of the garden for later weeding and mulching.

DIVIDE AND CONQUER

When you have a whole pile of plants to arrange, where in the world do you start? One simple step can help you impose some order on this chaos. Grab your favorite catalog or plant encyclopedia, then use it to help you divide your plants into three basic groups: shorties (the plants up to 18 inches tall), the tall guys (those 3 feet tall and over), and the in-betweens (18 to 36 inches tall). Set out the tall guys first, then the shorties in front, and tuck the in-betweens in wherever there's room.

GIVE ME SOME SPACE

I think the hardest part of designing a garden on the spot is knowing how far apart to put the plants. It's tempting to squeeze the puny-looking little guys together and give the

Black-eyed Susan
Rudbeckia hirta

A classic for summer gardens, with bright orange-yellow blooms

Blanket flower
Gaillardia x
grandiflora

Red and yellow
flowers on tough
plants that defy
heat and drought

big beauties plenty of space, but that can be exactly the
wrong approach! Plants that are bushy and blooming in
spring often die back, at least a bit, after flowering, while the
later bloomers, which look spindly now, will bush out and fill
up a surprising amount of space once things heat up. Also
keep in mind that your perennials will get bigger every year,
so unless you plan to dig and divide them in a year or two,
it's better to give them plenty of elbow room in the beginning.

➤ SAY NO TO ROWS!

I've said it before, but it bears repeating: Don't set your
perennials and bulbs in rows! They'll look stiff and awk-
ward—more like a field of corn than a flower garden. If
you have three plants that are alike, set them out at the
three points of a triangle (one in front and two behind,
equally spaced out from the front one, or vice versa). If
you're planting more than three, use a staggered or
checkerboard pattern: two
or more rows with the
plants offset in alternating
rows. If you follow this simple rule, your new garden
will have a much fuller and
more natural look right
from the get-go.

If I'm not exactly sure how much
space a particular perennial will
fill, here's the general rule of
thumb I follow:

☑ Plants under 1 foot tall—10 inches apart

☑ Plants 12 to 30 inches tall—18 inches apart

☑ Plants taller than 30 inches—2 to 3 feet apart

CHAPTER 2

DIG IN!

There's no doubt about it: Great gardens start
with great soil. But if you're stuck with
less-than-ideal earth, don't throw in the trowel!
This chapter's chock-full of great ideas for making
a great flower garden in just about any spot—
even if you *don't* feel like digging.

Bed-Building Basics

Making a good bed is the key to getting the best out of your perennials. Annuals can grow and flower in poor soil, but perennials seldom survive for more than a year or two if their beds are not to their liking. So put in a little effort now, and your investment will pay off with big, beautiful blooms for many years to come!

⬤ TIMING IS EVERYTHING

In most areas, fall is the ideal time to get started on your new flower garden. There's not much else to do this time of year, and the weather is usually quite pleasant. You can work at a comfortable pace, since you're not in a hurry to plant, and the soil will have time to settle before spring planting.

If you live in a hot-summer area, though, consider digging your new garden in late winter or early spring, then letting the site sit until fall. That way, you'll get your perennials settled in when the weather's likely to be mild and moist, rather than hot and dry.

The very first thing I learned about gardening was that a lawn has magical powers: All you have to do is start digging, and it gets bigger before your very eyes. Back when I set out to dig my first flower garden, it looked to me like the whole thing could fit in the back of a pickup truck. But by the time I'd spaded up just a few pieces of turf, I'd have sworn that big 'ol plot stretched into the next county!

⬤ GETTING AN EDGE

If you want a straight-edged bed, simply drive small stakes into the ground at the corners and stretch a string between them.

To mark the edge of your informal flower beds, use an old clothesline, electrical extension cord, or garden hose. That way, you can get the curves just right *before* you begin to turn over any soil.

Another way to outline the shape of your flowerbed is with small pieces of stale bread. They're easy to rearrange, and when you're done, the birds will feast on the crumbs!

 DON'T TURN IT UNDER

If you're going to plant your garden in an area where grass is now growing, you need to get rid of it, *pronto!* Over the years, I've seen too many folks try to turn the sod under, which often results in big trouble later on! The grass, weed seeds, and runners continually pop their ugly little heads up to the surface of the soil, where they sprout and become a troublesome bother, when all you really want to do is grow flowers. Believe me— spending a little time in this preparation stage will save you a whole lot of time and effort later on.

TOOL TIME Have a large area of grass to get rid of? Then consider renting a "sod cutter" for a day or two. This handy machine does a great job and can save you hours of hard work!

IT'S OUTTA HERE!

In a hurry to get your garden started? Then here's a tip— strip off the turf by slipping a sharp spade in horizontally, about an inch below the surface. You want to remove the top growth and the uppermost roots without taking off too much soil. Use the pieces to fill in any bare spots in your lawn, or shake off the loose soil and put them grass-side-down on your compost pile. (If you put the roots down, the pieces can quickly root into the pile, and you'll end up with a grass pile instead of a compost pile!)

SPRAY THAT GRASS AWAY

What if you don't have the energy to remove the grass, but you also don't want to wait months for the grass to get smothered (see "Smothering Instinct" on page 32)? Spraying the site with an herbicide might be the best route for you. Look for an herbicide that's described as "systemic": This means it will kill the roots as well as the plant tops. Otherwise, the tops may look dead, but the roots can still regrow and spread. Even with a systemic plant killer, it's best to wait a week or two to make sure all the growth is

Bleeding heart
Dicentra spectabilis

Arching sprays of pink and white hearts; beautiful with spring bulbs dead. Then if you do see any new growth—usually from the tough perennial weeds—simply spray again.

Once the sod is dead, you may be able to till it into the soil if the sod isn't too thick. Otherwise, you could strip it off with a spade or sod cutter (with either tool, it will be a much easier proposition than stripping live turf). Or, if it's really thin, leave it in place and plant right through it!

SQUEEZE, PLEASE

Any gardener worth his or her salt knows that if you work soil when it's too wet or dry, you can destroy its structure and turn your gardening into a real chore. So before you set out to work in the garden, give your soil a good, old-fashioned squeeze test! Simply dig up a handful of soil from the site and squeeze it. If it crumbles apart when you open your hand, it's too dry. (Water thoroughly, let the area sit for two to three days, and then test again.) If it clumps into a solid shape, it's too wet. But if it holds together without packing, it's just right—and you can get on with your digging!

Mixers & Elixirs

SOIL ENERGIZER TONIC

1 can of beer
1 cup of regular cola (not diet)
1 cup of dishwashing liquid
1 cup of antiseptic mouthwash
¼ tsp. of instant tea granules

Mix these ingredients in a bucket or container, and fill a 20 gallon hose-end sprayer. Overspray the soil in your garden to the point of run-off (or just until small puddles start to form), then let it sit for at least two weeks. This recipe makes enough to cover 100 square feet of garden area.

SPRAY WISELY

Always read the label carefully before spraying any herbicide, and follow all the directions to the letter. Systemic herbicides usually work best when the temperature is above 50°F and the weeds are actively growing; otherwise, the roots may not be killed, and you'll end up having to respray them several times.

➤ BED-BUILDING 101

Unless your soil is already loose and fluffy, I think the best way to prepare a new garden site is the good, old-fashioned way: by hand. Now, I hear you moaning already. But, believe me, it's not as hard as it sounds—the whole job will go easier if you do a little at a time. I like to spread the work over a week or two in the fall. Here's my surefire method:

1. Following the outline of your new bed or border, cut an edge with a sharp spade. Shove it all the way down each time, so that the top of the spade is even with the ground, then wiggle it back and forth a few times. This will give you a clear mark to go by.

2. Make parallel cuts, 6 to 8 inches apart, across the bed. When you're done, your plot will look like a piece of lined notebook paper.

3. Now start turning over the soil, working along one strip at a time. Keep going until you're tired, then stop for the day. You've earned a rest!

4. When you've dug up the whole plot, chop up any surface lumps, then spread organic matter or compost (see page 38 for directions) over the whole area.

5. Take a rest for a day or two, then mix the soil and amendments together. Top it off with my Soil Energizer Tonic (at left), and curl up with a steaming mug of cocoa and some mail-order catalogs until spring rolls around.

Bloodroot
Sanguinaria canadensis

Shade-loving wildflower with delicate white blossoms in spring

Grandma Putt's **WISDOM**

As a kid, I often got overwhelmed when I'd look at an expanse of garden I had to dig up. But I always got through it by following Grandma Putt's advice: "Back into your work." With any task, she explained—digging, weeding, mulching, or whatever—it's better to face the work you've already done, and keep your back toward what's still left to do. That way, you can admire what you've done so far, and you can always hope you're almost finished! An added plus to this approach when digging is that you aren't stepping on and packing down the already-loosened soil.

Layering's a Piece of Cake!

Of course, there's more than one way to start a flower garden. Instead of digging *down*, some gardeners prefer to build their beds *up*. This can be as simple as a single layer of mulch to smother the grass, or as complete as a whole aboveground garden—with no digging required! It's an ideal approach where the soil is too tough to work because of tree roots or rocks. Plus, it minimizes future maintenance, because you're not bringing up weed seeds that can sprout later on.

If you're planning to start a new garden by trucking in topsoil, keep in mind that more isn't always better. A foot of new topsoil is great for most sites, but if you're gardening under a tree, don't add any more than 8 inches of topsoil. Otherwise, you may smother the roots and weaken the whole tree.

SMOTHERING INSTINCT

For those of you who have back problems, can't handle a sod cutter, or who are just too lazy to remove the grass, I have a little secret: You can simply smother the sod out of existence! Keep in mind, however, that this process takes some time.

What you need to do is cover the ground with cardboard or several sheets of newspaper. Wet it down, add several inches of grass clippings, and then thoroughly hose down the whole thing. Keep adding mulch through the season to keep the layer several inches thick, and hand-pull any weeds that pop through. By the following year, the grass should be gone! Then you can dig or till as usual to loosen the soil for planting.

BED-BUILDING THE EASY WAY

Here's another easy way to get rid of a lawn that's standing in the way of your new flower garden. It takes about six months, but it's well worth the wait!

1. In late summer, the year before you plan to plant, mark out where you want your new bed or border to be.

2. Place a 1-inch-thick layer of newspaper on top of the area, and set rocks on the papers to hold them down.

3. Give the papers a good soaking, and keep them moist for the next several weeks.

4. In the fall, remove the rocks and spread 6 to 8 inches of leaves on top of the papers.

5. On top of the leaves, put a foot or so of good soil. I like to use a nice, sandy loam that I buy at the garden center. (And I have them deliver it!) If you've got access to a good supply of compost, that works well, too.

6. Sit back and relax while worms and other little organisms spend the winter hard at work, breaking down all those layers of good stuff. Come spring, that grass will be history, and you'll have a loose, rich flower bed that's a joy to plant in—with no digging needed!

Blue-eyed grass
Sisyrinchium angustifolium

Clumps of small, but abundant blue blooms for sunny spots

Two Simple Solutions to Weed Woes

Weeds can be a lot harder to get rid of than plain old lawn grass. If a healthy crop of dock and dandelions has settled in where you want to plant your daffodils and daisies, it pays to serve it with an eviction notice early in the spring, a whole year ahead of planting time.

Here are two methods I use to get rid of really stubborn weeds and make my soil richer in the process. It means giving up a whole growing season, but I figure that's a small price to pay for a weed-free flower bed!

The last straw. Cover the area with sheets of cardboard, or at least 2 inches of newspapers. On top of that, pile about a foot of straw. Wet it down once in a while to keep it from blowing away. But otherwise, give it the cold shoulder until next spring rolls around.

Black plastic sheet. Spread pieces of black plastic over your garden-to-be and weight

Try This!

Spreading newspapers to smother the grass can be a real adventure on a windy day. To make your life easier, have a large bucket of water handy, and dunk the papers in the water *before* you spread them out on the ground. The wet papers will stick together and stay where you put them, so you won't be chasing them into the next county!

them down with rocks. The sun will cook those weeds to a crisp! In the fall, remove the plastic and replace it with an 8- to 12-inch layer of leaves or straw for the winter.

Coping with Clay

If you have clay, you know it! In wet weather, it's everywhere—on your shoes, on and in your car, on your carpets—and when it's dry, you practically need a jackhammer to loosen it. Smart gardeners, though, know that clay has some good points, too. It holds on to whatever water there is, so it's the last kind of soil to need watering during a dry spell. Clay also holds lots of nutrients, so you'll spend less time and effort fertilizing your flowers. Read on to find tips for making the most of your clay soil—without breaking your back!

Soils that contain too much silt or clay are called heavy or clay soils. Once you try spading up a plot of clay soil, you'll understand right away why it's called *heavy soil!*

➤ SLIPPERY WHEN WET

The first commandment when it comes to working with clay soil? Don't even *think* about digging or tilling when the ground is wet! Besides making your job 10 times harder, working soggy clay soil can result in a compacted mess that's sticky when wet and hard as rock when dry—definitely not what you want for healthy, happy perennials and bulbs. So pick up a handful of soil and squeeze it: It should be moist enough to stick together when you squeeze it, but dry enough to break apart when you tap it lightly with your finger. If it's wet enough to stick to your hand, it'll stick to your tools, too! Wait a few days and test again before digging.

COARSE? OF COURSE!

Keep in mind that when it comes to improving clay soil, not all organic matter is created equal. Your best bet is coarse stuff, like straw, pine needles, chunky compost, or ground pine bark. These big pieces will keep the clay from clumping together, so air and water can enter the soil more easily and the roots of your perennials and bulbs can grow like gangbusters. Real fine material like peat moss, dehydrated cow manure, and sieved compost soaks up and holds water just like clay, so using these types of organic matter could actually make your soggy clay soil even soggier!

Don't Skimp on Sand

You'll hear a lot of different stories about the value of adding sand to clay soil, but here's the real scoop: Sand *can* help, *if* you add enough. Just like organic matter, sand won't do much good unless you really pile it on. Spread at least 3 inches of sand over the area, and work it into the top 6 inches of soil. Adding less than that *won't* turn your soil into concrete—that's an old wives' tale—but it also won't make a difference in helping loosen up tough clay.

PILE IT ON

Sure, ordinary digging or tilling can loosen up heavy soil a bit, but in a day or two, it's packed down again. The key to keeping clay from caking is to add organic matter—and *lots* of it! I'm not talking about a scattering on top of the soil—I mean giving your new garden a heaping helping of good stuff: compost, chopped leaves, pine needles, or whatever you can get your hands on.

To make a real difference, you want to add 6 to 8 inches of organic matter and work it into the top 12 inches of soil. Sounds easy on paper, but if you try to dig or till all

Blue false indigo
Baptisia australis

Showy spikes of blue flowers in late spring and early summer

When you're looking to loosen up your clay soil, make sure you ask for coarse sand, builder's sand, or sharp sand. If they try to sell you "play sand," shop somewhere else; it's great for filling sandboxes but way too fine to help loosen up your clay!

that together at one time, you've got a big job on your hands! A more gradual approach is generally best. Start by digging or tilling in 1 or 2 inches of organic matter in the fall, then the same amount again in spring. If the soil still feels heavy to you, plant annuals there for the summer, then work in another 1 to 2 inches of organic matter in fall and the following spring. By then, your soil should be in great shape for perennial plantings!

ADD SOME GYPSUM—OR NOT?

Talk to a bunch of gardeners who've spent years improving their clay soil, and sooner or later someone will mention gypsum (calcium sulfate). For some, gypsum works wonders; for others, it's a dud. You're likely to have the best luck with this material if you live where the soil is high in salt (generally in semi-arid areas or in beds that get splashed by roadway deicing salts in winter). Apply about 2 pounds of gypsum per 100 square feet in fall the year before you plant, and work it into the soil. Then do it again in spring. If gypsum is working for you, you should notice that your soil is distinctly more crumbly than it was before you started the first treatment.

Even if gypsum does work for you, don't expect the results to last. It's critical that you follow up with generous amounts of organic matter to help keep your clay soil in good shape for many years to come.

Blue fescue
Festuca glauca

Tufts of silvery blue foliage for the front of a bed or border

KISS MY GRITS!

Can't find coarse sand to break up your clay? The solution could be as close as your local feed store! Call them up (look under "Feed" in your phone directory) and ask if they have grit for sale. It usually comes in three grades: turkey (the largest), layer or grower (medium size), and chick or starter (the smallest and the kind I recommend). This pebblelike white material does a fantastic job of loosening up clay soil. Start by spreading 1 to 2 inches over your garden-to-be and digging or tilling it into the soil. Repeat once or twice if needed, until the ground feels nice and loose.

RAISING THE ROOTS

So far, I've given you plenty of clay-soil solutions that call for lots of digging or tilling. But what if you just don't have the time, energy, or inclination to do all that work? You can still have a great-looking perennial garden—just build your beds *up*!

It's easy to make a raised flowerbed: Simply top your existing clay with trucked-in topsoil or—even better—a blend of topsoil and compost. If you're making a raised bed in a spot that has existing grass or weeds, spread a layer of newspapers about 10 sheets thick over the area and wet it down, then dump the new soil on top. A 6-inch layer of topsoil usually does the trick, but you can add more if you like. A low "frame" of rocks, bricks, or landscape timbers will help hold the new soil in place.

NO MORE WET FEET

Besides giving your perennials lots of rooting room above the clay, building raised beds also dramatically improves drainage—a real plus in soggy sites. This way, your plants get the best of both worlds: a loose, well-drained layer for easy rooting over a generous supply of moisture and nutrients from the clay below. (For a list of plants that do well in wet soil, see "Perfect Perennials for Moist Soil" on page 218.)

Sandy-Soil Strategies

Sandy-soil gardeners take heart—gardeners stuck with clay soil would give anything to be in your shoes! But then, they don't know what you go through: the countless hours of watering and fertilizing to get *anything* to grow in that beach you call a yard. But don't worry; there's hope for you yet. Here are some ideas to help you make the most of your special soil conditions.

➤ SMART SITES FOR SANDY SOIL

If you're facing a yard full of sandy soil, it's smart to site your new flower garden with that in mind. Here are a few tips to remember:

❧ Choose a location close to your house, so that it's easy to reach the garden with a hose. That will save you the trouble of hauling hoses to distant parts of your yard every time you have to water.

❧ Shelter from winds can help reduce water loss, which can be a big help where the soil is already dry. Plant your perennials near a wall or fence, or grow tall ornamental grasses on the windward side of the garden to block the strongest breezes.

❧ Plant perennials and bulbs that are already adapted to dry conditions. They'll thrive in sandy soil with a minimum of fussing from you!

TOP 10

Perennials for Sandy Spots

Basket-of-gold (*Aurinia saxatilis*)

Blanket flowers (*Gaillardia*)

Butterfly weed (*Asclepias tuberosa*)

Evening primroses (*Oenothera*)

Moss phlox (*Phlox subulata*)

Pinks (*Dianthus*)

Rock cress (*Arabis caucasica*)

Wormwoods (*Artemisia*)

Yarrows (*Achillea*)

Yuccas (*Yucca*)

Sand or Clay—the Answer's the Same

Believe it or not, the same advice I gave for improving clay soil also applies to sandy soil: Add organic matter, and *lots* of it! I want you to spread 3 to 4 inches of organic matter over your garden-to-be in the fall, then dig or till it into the top 6 to 8 inches of soil. Repeat the process in the spring, then go ahead and plant your perennials!

 Mix It Up

The *kind* of organic matter
you add to your new flower
garden can make a big difference in the long run. Fine-
textured stuff, like finished
compost, grass clippings, and
peat moss, will definitely
help hold water in the soil, so
you'll want to add some of
that. But sandy soil also contains lots of air, which in turn
provides ideal conditions for
soil microorganisms—and
those little critters can chew up all your nice organic matter
in the blink of an eye! So it's smart to also add some tough,
long-lasting organic material, such as chopped straw, ground
pine bark, or sawdust. I'd suggest adding equal parts of fine
and tough organic stuff to your sandy soil, so you'll get the
benefits immediately and for several years to come.

JERRY'S GEMS

Soils that contain too much
sand are called *light* soils. They
are very easy to work, and they
usually warm up first in the
spring, so your perennials and bulbs get a
jump start on the growing season. The problem with these soils is that they are often
unable to hold enough moisture for growing
plants—water runs through them as fast as it
does off a duck's back! As a result, you're
fighting a never-ending (and, quite often, losing) battle to keep enough moisture in the soil.

 Lay on the Clay

For a practically permanent benefit, consider adding clay to
your sandy soil. Then you'll have the best of both worlds:
The clay will hold water and nutrients while the sand will
allow excess water to drain away. Find a supplier that can
bring high-clay topsoil by the truckload (look under "topsoil" in the Yellow Pages), then work a 1-inch layer into the
top 4 to 6 inches of your existing sandy-soil bed.

 Flip Your Lawn, Not Your Lid!

Already have decent grass growing where you want your
flower garden? Then you have a great, homegrown source of
organic matter for bulking up your sandy soil. In the fall,
strip the sod with a spade or a sod cutter, then lay it back

Blue flag
Iris versicolor

Elegant blue
blooms; thrives
in sun and
soggy soil

Blue vervain
Verbena hastata

Tall clumps
with narrow spikes
of flowers

over the site, root-side-up. Cover the whole area with a layer of newspaper (six to eight sheets thick should do the trick), then water everything thoroughly. Cover with 2 inches of mulch and let it sit until spring. When you're ready to plant, simply pull back the remaining mulch as you dig each hole, then put the mulch back around each settled plant. After planting, give the whole site a good drenching, add another 1 to 2 inches of organic mulch, then stand back and watch your perennials take off!

POST-PLANTING POINTERS

Chances are, you're going to need to provide extra water to your perennials in sandy soil, even if you add lots of organic matter at planting time. That doesn't mean you have to spend your summers permanently attached to your hose, though! If you lay some soaker hoses in place as soon as you plant, then watering sandy beds and borders will be a breeze. These handy hoses have tiny pores all along their sides, so they ooze water along their length, supplying water right to the root zone of thirsty perennials. Cover the hoses with mulch, and no one but you will know about your secret watering weapon!

*B*ulking up your sandy soil with compost or clay before planting is a great start, but don't think you're done there! No sireee! It's important to keep up your good work by adding more every time you get a chance. Each time my Grandma Putt set out a new perennial, dug a hole to plant bulbs, or lifted a clump to divide it, she scratched a few handfuls of clay or organic matter into the bottom of the hole to keep her soil in tip-top shape.

CHAPTER 3

MORE PLANTS FOR LESS DOUGH

Filling your garden with flowers doesn't have to cost you a
bundle—if you know how to spend your money wisely.
Over the years, I've learned an awful lot about the best ways to
get the perennials and bulbs I want to try. Some I buy,
some I've gotten by swapping plants with other gardeners,
and some I've even grown myself! Read on, my friends, and
see which way—or ways—might work best for you.

Shop Smart

Buying your perennials and bulbs is the quickest way to get a new garden started, but it can get pretty pricey, too. Make the most of your plant-buying pennies with these smart shopping tips.

Butterfly weed
Asclepias tuberosa

Clusters of
bright orange
blooms; a favorite
of Monarch
butterflies

➤ BIGGER ISN'T ALWAYS BETTER

Nowadays, you can find plants for sale in spring just about anywhere—from the usual nurseries and garden centers to huge home centers and even grocery stores. Chain stores often have great prices on plants, since they can contract with growers for large quantities and pass their savings on to you. On the downside, though, their selection is usually pretty limited, and there's a fair chance that the plants haven't been well cared for. (Rather than invest in skilled labor to keep the plants looking good, it's usually just easier for these outlets to toss the plants out as they start to look bad.) At the other end of the spectrum are high-end nurseries with fancy signs and spectacular display gardens—and prices to match!

The chain stores are worth frequent visits, since you may get lucky and get to pick from a fresh delivery of healthy plants. And, the displays and signage at the bigger nurseries can provide lots of good ideas and information. But for my main plant shopping, I do most of my business at local mom-and-pop operations. These smaller outlets generally offer the best value: Maybe the glitz isn't there, but the plants get good care, and the personal service just can't be beat!

➤ GO POSTAL FOR PERENNIALS

More and more folks are trying out mail-order plant sources, and it's easy to see why. Those glossy, photo-packed catalogs are enough to make even the most jaded gardener want to grab his or her checkbook. But before you blow your whole plant-buying budget shopping by mail order, here are a few things to keep in mind:

Consider shipping costs. What looks like a good deal at first may not be, once you add the shipping and handling charges to your order. If you're going for price alone, buying locally may be a better bet.

Don't expect big plants with big root systems. One way mail-order sources try to keep shipping prices reasonable is to ship plants bare-root (with moss, sawdust, or some other lightweight packing material around the roots, instead of soil). These perennials can settle in quickly and per-form well after planting, but it can be a bit of a shock to see those scrawny little sprigs when you open the box!

Be prepared to plant. Even the best pack-ing and fastest shipping can cause perennials some stress, so get them unpacked and in the ground as soon as possible. If you aren't home during the day, consider hav-ing your plants delivered to your workplace, or to a neighbor's house, so they won't sit outside in the hot sun (or the pouring rain). Also, it's smart to have the soil prepared in advance, so you'll be ready to plant right away. Most mail-order nurseries will wait to ship until the weather in your area is suitable, but if your plants arrive at a bad time, pot them up and keep them in a protected place until the weather settles.

Try This!

If you're buying from a mail-order nursery for the first time, try a test order of three or four plants. That should give you an idea of their quality (or lack thereof). If you are pleased, you can always try a larger order later on; if not, at least you didn't gamble (and lose!) your whole garden.

Bulbs in the Mailbox

When you're buying bulbs, mail-order sources are generally your best bet. The prices are great—especially if you order early—and your bulbs will be delivered at the right planting time for your area. Local retailers will have a more limited selection, and their bulbs may be damaged from frequent handling.

*W*hen I was a kid, I always picked the plants with the most flowers when I went shopping for annuals with my Grandma Putt. But Grandma would make me put them back. Instead, she'd select annual plants with the fewest open blooms, saying they'd settle in better.

But when we went shopping for perennials, the rules were often reversed! Grandma liked to pick out her pots of perennials when they were flowering, so she could see the flower color for herself. She knew that the tags in the pots don't always tell the true story: Sometimes they get switched by careless shoppers, or the nursery itself may make a mistake. But when the plants are in bloom, you know exactly what you're getting.

THINK SMALL

Bigger plants aren't necessarily better—and they sure as heck aren't cheaper—than smaller ones. Sure, those large, lush perennials will make your garden look great from the get-go. But think of it this way: For the price of one big plant, you can often buy two, three, or even four smaller pots of the same variety! These little guys will settle in surprisingly quickly, generally catching up to the big bruisers by midsummer and often blooming even better by season's end.

Canada wild ginger

Asarum canadense

Good-looking groundcover for shady gardens

SHOP THE SALES

Sales sponsored by local plant societies are great, but often-overlooked, sources of perennials. Watch the community calendar section of your newspaper for announcements of sales open to the public. Aficionados bring divisions of their own favorite plants, then the society sells them to raise funds for their various projects. You can get some really choice plants at reasonable prices—as well as excellent gardening advice—from the society members manning the sales tables!

DON'T BE THE FIRST ON YOUR BLOCK

Wherever you shop, avoid the temptation of trying the latest and greatest "new" perennial. True, these bodacious beauties can be simply stunning—but so can their price tag! If there's a new plant that really catches your eye, wait for a year or two (at least) before plunking down your hard-earned cash. By then, the novelty will have worn off a bit, and the price should be more reasonable.

Share and Share Alike

There's something about gardening that brings out the generosity in people. True gardeners love to share their favorite plants with others, and what could be nicer than to get another special plant in return? Participating in a plant swap with friends, neighbors, and co-workers is a fun and rewarding way to expand your gardens without spending your whole week's paycheck!

TOOL TIME

Sometimes, the best gardening tool isn't a trowel or spade—it's a friend at your local garden center! As you shop at various places, pay attention to the staff and how they relate to you and other customers. Keep your eyes open for someone who seems friendly and is willing and able to answer all (or most) of your questions.

When you find salespeople you click with, take the time to introduce yourself and find out their names. Then make a point to say hello each time you shop there. The more they get to know you and your shopping habits, the more they can help you choose plants that are suited to your style, budget, and growing conditions. They can also tell you when new shipments are due in, and perhaps even when a sale is planned!

In return, though, be considerate of their time. They have a lot of other people to help, too, so don't monopolize their time or expect them to plan your whole garden for you! If possible, plan your shopping trips on a weekday, or early in the morning, when fewer other customers are out and about.

One of Grandma Putt's favorite sayings about perennials was: "The first year they sleep, the second year they creep, and the third year they leap!" She'd use this to remind herself that it took a new plant at least three years to really show what it could do. A perennial that looked tidy and controlled for the first year or two could suddenly be surrounded by dozens of runners or seedlings the next!

So when Grandma Putt received a new perennial as a gift, she'd first check her books to see what to expect. If she wasn't sure of the plant's inclination to spread itself around, she'd set it in the corner of the vegetable garden for several years, where she could keep a close eye on it. If, and only if, it behaved itself, was it then allowed to join the other perennials in her flower garden!

Cardinal flower
Lobelia cardinalis

Moisture-lover
with rich red
flowers that attract
hummingbirds

SWAP SMART

Whether you are participating in an already organized plant swap or setting up one of your own, it's important to be prepared. It's best to have your offerings potted up at least two weeks (and ideally longer) before you plan to trade, so the plants have a chance to recover from the shock. It's no fun to give or receive a droopy, bedraggled-looking plant that was yanked out of the ground the night before the swap!

It's also important to include a label with the plant's name, and ideally your name, too, so the recipients know what they are getting and who to come to with thanks or questions. Including information on the height and flower color, along with a few growing tips—for example, "likes full sun, wet soil"—is helpful, too!

BEWARE OF GARDENERS BEARING GIFTS

Plant swaps and gifts of plants from friends and neighbors can be a real blessing, if you're a new gardener looking for sturdy, easy-care perennials to fill your beds and borders. But before you let any and every new addition loose in your garden, keep this in mind: If the giver has enough to share, that likely means that the original plant has produced plenty of seedlings or offsets. And that can translate into a garden thug—a perennial that might end up taking over your garden if you don't keep digging it out and finding new homes for the offspring! (See "Top 10 Fast-Spreading Perennials" below for a list of plants often found at plant swaps. They sure are pretty—but they're also aggressive spreaders, so buyer beware!)

If you're going to pick up plants at swaps and accept gift plants, here's my suggestion: Consider setting aside an out-of-the-way spot in your yard where you can grow these plants for a few years. That will give you some time to learn about the plants and their habits before either moving them into your flower garden or else disposing of them discreetly!

Grow Your Own

Need lots of perennials, but don't have lots of money? With a little know-how, it's easy to turn one packet of seed or a single starter clump into dozens of new plants!

A GROWING INVESTMENT

Sowing seed is a great way to get a garden full of flowers without going broke in the process. For less than three bucks, you can buy a packet of seed and easily end up with 30 bucks worth of plants. That's a 1000 percent return on your money!

Most perennials are a snap to start—just sow the seeds indoors in pots filled with moistened seed-starting mix, then set them under plant lights or on a sunny windowsill. If you're too busy starting annuals to sow perennial seeds indoors in late winter and early spring,

TOP 10 | **Fast-Spreading Perennials**

Bee balm (*Monarda didyma*)

Bugleweed (*Ajuga reptans*)

Chameleon plant (*Houttuynia cordata* 'Chameleon')

Gooseneck loosestrife (*Lysimachia clethroides*)

Mexican evening primrose (*Oenothera speciosa*)

Obedient plant (*Physostegia virginiana*)

Ribbon grass (*Phalaris arundinacea* 'Picta')

Tansy (*Tanacetum vulgare*)

Tawny daylily (*Hemerocallis fulva*)

Wormwoods (*Artemisia*)

wait until early to midsummer for the perennials. They'll germinate quickly in warm weather, and you can have garden-size plants by fall and flowers the following summer.

FLOWERS IN A FLASH

Contrary to popular belief, many perennials are just as easy to grow from seed as annuals. And even better, quite a few can bloom the very first year if you start their seeds indoors in late winter. Check out "Top 10 Early Bloomers" at left for some varieties to try if you're looking for flowers in a flash.

SEEDLINGS IN THE NURSERY

You don't need a greenhouse to grow perennials from seed, but it does help to have a special nursery area to get your baby plants off to a strong start. Pick a sunny spot that's out of the way but still close enough to the house that you can keep an eye on it. It doesn't have to be big—even a 3-foot-square bed can hold quite a few seedlings. I like to build a raised bed by setting 1 x 6 or 2 x 6 lumber on its short side and nailing the corners together, then filling it with a 50-50 mix of good topsoil and compost.

You can plant perennial seeds directly into your nursery bed, or sow them in pots first and then transplant the seedlings into the bed. Don't be concerned about having enough space for them. The seedlings will be growing there for only a matter of months, so you can set them just a few inches apart. Put a small fence around the bed to protect the youngsters from marauding critters, and watch out for slugs and snails; those slimy scalawags simply love to feed on tender

TOP 10 Early Bloomers

Arkwright's campion
(*Lychnis* x *arkwrightii*)

Black-eyed Susans
(*Rudbeckia*)

Blue lobelia
(*Lobelia siphilitica*)

'Cannon J. Went' toadflax
(*Linaria* 'Cannon J. Went')

Checkerbloom
(*Sidalcea malviflora*)

Jupiter's beard
(*Centranthus ruber*)

Purple coneflower
(*Echinacea purpurea*)

'Southern Charm' mullein
(*Verbascum* 'Southern Charm')

'Summer Pastels' yarrow
(*Achillea* 'Summer Pastels')

Zebra hollyhock
(*Malva sylvestris* 'Zebrina')

young seedlings. Keep your baby perennials well watered and mulched, and these small-fry will soon be big enough to hold their own in your regular flower gardens. Move them into beds and borders in fall, or let them stay where they are until early spring. After they've been moved, top off your nursery bed with a bit more soil and compost, and you'll be ready for another round!

Nursery beds are handy for bulking up clumps of perennials for dividing later on. Say, for example, that you need three clumps of daylilies or hostas, but you can only afford to buy one plant. Buy the biggest clump you can, then plant it in your nursery bed. The following spring, dig up the clump and divide it. If you have all the divisions you need, plant them right into your garden; otherwise, set them back in the nursery bed and repeat the process the following spring. Pretty soon, you'll have doubled or tripled your plant collection—without paying any more money. And that, my friends, is what it's all about!

Carpathian
harebell
*Campanula
carpatica*

A low-growing
perennial with
blue summer
flowers; a beauty
for beds and
borders

CHAPTER 4

PLANT IT!

So what are you waiting for? Let's get this garden party started! Whether you've got potted perennials, bare-root plants, or bulbs to get in the ground, I've got plenty of terrific tips, tricks, and tonics to make your planting go perfectly.

Potted Perennials

If your new perennial plants or seedlings are growing in pots or flats, getting them into your garden is a snap. If possible, pick a cloudy day to do your planting, so your perennials won't be stressed out by the hot sun. Then read on for more tips.

 SPRING OR FALL? IT'S YOUR CALL!

Growing perennials in pots offers you the most flexibility when it comes time for planting, since you can set them out pretty much any time the ground isn't frozen. Early spring and early fall are ideal planting times in most areas, though. The best fall-planting conditions are a warm, long fall, followed by a hard, freezing winter. But if your area tends to see a lot of alternating freezing and thawing in winter, you would be wise to choose spring planting—it's a better bet for you and your plants.

DIVIDE AND CONQUER

Here's a super money-saving tip: Buy potted perennials at end-of-the-season sales, then bring them home and divide them before planting. By the next season, you'll have two, three, four, or even more great-looking perennials for less than the normal price of one clump!

*W*ay back when I was still a youngster, my Grandma Putt showed me how to remove a plant from a pot until I got it right. Yes, there is more to it than simply pulling on the stem! To remove a perennial from its pot, follow these three easy steps:

Step 1: Water thoroughly, or soak the whole pot in water 30 minutes before transplanting. This will help the roots hold together and slip out of the pot more easily.

Step 2: Slip one hand over the top of the pot, so the base of the plant is between your fingers.

Step 3: Tip the pot over onto that hand, then use your other hand to slide off the pot. If it doesn't come loose right away, tap it gently on a table. Whatever you do, don't tug on the stems, or you'll end up with a torn plant in your hands!

Checkered lily
Fritillaria meleagris

Spring bulb with
nodding white
or maroon bells
with deep purple
markings

 ## SERVE 'EM SOUP

Ready to plant? Dig a hole slightly larger than the width of
the pot, then remove the perennial from its pot. Use your
fingers to loosen the soil on the sides of the root ball. Place
the plant in the hole, and half fill around the roots with the
soil you removed to make the hole. Add enough water to
make a "soup," then let the water soak in for a few minutes.
(This step settles the soil and eliminates air pockets, which
can damage developing roots.) Finish filling the hole with
soil, and water again generously. Then stand back and watch
your perennials take off!

THE KINDEST CUT

When you unpot your perennials, take a good look at the
roots. If you see circling or matted roots, simply loosening
them with your fingers won't do the job. Instead, use an old
kitchen knife to cut slits 1 inch deep every 3 to 4
inches around the root ball,
from the top right down to the
base. If the roots are really tangled, you can also slice off the
whole bottom inch or two from
the root ball. That sounds harsh,
but you'll really do the plant a
favor! Cutting the roots encourages them to branch out into
the surrounding soil, where
they'll find the water and food
they need for the plant to thrive.

Mixers & Elixirs

FLOWER POWER TONIC

Whenever Grandma Putt brought a new perennial to her garden, she gave it a little extra-special TLC. First, she'd fill the hole with plenty of
organic matter, and then follow that up with a
dose of her Flower Power Tonic. That got them
up and growing on the right root!

2 lbs. of dry oatmeal
2 lbs. of crushed dry dog food
1 handful of human hair
½ cup of sugar

Mix all of these ingredients in a 5 gallon bucket.
Work a handful of this mix into the base of each
hole before planting your prized perennials.

MAKE YOUR MARK

I know it's here somewhere—
but where did it go? If that
sounds like you in the garden,
then be sure to mark each

OUT OF MY DEPTH

Proper planting depth is a key part of growing great-looking, perky perennials. But you don't have to memorize complicated depth charts. Just follow these simple guidelines for beautiful blooms year after year in your garden.

Perennials	Planting Guidelines
Most common perennials, including carnations (*Dianthus*), phlox (*Phlox*), Shasta daisies (*Chrysanthemum x superbum*)	These plants have a fibrous (many-branched) root system. They want their crown (the point where the stems and roots join) just at or a smidge above the soil surface.
Bleeding hearts (*Dicentra*), peonies (*Paeonia*)	Plant deep enough so that the tips of the new eyes (buds) are about 2 inches below ground level.
Baby's breath (*Gypsophila paniculata*), hollyhock (*Alcea rosea*)	These perennials have long taproots, so plant them with their crown just below ground level.
Bearded iris (*Iris* Bearded Hybrids)	Set the thick rhizome flush with the soil surface, because they need the kiss of the sun to thrive.

planting site with the name of the perennial you set there. Some of them start growing later in the spring than others; balloon flowers (*Platycodon grandiflorus*), for instance, are particularly late risers. If you don't know what you planted where, you may accidentally dig up something that hasn't started growing yet!

TRANSPLANTING'S AS EASY AS 1, 2, 3

Planting out perennial seedlings? First, get them acclimated to the great outdoors by setting them outside for longer periods each day over the course of a week or so. Then follow these simple steps to transplanting success:

1. Water the plants thoroughly 24 hours before transplanting them.

Transplant Tonic

½ can of beer
1 tbsp. of ammonia
1 tbsp. of instant tea granules
1 tbsp. of baby shampoo
1 gal. of water

Mix all of the ingredients together. Use 1 cup of the tonic for each perennial you are transplanting.

2. Dig a small hole, set the plant in, and gently firm the soil around the roots.

3. Water thoroughly, then give each plant a good dose of my Transplant Tonic, at left.

SEEDLINGS OVER EASY

To remove perennial seedlings growing in flats, slice downward into the soil between the plants with an old knife or narrow-bladed spatula. Lift out each plant with a block of soil surrounding its roots, and set the soil block in the planting hole. Fill in with soil and water thoroughly.

PLANTING PEAT POT PERENNIALS

When setting out perennials in peat pots, remove the top edge of the pot to prevent it from drawing water away from the roots as it dries out. Thoroughly moisten the pot and its contents to help the roots develop properly. Set the moistened pot in the planting hole, and press the soil up around it. The pot will break down in the soil and improve the soil around the plant.

No Soil? No Problem!

Have you ever bought perennials by mail? If you have, then you were probably quite surprised when all you received was a tangled mass of roots topped by a small tuft of foliage. **Fortunately, it doesn't matter how much foliage perennials have, it's the roots that count. These plants may look downright unpromising, but give them a good start, and they'll repay you with bountiful blooms for many years to come!**

TIMING IS EVERYTHING

Bare-root perennials are shipped when they are dormant (not actively growing), so their shipping season is fairly limited. Most mail-order nurseries will ship when they think it's best for your area. North of Zone 6, that's most likely early spring; in warmer areas, fall planting can work wonders. Wherever you live, the idea is to give your new perennials a generous period of mild, moist weather so that they can send out a good root system before summer's heat encourages a lot of leafy growth.

If you can't plant out your bare-root perennials within three days after they arrive, plant them in pots. Then, when you're ready to get them in your garden, plant them just like you would regular potted perennials.

MAKE THEIR BED AHEAD OF TIME

The key to success with bare-root perennials is planting them as soon as possible. So it's smart to make sure their new bed is ready and waiting well before they arrive. Otherwise, you'll be rushed to dig a new garden—and both you and your new perennials will suffer!

IN THE MEANTIME

Sometimes, despite your best-laid plans, you might not be able to plant your new bare-root perennials immediately. What then? At least open the box and inspect the shipment. Open the wrappings around each plant and check the roots. If the packing material around the roots seems dry, sprinkle it with a little water, then loosely rewrap the roots. Keep the packing material slightly damp and the plants out of the sun.

Christmas fern
Polystichum acrostichoides

Clumps of evergreen foliage for year-round interest in shade

➤ FIVE STEPS TO PLANTING SUCCESS

Ready to plant? Remove the wrappings around your bare-root perennials, as well as any packing materials, then follow these simple steps:

1. Clip off any broken or discolored roots cleanly with sharp shears, then soak the remaining roots in my Root Revival Tonic (at left) for one day before planting.

2. Dig a planting hole that's large enough to hold all the roots without bending them.

3. If the plant has many roots, replace some of the soil to make a mound in the center of the hole. The top of the mound should be close to the level of the surrounding soil, so the plant's crown (where the top growth joins the roots) will be at the right level after planting. Spread the roots as evenly as possible over the mound, then fill in around the roots with the remaining soil.

4. If the plant has one main root, hold the crown at the right level with one hand while you fill in around the root with the soil you removed from the hole.

5. After planting, firm the soil around the crown, then water the plant generously.

➤ LET THE SUN SHINE

If you buy bearded irises by mail, look for them to arrive in late summer as bare-root rhizomes with relatively close-cropped leaves. These thick, fleshy roots call for a slightly different planting strategy than other bare-root perennials—be sure to expose the rhizomes to sunlight to help them

---

Mixers & Elixirs

ROOT REVIVAL TONIC

¼ cup of brewed tea
1 tbsp. of dishwashing liquid
1 tbsp. of Epsom salts
1 gal. of water

Let bare-root plants sit in this tonic for up to 24 hours. This will revive the plants and get them up and rarin' to grow.

Clustered
bellflower
*Campanula
glomerata*

Clusters of
purplish blue
blooms atop
tall stems

grow. (See "Tuber U" on page 271 for more information on rhizomes, bulbs, corms, and tubers.)

First, dig a hole wide enough to accommodate each long rhizome, then build up a little ridge of soil in the center of the hole. Set the rhizome flat on top of the ridge, so it is about even with the soil surface in the rest of the garden. Let the smaller roots hang downward, spreading them out on each side of the ridge as best you can. Holding the rhizome in place with one hand, scoop soil back into each side of the ridge to cover the roots (but not the rhizome) and pack it down firmly.

Bulb-Planting Basics

If the promise of a colorful spring garden finds you out-of-doors on a crisp November day, don't be daunted by the bushels of daffodil bulbs, boxes of tulip bulbs, and bags and bags of teeny-weeny crocus corms all around you. With the right tools, tucking away those bulbs for the winter will be a snap!

➤ HANDLE WITH CARE

Bulbs may not look like they are alive, but inside each one is a small-but-perfect plant waiting to bloom—unless it gets treated too

Mixers & Elixirs

BULB BATH

To keep your bulbs bug-free, treat them to a nice warm bath before putting them into their planting bed. Here's what you'll need:

2 tsp. of baby shampoo
1 tsp. of antiseptic mouthwash
¼ tsp. of instant tea granules
2 gal. of warm water

Mix all of the ingredients in a bucket, then carefully place your bulbs into the mixture. Stir gently, then remove the bulbs one at a time and plant them. When you're done, don't throw the bath water out with the babies. Your trees, shrubs, and evergreens would love a little taste, so don't let it go to waste.

Columbine
Aquilegia hybrid

Long-spurred,
early-summer
flowers in a
rainbow of colors

roughly. Never handle bulbs carelessly or drop them into the bottom of a box or shopping bag; you'll bruise more than their egos, and chances are, they won't recover.

THROW IN THE TROWEL

A sturdy garden trowel makes a super-handy bulb planter. To use it like the pros do, grab the handle so the inner curve of the blade faces you, pointing downward. Then stab straight down into the soil like you're using an ice pick. (When plunged to the hilt, the blade should sink to about 8 inches, the perfect depth for planting larger bulbs.) Just pull back on the trowel to open a pocket in the soil, tuck the bulb in with the pointed end up, remove the trowel, and smooth the soil down. This technique allows you to get a good rhythm going and plant a lot of bulbs in a short period of time.

TOOL TIME

Sold in garden centers and nursery catalogs, bulb planters come in two versions: a handheld planter and a stand-up model with a long handle. Both make it easy to dig neat, circular holes of the proper depth for bulbs. Their cone shape pulls out a plug of soil as you withdraw the tool. You just plop the bulb in the hole and replace the soil. Some gardeners swear by their bulb planters, while others think they're too much fuss. Why not try one on for size and see for yourself?

TRENCH 'EM

Have more than a handful of bulbs to plant? Things will go much quicker if you dig one larger hole that can hold several bulbs, instead of many smaller holes. Use a trowel or spade to dig a trench to the proper depth. (Hint: If you place the soil on a sheet of plastic until you're ready to replace it in the trench, you'll make a neater job of it!) Then place the bulbs in neat, evenly spaced patterns, and replace the soil.

BEAUTIFUL BULBS *AU NATUREL*

One fun planting technique for bulbs is called "naturalizing," which means planting them in grassy areas (like your lawn). It works great for small bulbs such as crocuses, as well as some larger ones, like daffodils. Here are two easy planting techniques to try:

❧ Stick the blade of a spade a few inches deep into your lawn, then push forward on the handle to open a pocket. Tuck a few bulbs in the pocket, slide out the spade to close the pocket, and step on the area to firm the soil back down.

❧ Use your spade to cut three sides of a square in the turf. Peel back the grass "carpet" (the uncut side will act like a hinge), plant the bulbs in the exposed soil, then roll the sod back into place and firm it with your foot.

BEST BULB-PLANTING DEPTHS

Use these planting depth guidelines to help ensure a beautiful batch of blooming bulbs.

Bulb	Planting Depth	Bulb	Planting Depth
Checkered lily (*Fritillaria meleagris*)	4-5"	Grecian windflower (*Anemone blanda*)	3-4"
Crocus (*Crocus*)	3-4"	Hyacinth (*Hyacinthus orientalis*)	4-6"
Crown imperial (*Fritillaria imperialis*)	6-8"	Lilies (*Lilium*)	3 times the diameter of the bulb
Daffodils (*Narcissus*)	5-7"	Siberian squill (*Scilla siberica*)	3"
Drumstick allium (*Allium sphaerocephalon*)	4-5"	Snowdrop (*Galanthus nivalis*)	3-4"
Dutch iris (*Iris* Dutch Hybrids)	4-6"	Striped squill (*Puschkinia scilloides*)	3"
Giant onion (*Allium giganteum*)	7-8"	Summer snowflake (*Leucojum aestivum*)	4-5"
Glory-of-the-snow (*Chionodoxa luciliae*)	3-4"	Tulips (*Tulipa*)	6-8"
Grape hyacinth (*Muscari armeniacum*)	3-4"	Wood hyacinth (*Hyacinthoides hispanica*)	3"

Mixers & Elixirs

BULB BREAKFAST

10 lbs. of compost
5 lbs. of bonemeal
2 lbs. of bloodmeal
1 lb. of Epsom salts

Mix all of the ingredients together in a wheelbarrow. Before setting out your bulbs, work this hearty breakfast into every 100 square feet of soil in your bulb-planting areas.

Don't neglect individually planted bulbs, either. Work a handful of compost and a teaspoon of bonemeal into the soil in each hole before setting in the bulb.

Columbine
meadowrue
*Thalictrum
aquilegifolium*

Tall stems topped
with purple-pink
clouds in late
spring and early
summer

BIT BY BIT

My all-time favorite bulb-planting tool is a planter bit. It looks like a huge drill bit, and it fits any ⅜-inch or larger electric drill. This bit makes a perfect 3-inch-round hole so quick, you won't believe it! Planter bits are available from garden catalogs or from my website, www.jerrybaker.com.

GROUND 'EM!

Don't keep tulips, daffodils, hyacinths, and other spring-blooming bulbs past the fall season to plant in spring, because they won't flower for you. They need a good, long time to settle in and get their roots established before they bloom, so get them in the ground in fall to have beautiful flowers in the spring!

ASHES ARE THE ANSWER

If you have a fireplace in your home and have been wondering what to do with the ashes, try this—add them to your bulb bed before you plant. You can apply up to 15 pounds of ashes per 100 square feet. They're a great source of potassium, which'll help your bulbs develop good, strong stems that don't need staking.

LAYER BULBS FOR LONGEST BLOOM

Want several months of beautiful bulb blooms without tearing up your whole garden to plant them? Try digging up just one area and planting several layers of bulbs in the same spot, with late bloomers at the bottom and early risers near the top. Here's how:

1. Dig a planting area about 8 inches deep. Set in the bulbs of the latest bloomers you've chosen (usually late tulips or lilies).

2. Put back enough soil to barely cover the tips of those bulbs, then set in the next layer (early and midseason tulips work well here, and so do daffodils).

3. Repeat the process of adding more soil, then setting in the top layer of smaller bulbs (perhaps a mix of snow crocuses for super-early color and squills for a little later).

4. Finish by mulching with leaves, shredded bark, or wood chips, and scatter moth crystals over the top to keep the varmints away.

Grandma Putt's WISDOM

I remember spending many a fall day on my hands and knees, helping Grandma Putt plant bulbs that would bring beautiful color in the spring. She always told me to make sure the bottom of each bulb was in firm contact with the bottom of its planting hole. If it isn't, then there will be an air pocket between the two. The roots won't develop properly, and the bulb will rot—a sad return for all that effort!

CHAPTER 5

NEW GARDEN— NOW WHAT?

You've got your new perennials and bulbs in the ground—good for you! Now what do you do? Read on, my friends, for a few more practical pointers on getting your new plantings off to a great start.

Post-Planting Hints and Tips

After putting all that time and effort into planning and planting your new flower garden, of course you want it to look its best. Here are some ideas for immediate after-planting care, as well as some suggestions for sprucing up the area for good looks and easier maintenance all season long.

Common
blue violet
Viola papilionacea

A spring-flowering
cutie with delicate
purple-blue
blooms

➤ PUT ON THEIR SHADES

Hopefully, you picked a cloudy day to plant your new garden, so your perennials were spared the stress of hot sun on their first day. But if the next few days bring strong sunshine, your plants would really appreciate some shade, especially if they've already leafed out and are actively growing. (If you've set out bare-root plants or bulbs, post-planting shade isn't an issue, because they are underground.)

To shield newly planted perennials, cover each one with a sheet of newspaper (weigh down the edges with rocks so the paper doesn't blow away). Or set a bushel basket, or some other slatted cover, over each clump. You want the plants to get some light—just not strong, all-day sun. After two or three days, it's okay to remove the covers; your perennials should be able to take on the sun by then.

➤ KEEP THE WATER COMING

Watering new plantings is undoubtedly the most important step in getting perennial plants off to a good start. If you don't get any rain, you may need to water every day for the first week. After that, cut down to every three to four days for several weeks, then water your plants once a week for the rest of the growing season.

GOT WATER?

What if you don't have time to water your new garden every day? A plastic milk jug with a few tiny holes punched in the base makes a handy temporary irrigation system. Simply set one perforated jug next to each new plant, fill each jug with water, and replace the cap. Refill the jugs every day or two.

➤ PILE IT ON!

Mulching your new flower garden will go a long way toward minimizing future maintenance. Besides keeping the soil cool and evenly moist—which encourages great root growth—mulches smother weed seeds. And, if any weeds do pop through, they'll be easy to pull from the loose soil. For extra benefit, spread a 1-inch layer of compost first (this will give your perennials and bulbs a nice nutrient boost). Top that with another 1 to 2 inches of organic mulch, such as shredded bark, pine needles, or chopped leaves.

JERRY'S GEMS

When applying mulches, avoid piling them right against the stems of your perennials; otherwise, these moisture-holding materials can cause stems to rot. To be safe, leave a mulch-free zone about 2 inches out from the base of each plant.

➤ MULCHING MADE EASY

Mulching can certainly save you lots of labor in the long run, but it can also take a fair amount of time to mulch a new garden—especially if you're mulching large areas with many small plants. To make the job go faster, set an upside-down flowerpot over each plant, then use a shovel or pitchfork to toss the mulch evenly over the whole area. Remove all the pots, and you have a perfectly mulched garden in a snap!

Common yarrow
Achillea millefolium

Flat-topped flower clusters in summer; super for cutting

Feed Me!

Newly planted perennials have limited root systems, so they may not be able to search out all the nutrients they need. You can help them along by feeding them regularly through their first growing season. Regular doses of a liquid fertilizer, such as my Perennial Planting Potion (at right), will provide a generous supply of food for healthy, first-year growth.

NAME THAT PERENNIAL

What are you supposed to do with all those name tags that come with your perennials? It's easy to toss them out or lose them—after all, you'll remember what you've planted, right? Well, take it from me: You won't remember for as long a time as you think you will! If you're really organized, make up a gardening notebook to hold your planting plan, then tape all the plant tags to the pages. Not only will you know exactly what you've planted and where it is, but you'll also have a handy place to keep notes about each plant's performance.

Not quite that organized? Then at least keep the tags with your perennials as you plant them. I like to stick them in deep, so only the top $1/2$ to 1 inch of the label is above the soil. They seem to last longer that way, and you won't be looking at a forest of plastic labels while waiting for your perennials to fill in.

Mixers & Elixirs

PERENNIAL PLANTING POTION

To get your perennials growing on the right foot, feed them this potion:

$1/2$ can of beer
$1/4$ cup of ammonia
2 tbsp. of hydrogen peroxide
1 tbsp. of dishwashing liquid
2 gal. of warm water

Mix all of the ingredients together. Pour the potion into the planting holes, and sprinkle it over your blooming beauties throughout the summer.

LIVING ON THE EDGE

There's nothing like a nice, neat edge to make even a new flower garden look great. The most popular type of edging starts as a simple trench, typically 2 to 4 inches wide and 4 to 5 inches deep, between the flowerbed and the lawn. Using a square-edged spade or long-handled, half-moon edging tool, dig straight down along the outer edge of the garden to remove the soil and create the trench. For even more protection from creeping lawn grasses, dig the trench slightly deeper, then slip a metal or plastic edging strip along the edge so that its top is about an inch below the surface of the lawn.

First-Year Fillers

Planting a new perennial garden is lots of fun, but it's even more enjoyable seeing it in all its glory, with loads of knock-your-socks-off blooms. Newly planted beds of properly spaced perennials can be a little sparse, though, so to get them looking good quicker, consider some of these surefire strategies for fast results.

TOP 10 First-Year Flowers

Ageratum
(*Ageratum houstonianum*)

Cleome
(*Cleome hasslerana*)

Cosmos
(*Cosmos*)

Flowering tobacco
(*Nicotiana*)

Impatiens
(*Impatiens*)

Mealy-cup sage
(*Salvia farinacea*)

Rose periwinkle
(*Catharanthus roseus*)

Snapdragons
(*Antirrhinum majus*)

Verbenas
(*Verbena*)

Zinnias
(*Zinnia*)

ANNUALS TO THE RESCUE

Keep in mind the cardinal rule of perennials: First year they sleep, second year they creep, and third year they leap. The first year, you probably won't see much activity, because your plants will be busy setting down their roots. The second year will bring more blooms, but it takes until the third year to get that flower-filled, lush perennial garden you were hoping for. So, remember two words: Be patient!

To get through the first few lean years, turn your attention to those old garden standbys, flowering and foliage annuals. Available in an amazing array of heights and colors, annuals make perfect temporary fillers while you're waiting for your perennials to do their thing.

LEAF THEM ALONE

When choosing annuals as fillers, don't over-look the possibilities of having fun with foliage. In sunny spots, the silvery leaves of dusty millers (*Senecio cineraria*) make a great accent against any other foliage or flower color. In shadier spots, the multi-colored leaves of coleus (*Coleus blumei*) can be fun for brightening up the gloom!

 SAMPLE SOME SELF-SOWERS

Self-sowing annuals can be especially useful for filling bare spots in new perennial plantings. These generous beauties will pop up wherever there's room, then gradually die out after a few years, when the perennials have filled in and covered the soil. Good choices for freely seeding fillers include love-in-a-mist (*Nigella damascena*), Brazilian vervain (*Verbena bonariensis*), and larkspur (*Consolida ajacis*).

VEGGIES ON THE SIDE

Why not have your new perennial garden do double duty for a couple of years? First-year fillers don't *have* to be flowers: Edibles, like vegetables and herbs, can look great among perennials, too! For veggies, try 'Bright Lights' Swiss chard for its colorful, upright leaf clumps, or a lower-growing but equally good-looking red-leaved lettuce, such as 'Red Sails'. Eggplants and peppers both offer colorful and tasty fruits, while cherry tomatoes can be beautiful at the back of the border. Among herbs, purple-leaved basils, like 'Purple Ruffles', are fabulous for foliage color, while dill and pot marigolds (*Calendula officinalis*) provide loads of flowers.

BE AN ARTFUL GARDENER

New perennial planting beds can be super places to show off a few pieces of fun garden art. Let your imagination run wild—"plant" a mirrored-glass gazing ball, a whimsical wooden cutout of a kneeling gardener, or even a collection of old watering cans along with your perennials. Don't use anything so big that it will shade out the plants, of course, but beyond that, the possibilities are endless! As the perennials fill in, move the decorative items to other areas of your yard so you can enjoy them in a different setting.

Try This!

I f you can afford to buy some extra perennials right off the bat, consider setting the clumps closer than you normally would at planting time, so they'll fill in faster. At the end of the first or second year, lift the clumps, replant some of them, and use the extras to make a new garden in another spot.

Coral bells
Heuchera sanguinea

Clumps of
evergreen foliage
and spikes of
coral-red bells
in summer

PART 2

LET'S GET GROWING!

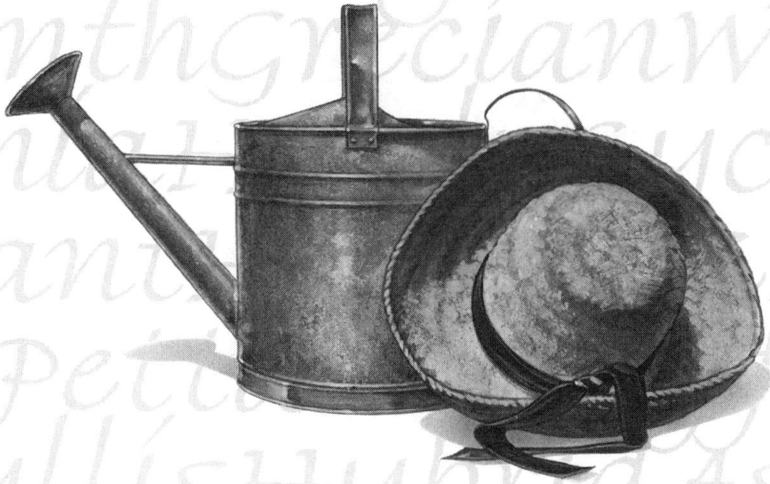

CHAPTER 6

FEEDIN', WEEDIN', AND WATERIN'

I'm sure you know that a successful perennial garden needs love and attention long after the planting's done. So as you wander down your garden path, take a good long look at your plants to see how those beautiful bulbs and perky perennials are doing. Then take a look through this chapter to find out how to give your garden beauties the tender loving care they need to produce bright, bountiful blooms.

Mulch Magic

What if you could minimize weeding and watering, improve your soil, encourage good growth during the summer, and protect your perennials in winter with just one simple step? Sound too good to be true? Well, it's not! All you need is a little mulch!

 WHAT'S THAT MULCH?

There's nothing like nicely mulched flowerbeds to give your yard that professionally landscaped look. Here's how to use some of the most common mulch materials:

Grass clippings: Spread them regularly in thin layers (up to 1 inch at a time) over your perennial gardens to a depth of 3 to 4 inches, or mix them with leaves and spread them all at one time.

Leaves: Deciduous leaves make a great-looking mulch for flower gardens. Evergreen needles can also be useful, but they take longer to decay. Pine needles are nice because they are usually soft to the touch; sharp spruce needles can be really unpleasant when you have to work in the soil!

Chipped or shredded woody waste: Spread this material about 3 inches deep for a good-looking, long-lasting mulch.

 BE SAFE—WAIT

Grass clippings are plentiful and free, and they make a marvelous mulch for all parts of your garden. One word of advice, though—don't use clippings from lawns that have been recently treated with an herbicide, or you run the risk of killing off your perennials. Wait four weeks—ideally, six

Crested iris
Iris cristata

Spreading carpets of spiky green leaves and blue spring blooms; great for shade

One secret I've learned over the years is that a 3- to 4-inch-deep layer of grass clippings will save you a heck of a lot of work and water in your planting beds. But before you mulch with clippings, put down newspaper (about three layers of individual sheets) to act as a weed barrier and help retain water.

TOOL TIME

One of the few modern yard luxuries I allow myself is a leaf shredder. I really enjoy shredding up leaves to make a nice mulch for my perennials and bulbs. I heartily recommend getting one, if you can afford it. If not, then you can always spread the leaves out on your lawn and mow over them with your lawn mower. You'll get the same result at a fraction of the cost!

weeks or more—before you collect clippings from a treated lawn to use as mulch.

WEED OUT THE WEEDS

Yes, mulch is great for minimizing future weeding—but don't expect it to get rid of the weeds that have already laid claim to your garden. Careful weeding, particularly of troublesome perennials like dandelions, quack grass, and thistles, is a must before you apply any mulch. Otherwise, these pesky plants will come right up through the mulch, and you'll just have to deal with them later on.

MULCH GROWS ON TREES

One of the best mulches for flower gardens is chopped-up leaves. They are loose and fluffy, so they won't pack down like whole leaves can, they look good, and they break down readily into soil-building humus. But best of all, they're readily available—and free!

If the trees in your yard don't generate enough fallen leaves, don't be shy about asking your neighbors to dump their leaves in your yard. You'll be glad you did—and so will they!

Crimson flag
Schizostylis coccinea

Starry red, late-summer flowers; ideal for wet spots in warm climates

Don't Pile It On

Whichever mulch you choose to use, be careful not to pile it against the crowns of your perennials, or it may cause them to rot. To be safe, keep these moisture-holding materials at least 2 inches away from the base of the stems.

MUCH ADO ABOUT MULCH

To get the most benefit from mulch, you need to use an *organic* material—something that's derived from a living, or formerly living, thing. This includes chopped leaves, compost, pine needles, wood-based mulches, and so on. Don't be tempted to use gravel or crushed stone as a mulch in your flower garden. Rock mulches may look nice at first, but they'll make later maintenance a pain in the neck. (Just imagine trying to dig up and divide the perennials or plant more bulbs with all those rocks around!) Plus, rock-based mulches won't add nutrients or humus to your soil like organic mulches will.

> ### Mixers & Elixirs
>
> #### ROOT-ROUSING TONIC
>
> *1 can of beer*
> *1 can of regular cola (not diet)*
> *1 cup of dishwashing liquid*
> *1 cup of antiseptic mouthwash*
> *$1/4$ tsp. of instant tea granules*
>
> Mix all of the ingredients in a large bucket, then pour into a 20 gallon hose-end sprayer and spray liberally over all of your flowerbeds.

One exception to this rule is mulching around lavender plants. These Mediterranean herbs demand good drainage and don't appreciate the extra moisture from organic mulches. A 1-inch layer of white sand or gravel right around the base of each lavender plant will help keep these aromatic herbs healthy and dry.

PEST CONTROL UNDERCOVER

I'm going to let you in on a little professional landscaping secret—it really doesn't matter what type of wood chips, bark chunks, or shavings you use in your flowerbeds, as long as you put shredded cedar or eucalyptus mulch underneath them! For some reason, these aromatic woods seem to discourage insects from setting up shop when they're either worked into the soil or laid on top of it. After mulching your beds with these or any other wood-based mulches, overspray the beds with my Root-Rousing Tonic (above) to feed the roots underneath.

Hold Off on Peat Moss

One organic material that *doesn't* make a good mulch is peat moss. When it dries out, it forms a tight crust that actually prevents water from reaching the soil, and it takes practically forever to get wet again. So save your peat moss for working into the soil *before* planting, where it will do the most good.

MULCHES, MULCHES EVERYWHERE!

Sometimes, the best mulches turn up where you least expect them! Sure, you can find conveniently bagged bark mulch at your local garden center or make your own chopped leaf mulch and compost at home. But how about asking your barber for the hair trimmings he sweeps up from his floor each day? Or maybe you have a chocolate factory nearby, which is a great source of cocoa bean hulls, or a nut-processing business for a ready supply of peanut shells. These locally available materials are often much cheaper than bagged mulches, since you aren't paying for any shipping costs.

DON'T BABY YOUR BULBS

Bulbs need low temperatures to develop good roots and buds. So don't mulch them too early, or you'll cause premature leaf growth, which will weaken them. New plantings of tulips and daffodils benefit the most from mulching; older beds, in milder climates, really don't need it.

YOU'VE GOT MULCH!

One plentiful—and free—source of mulch material is as close as your mailbox! Shredded junk mail, office paper, and newspapers all make super mulches for your flower garden. Spread a layer of shredded paper up to 3 inches thick, then top it with a better-looking mulch to improve the appearance and keep the paper from blowing away. The local earthworms will love you!

TIMING IS EVERYTHING

The best time to mulch your perennials is after a heavy rain, but before the weather gets too hot. Never apply mulch when the ground is dry. If you do, the mulch will absorb any rainwater that happens to come along and allow it to evaporate before it can soak into the soil, where it will do the most good.

Make the Most of Compost

Any organic gardener will tell you that compost is the best darn, humus-building material you can give your perennial garden! There are as many ways to make compost as there are gardeners who make it. But don't let that scare you away from giving composting a try. The important thing isn't so much *how* you do it but *that* you do it! The composting tips in this section will get you on track to making that perfect batch of "black gold."

COMPOST CAN-DO

Composting is the process of turning clippings, leaves, and other yard and garden materials into a rich soil additive for use in gardens or around plants and shrubs. There's really nothing to it—just pile up lawn trimmings, vegetable parings, and other organic refuse, and wait for it to decompose. Compost piles work by generating heat and biological activity to decay organic materials. In return for your efforts, you

Crocosmia
Crocosmia x
crocosmiiflora

Clumps of
can't-miss color for
late-summer beds
and borders

get a great multipurpose garden booster! Here's just a few of the fabulous benefits of compost:

✔ Helps sandy soil hold more water

✔ Breaks up clay soil, improving drainage

✔ Makes a super mulch

✔ Provides a small but steady supply of nutrients to your growing plants

✔ Builds up humus levels in the soil

✔ Makes a great addition to potting soil for all your container perennials

Mixers & Elixirs

COMPOST BOOSTER

1 can of beer
1 can of regular cola (not diet)
1 cup of ammonia
½ cup of weak tea water*
2 tbsp. of baby shampoo

Pour this mixture into your 20 gallon hose-end sprayer, and saturate your compost pile every time you add a new foot of ingredients to it. This'll really get things cookin'!

*Soak a used tea bag in a mix of 1 gallon of warm water and 1 teaspoon of dishwashing liquid until the mix is light brown.

THE COLORS OF COMPOST

To get the best compost, you need to mix balanced amounts of high-nitrogen ("green") materials along with high-carbon ("brown") materials. Here's a quick rundown to help you keep track:

Greens: Coffee grounds, fruit wastes, grass clippings, hair, green leaves, manures, seaweed, vegetable scraps, eggshells, and weeds.

Browns: Corncobs, cornstalks, dead flower and vegetable stalks, hay, shredded paper, pine needles, sawdust, and straw.

COMPOST OVER EASY

Turn over your compost pile every 10 days to two weeks with a pitchfork; at a minimum, you should turn it over at least three times during a season. When the mix is dark and crumbly, it's ready to use in your garden!

COMPOST KNOW-HOW

You can put just about any material in your compost pile as long as you keep turning it often enough to let the airborne bacteria get at it. Before long, your pile will heat up, which not only will help with the decomposition, but also will eliminate a lot of the odors. Here are things you can (and should) add to your compost pile, as well as materials you definitely should *not* include.

Compost These

- ☑ Bonemeal
- ☑ Coffee grounds
- ☑ Eggshells
- ☑ Farm animal manure
- ☑ Fish scraps
- ☑ Granite dust
- ☑ Grass clippings
- ☑ Leaves
- ☑ Rock phosphate
- ☑ Seaweed
- ☑ Soft prunings
- ☑ Soil
- ☑ Used tea leaves and tea bags
- ☑ Vegetable and fruit peels and scraps
- ☑ Young weeds

Do NOT Compost These

- ☑ Diseased or pest-infested plants (which will only spread the problem wherever you use the compost)
- ☑ Dog and cat droppings (which can carry diseases that can spread to humans)
- ☑ Oils, fats, or meat products
- ☑ Poisonous plants (like poison ivy)
- ☑ Weeds that have gone to seed (You'll end up spreading weed seeds with your compost!)

Crown imperial
Fritillaria imperialis

Clusters of yellow or orange bells topped with a tuft of green leaves; a real attention-getter

STEP-BY-STEP COMPOST SUCCESS

Never made compost before and not sure where to start? Follow these simple steps for top-quality compost:

Step 1: Dig up the sod in an area that's 3 to 4 feet square, turn it over, and then wet the area slightly.

Step 2: Using chicken wire or square-mesh wire fencing, build a circular or square-sided bin the same size as your dug-up area to keep your compost materials in place.

Step 3: Build the bottom layer of the pile out of sod or grass clippings, making it about 6 inches high.

Step 4: On top of the sod or clippings, spread a layer of straw, chopped leaves, or other "brown" material about 4 inches thick, and saturate it to the point of run-off.

Step 5: Spread a 2-inch-thick layer of grass clippings, farm animal manure, or other "green" material on top of the "brown" layer.

Step 6: Top that with an inch-thick layer of topsoil.

Mixers & Elixirs

COMPOST TEA

This solution is great as an all-around perennial pick-me-up. Simply put several shovelsful of compost or manure into a large trash can, and fill the can to the top with water. Allow the mixture to sit for seven days, stirring it several times each day. To use, dilute with water until it is light brown. Give each plant about a cup of this tea every two weeks, and your feeding worries will be over!

Keep alternating the layers of brown/green/topsoil until your compost pile is about 4 feet tall. Keep the pile moist, but not soggy, and cover it with a sheet of black plastic so that the nutrients don't leach out. Add a can of beer or regular cola (not diet) for each 5 bushels of material to jump-start the process, or sprinkle the pile occasionally with my Compost Booster (see page 76).

NOT TOO WET, NOT TOO DRY

A compost pile that's too dry won't heat up and decompose. And if it's too wet, it'll smell. My general rule is to keep your compost pile as wet as a damp sponge. If it gets too wet, mix in an armful or two of dry material, such as chopped leaves or straw.

🪣 SMOOTH OR CHUNKY?

"Chunky" compost is fine for digging into the soil or using as mulch for your perennials and bulbs. But if you want finer material for adding to perennial potting soil, build a basic sifter and use it to screen out the lumps. My sifter is a 3-foot by 2-foot frame made of two-by-fours with a piece of wire mesh stapled to the bottom. I lay the sifter across the top of my wheelbarrow, toss in a shovelful of compost, and shake the sifter to separate the coarse and fine material. Toss the coarse stuff into an in-progress compost pile.

🪣 BIN THERE, DONE THAT

For some folks, their compost pile is just that—a pile. Others prefer to corral their compost materials in a tidy bin. Besides making things look neater, a bin can help speed up the composting process. Either way, it's best to place your composting zone in an area that's out of sight of both you and your neighbors, but still within easy reach of your house and garden. Don't place your compost pile too near trees, or their roots will quickly take over your pile! Plan on having at least two piles or bins—and ideally three—going at any given time: one being built, one "cooking," and one ready to use.

🪣 COMPOST CONCEALER

Need a way to camouflage your compost? Surround it with a hedge of evergreens or tall perennials, or place a trellis around it and train ornamental vines, such as clematis, morning glories, or gourds to grow over the sides.

Cyclamen
daffodil
*Narcissus
cyclamineus*

Gracefully nodding
yellow or white
trumpets in spring

Try This!

Need compost in a hurry? Smaller pieces compost much more quickly, so run all of your compost ingredients through a shredder before adding them to the pile. This simple step can cut composting time dramatically—from two to three months down to two or three weeks!

🪣 BIN BASICS

My favorite material for easy bin building is sections of chain-link fencing, but you can use flexible wire fencing, concrete blocks, boards, discarded shipping pallets, or whatever's handy. Whatever you use, having air spaces in the sides is a must. Figure on a bin that's about 4 feet tall, wide, and high. Be sure to leave one side open (or make it removable) for easy access to the compost. You will also need a cover for your bin. A sheet of exterior plywood, painted or wrapped in plastic, will last three or four years; a plastic tarp alone will last a year or two.

Drinks All Around!

Just like people, plants need water to survive. But there's a right way to water your perennials and bulbs, and there's a wrong way. Watering them wisely can make the difference between a lush garden brimming with blooms, and a pathetic patch of weeds with a few scrawny flowers struggling to survive. My tried-and-true watering techniques will help keep your beautiful bulbs and perfect perennials alive and kicking!

🪣 WEATHER-WISE WATERING

Watering wisely means paying attention to your plants, instead of just dumping water on them on a set schedule. A general rule of thumb is that perennials need 1 to 1½ inches of water every seven to 10 days, either from rain or from irrigation. If you get a rainy spell, or a week or two of

Daffodil
Narcissus hybrid

A spring classic with yellow, white, pink, or orange trumpets; yellow or white petals cloudy weather, you probably won't have to worry about watering at all. But if the weather is hot and sunny, or if a stiff breeze sets up for a few days, you'll have to water much more often.

SOAK, DON'T SPRINKLE

The first rule of wise watering is to make sure you water deeply. Frequent, shallow watering does more harm than good, because it encourages your perennials to keep their roots close to the soil surface. This can mean trouble during prolonged dry spells!

So whenever you water your perennials and bulbs, slow and steady is the key. Thoroughly soak the top 6 inches of soil, then hold off on further watering until the top 2 inches dry out again. This will encourage your plants to send their roots down deep, so they'll be better able to deal with whatever dry weather Mother Nature sends your way.

HOLD OFF ON THE HOSE

The *least* effective method for watering your perennial garden is with a handheld hose nozzle or watering can. Watering with a nozzle can really tear up the soil surface, getting your flowers all dirty, and causing crusting when the soil dries. And more often than not, either method can result in poor water distribution over your garden—some plants get watered too much, while others are missed completely. Plus, they both require a very patient person to do as thorough a job as a soaker hose or oscillating sprinkler would do. Who really wants to spend half a day standing around with a hose in their hand, or running back and forth from the spigot to the garden with a watering can? I'm sure we can all think of better things to do!

Try This!

The secret to knowing *when* to water is right at your feet! To check the soil moisture, pull back the mulch in a small area, then dig down a few inches with your trowel. If the top 2 inches are dry, it's time to water. Don't wait until your perennials start wilting to water them: In time, that will lead to poor flowering, discolored foliage, and stunted growth. And the result of all that is a pretty pathetic perennial garden!

SHAKE YOUR BLOOMERS

If your flowers get wet from rain or watering, it's smart to shake them gently to remove the water. Otherwise, the droplets can cause spotting on the petals (especially on light-colored flowers), and the moisture can encourage disease development on the buds and blooms.

*G*randma Putt always made it a point to water her flower gardens in the morning. That way, they were juiced up and ready to handle the heat of the day. Plus, she explained to me, morning-watered plants have ample time to dry off before bedtime. She knew that perennials and bulbs that go to bed wet are far more likely to develop disease problems down the road than dry plants will!

SPRINKLER SECRET

If you decide to water your perennial garden with a sprinkler, use what professional landscapers use—an oscillating type. These sprinklers cover a large area and produce rain-like drops of water. Don't use a rotating sprinkler—it tends to break up the soil surface and covers only a small area. Run your sprinkler for at least four hours in each area to give the soil a good soaking.

SOAK THE SOIL, NOT THE STEMS

When we talk about watering our plants, what we should really be talking about is watering the soil around our plants. *This* is where the water really counts, not on the leaves! And the best way to get the water right to the soil is with a soaker hose.

Soaker hoses are the easiest type of watering system to install. They look similar to regular garden hoses, but are usually black, with many tiny holes in their walls. When you attach them to a regular hose and turn on the spigot, water gently oozes out and soaks a 2- to 3-foot-wide area along the length of the hose.

It's easiest to lay soaker hose in early spring, before your perennials and bulbs are up and growing. You can snake it back and forth among the clumps in a serpentine pattern, or run the hose along the front edge of the bed— about 18 inches in from the edge—then give it a U-turn and run it back to the other end of the bed. Cover the hose with mulch to hide it from view. At the end of the season, simply lift, drain, and store the hose indoors for the winter.

BULBS NEED WATER, TOO!

Most years, there's enough rain in the spring to provide spring-flowering bulbs with the water they need to send up their beautiful blooms. But if Mother Nature is stingy with the April showers, or if she's feeling sulky and cooks up a prolonged dry spell, you'll have to help out your bulbs by supplying the water yourself. Even after spring bulbs have stopped blooming, they're still producing foliage. If those leaves dry out and die before they mature properly, your bulbs will put on a poor show next year. Whatever you do, don't be a fair-weather friend and neglect your bulbs after they've done their best for you!

HOLD YOUR HOSE

To keep your soaker hose where you want it, secure it to the ground with upside-down U-shaped pieces of wire coat hanger. Simply cut off the hook and "neck" where the wires come together, then make another cut in the middle of the long side of the hanger. You'll end up with two large wire "hairpins." Push these pins down over the hose and into the soil to hold the hose firmly in place.

Daffodil garlic
Allium neopolitanum

Clusters of sweetly scented white flowers in late spring; nice as a cut flower

JERRY'S GEMS

It's important to thoroughly check out your entire watering system at the start of each growing season. It's easy for a bit of dirt or other debris to find its way into a soaker hose and clog one or more of the holes. Plus, sprinkler heads can quickly become clogged by hard-water deposits (soak these parts in vinegar to remove the caked-on minerals). If you give everything the once-over in spring, as I do, you'll be in great shape to keep your perennials and bulbs well-watered all season long.

Feeding for Fabulous Flowers

Keeping your perennials and bulbs at their bountiful best takes more than water, of course—they need food, too. The key here is moderation, though; you don't want to overdo it. Simply pick the right food or tonic for the plants you're growing, apply it properly, and then be prepared for the best-looking flowers on the block!

FERTILIZER 101

Just what do those mysterious numbers on fertilizer bags mean? Well, they're *not* the odds on your flowers living or dying! They simply indicate the percentages of nitrogen, phosphorus, and potash in the mix. For example, if the label says 5-10-5, that means the fertilizer has 5 parts nitrogen to 10 parts phosphorus to 5 parts potash (or, in other words, twice as much phosphorus as nitrogen and potash). Here's why these nutrients are important for your perennials and bulbs:

• **Nitrogen** promotes vigorous leaf growth, helps in chlorophyll formation, and is a building block for protein.

• **Phosphorus** hastens plant maturity, promotes cell division, stimulates healthy root formation, and plays an important part in other vital plant processes.

• **Potash** is essential for photosynthesis, strengthens plant tissues, and provides disease resistance and winter hardiness.

ONE FOOD FOR ALL

I'm often asked if there is any one fertilizer that's good for all flowers. The answer is yes—any garden food that's low in nitrogen and high in phosphorus and potash will do the trick. For beautiful bulbs and perennials, add some bonemeal to the soil, too. During the growing season, you can also add liquified table scraps (see "Daily Drink from the Kitchen Sink," at right) to your flowerbeds.

Dahlia
Dahlia hybrid

Summer and
fall flowers
in every shape,
size, and color

DAILY DRINK FROM THE KITCHEN SINK

Give your perennials this fortified daily drink and watch them grow to new heights! Take any combination of plant-based kitchen waste—like table scraps (no meats or fats), potato peelings, and banana peels—and put them in your blender. Fill it with water, blend it all up, and pour it around the base of your perennials.

KEEP IT LIGHT

Perennials have a long growing season, so they gradually rob the soil of its natural fertility. But if you only dump on one big batch of fertilizer, the plants will pig out and end up growing much too tall with fewer flowers. To keep up with their needs effectively, feed them *lightly* but more *frequently* to provide a continuous supply of nutrients, and you'll end up with healthier plants that are much less likely to need staking.

If you worked lots of compost or peat moss into your soil at planting time, a 5-10-5 fertilizer will work fine. Put little rings of it around each perennial out at the tips of the farthest shoots, once in midspring, and again in midsummer. If your soil isn't particularly rich in organic matter, then feed with fish emulsion (apply every two weeks at half of the recommended rate, mixed with a cup of beer, and a tablespoon of dishwashing liquid per gallon of water). Or use another natural organic fertilizer, such as my Year-Round Refresher Tonic, on page 86.

Mixers & Elixirs

FLOWER FEEDER TONIC

1 can of beer
2 tbsp. of fish emulsion
2 tbsp. of dishwashing liquid
2 tbsp. of ammonia
2 tbsp. of hydrogen peroxide
2 tbsp. of whiskey
1 tbsp. of clear corn syrup
1 tbsp. of unflavored gelatin
4 tsp. of instant tea granules
2 gal. of warm water

Mix all of the ingredients together. Feed all of your perennials and bulbs with this mix every two weeks in the morning for glorious blooms all season long.

TONIC TALK

As you read through this book, you'll see dozens of recipes for everything from feeding tonics to pest and critter controls. And you'll notice that many, if not most, of the recipes contain common household products. In case you're wondering what makes these ingredients so useful for garden tonics, here's a quick rundown for future reference:

Mixers & Elixirs

YEAR-ROUND REFRESHER TONIC

Use this elixir every three weeks from spring through fall to keep your flower gardens gorgeous. (In warm climates, you can use it as a year-round tonic.)

1 cup of beer
1 cup of baby shampoo
1 cup of liquid lawn food
½ cup of molasses
2 tbsp. of fish emulsion
Ammonia

Mix the beer, shampoo, lawn food, molasses, and fish emulsion in a 20 gallon hose-end sprayer, and fill the balance of the jar with ammonia. Then spray away!

Ammonia: A mild, immediately available source of nitrogen that helps encourage lots of leafy plant growth.

Beer: An enzyme activator that helps to release nutrients that are locked in the soil; plus, it promotes the activity of soil organisms.

Molasses: A source of sugar that stimulates chlorophyll formation in plants.

Shampoo and soap: Softens soil and, when used on foliage, removes dust, dirt, and pollution to improve photosynthesis.

Tea: Contains tannic acid, which helps plants digest their food more quickly.

WHAT'S THE SCOOP ON BULB FOOD?

When checking out the fertilizer offerings in your local garden center, you'll probably see some products labeled specifically as "bulb food." This is usually ordinary garden fertilizer that has a liberal supply of bonemeal added to it.

And no, it's not necessary to buy special "bulb food" for your bulbs. When you plant your bulbs, simply work a handful of compost and a teaspoonful of bonemeal into the soil in each hole before setting in the bulb. After that, try this bulb booster: Mix 2 pounds of bonemeal with 2 pounds of wood ashes and 1 pound of Epsom salts. Sprinkle this mixture on top of flowerbeds where bulbs are growing in early spring, just as the foliage starts to break out of the ground.

MAKE MINE MANURE

In my humble opinion, good old-fashioned manure is still the best all-around fertilizer. If you don't have the time to wait a year or two for it to age before using it, you can always buy handy, ready-to-use, dried manure at your local garden center.

BONE-AFIDE FEEDING SECRET

Here's a little secret I discovered years ago—believe it or not, dry dog food contains many of the same nutrients, such as bonemeal and bloodmeal, found in organic fertilizers! So grab a handful and work it into the soil for an added energy boost when planting, or sprinkle it around your growing perennials.

Daylily
Hemerocallis hybrid

A must-have for summer color in sunny gardens; sturdy and dependable

OLD-FASHIONED FERTILIZERS

When my Grandma Putt needed to fertilize her flowers, she used practically anything she could find around the farm. Here's a sampling of a few of her old-time favorites (and mine, too):

Eggshells: Soak crushed eggshells in water for 24 hours, then water your plants with the mixture to provide much needed calcium.

Fish: Any and all fish parts, buried or composted, are a great nutrient source.

Hair: Both human and animal hair provide many nutrients, including iron, manganese, and sulfur. Work it into the soil or add it to your compost pile.

Mud: Pond mud and ditch scrapings can be used as fertilizer because of the rich accumulation of nutrients in the muck.

Mixers & Elixirs

FERN FOOD

Ferns are fabulous fillers for shady spots in perennial gardens. To keep your outdoor ferns looking lush, give them a dose of this milky brew.

2 cups of milk
2 tbsp. of Epsom salts

Combine the milk and Epsom salts in your 20 gallon hose-end sprayer, and give your ferns a generous drink until they are saturated.

DIAGNOSING DEFICIENCIES

When perennials are lacking in nutrients, their leaves usually tell the story. Here's a rundown of common foliage symptoms, the deficiencies that cause them, and what you can do to get your perennials perky again!

Symptoms	Deficiency	Remedies
Entire leaf surface pales to yellow; severe dwarfing or stunting soon follows.	Nitrogen (N)	Work aged manure into the soil before planting; during the growing season, apply my Year-Round Refresher Tonic as needed (see page 86).
Leaf edges turn yellow, tips turn brown and dry; sometimes there is a purplish cast. Leaves fall off.	Phosphorus (P)	For a quick fix, spray the foliage with seaweed extract. A long-term solution is to work bonemeal or rock phosphate into the soil.
Leaves spotted or mottled with yellow; leaf edges turn yellow or brown. Purplish tinting along the veins extending into the leaf tissue.	Potash (K)	Apply muriate of potash or potassium sulfate in spring. Or apply wood ashes at the rate of 50 pounds per 30- by 50-foot area.
Leaf tissue darkens from base outward and dies because feeder roots have died.	Calcium (Ca)	Dust soil with garden lime (calcium carbonate), or use dolomitic lime if your plants also need magnesium.
Leaves turn yellow between the veins; veins stay green or faintly yellow.	Iron (Fe)	Apply 1 tablespoon of my Liquid Iron or chelated iron per quart of water per plant.
Leaf centers turn yellow or reddish. Dead spots appear between the veins.	Magnesium (Mg)	For each plant, apply 1 tablespoon of Epsom salts mixed into enough water to dissolve it.
Leaves at the top of the plant turn yellow in the center, between the veins; no reddening.	Manganese (Mn)	Mix 1/2 tablespoon of manganese sulfate per quart of water per plant.
Leaf veins lighter in color than the tissue in between.	Sulfur (S)	Apply agricultural sulfur according to package directions.

Weeding Made Easy

Weeding woes don't have to take all the fun out of your flower gardening! Follow my simple suggestions for keeping these pesky plants to a minimum, and you'll have a great-looking perennial garden with a minimum of muss and fuss.

 DON'T WAIT FOR WEEDS

Where weeds are concerned, putting off until tomorrow what you should do today is a recipe for disaster. Starting right now, make a habit of pulling any weed as soon as you see it. If you wait, it's just going to get bigger, and in the meantime, it's stealing water and nutrients that your perennials and bulbs could be using to give you more flowers. Plus, pulling a few weeds here and there each time you walk around your garden will save you from marathon weekend weeding sessions. And believe me, they can be real killers!

 MAKING ¢ents Steak knives make super weeding tools! Buy them when they're on sale (like at dollar-days sales), and you'll have a cheap, long-lasting, and easy-to-wield weapon in the war against weeds.

SHALLOW'S THE WAY TO GO

Always use special care when cultivating, to avoid damaging bulbs or the roots of your perennials. If you're using a hoe, make short, shallow, scraping motions instead of chopping deep down into the soil.

Also keep in mind that when weeds grow very near other plants, their roots become intertwined. So when you are pulling out a weed, take care not to also pull out the perennial or bulb you're trying to protect.

MINIMIZE WEEDS WITH MULCH

I rarely need to use weed killers in my flower gardens as long as I have an adequate amount of mulch down to cover

Dogtooth violet
Erythronium dens-canis

Small, beautiful yellow blooms in spring over brown-mottled green leaves

the soil. Grass clippings, chopped leaves, shredded bark, and peanut or cocoa shells all fit the bill. Then all I need to do is pull or dig out the occasional weed.

 COVER UP

Mother Nature hates bare soil, so if you don't cover it, she will! If you're not going to use mulch, then use plants—either set your perennials a little closer together, or sow or plant annuals in between your perennials until the bigger plants fill in.

SPRING INTO WEED CONTROL

When you're cleaning out your flowerbeds in spring, make sure you remove all the weeds you can see *before* adding a fresh layer of mulch. Don't count on the mulch to simply smother the weeds, because it won't!

JEEPERS! CORRAL THOSE CREEPERS!

Double daffodil
Narcissus hybrid

Petal-packed blooms for the spring garden

Keep spreading perennials from turning into weeds by corralling their roots with a collar. Within a year after planting, dig a narrow, but deep, trench—8 to 12 inches should do the trick—around potential problem perennials like bee balm, mints, and loosestrife. Line the trench with pieces of heavy plastic or metal roof flashing, leaving about an inch sticking above the ground to keep the roots from sneaking out.

SEND WEEDS TO A SALTY GRAVE

Need to get rid of those tough weeds growing through cracks in patios and garden walkways? Pour some salt on them! Just be sure to do this on a dry day, when there is no rain forecast, or the salt will wash away. In a day or two, the weeds will curl up and die from dehydration, and you can easily pull them out.

Another option is to pour boiling water on walkway weeds. Be sure to pour it slowly and carefully to keep it from splashing on you!

WATCH OUT!

Some perennials self-sow so freely that they become their own worst weed enemy. Fortunately, it's not hard to keep these overgenerous perennials in check—simply snip off their spent flowers before they have a chance to set seed. Here are a few self-sowing perennials to keep your eye on, so they don't get out of hand:

Black-eyed Susans (*Rudbeckia*)

Bronze fennel (*Foeniculum vulgare* 'Purpureum')

Common yarrow (*Achillea millefolium*)

Coreopsis (*Coreopsis*)

Feverfew (*Tanacetum parthenium*)

Foxgloves (*Digitalis*)

Garlic chives (*Allium tuberosum*)

Golden marguerite (*Anthemis tinctoria*)

Hollyhock (*Alcea rosea*)

Jupiter's beard (*Centranthus ruber*)

Mullein (*Verbascum*)

Purple coneflower (*Echinacea purpurea*)

Purple loosestrife (*Lythrum salicaria*)

Rose campion (*Lychnis coronaria*)

Switch grass (*Panicum virgatum*)

Tufted hair grass (*Deschampsia cespitosa*)

Mixers & Elixirs

WEED WIPEOUT

Zap those hard-to-kill weeds with this lethal weapon:

1 tbsp. of gin
1 tbsp. of apple cider vinegar
1 tsp. of dishwashing liquid
1 qt. of very warm water

Mix all of the ingredients together in a bucket, then pour into a hand-held sprayer to apply. Drench weeds to the point of run-off, taking care not to get any of this elixir on the surrounding plants or grass.

 PUT POISON IVY IN THE BAG

Poison ivy popping up in your flowerbeds? Think twice before you grab it, and you could save yourself a whole lot of itching later on. To shield your skin, take an old, plastic bread bag and insert your hand and forearm. Use your plastic-protected hand to pull out the poison ivy, then use your other hand to roll the free end of the bag down over your arm and hand. Presto—poison ivy in a bag!

Give 'Em a Pinch

Pets aren't the only ones who look better with good grooming—it can help your perennials, too! A well-timed pinch (or snip) can keep plants healthier, minimize staking and weeding chores, and ensure that you have the best-looking garden on the block.

PERENNIAL PRUNING POINTERS

Long fingernails—or a good, sharp pair of hand pruners—can be a busy gardener's best friend! Pinching or cutting back some perennials in early summer encourages them to produce more compact, bushier growth, so your plants are sturdier and won't need staking. Plus, you get more blooms, since there are more shoots to form flowers. Pinching or cutting back can also delay blooming for a bit, which is a plus if you're looking for later color in your beds and borders.

Cutting perennials back by about half in *early summer* will have the most noticeable impact on the size and bushiness of your plants. Pinching off the top 2 inches or so of

Double tuberose
Polianthes tuberosum

If you love fragrant flowers, this bulb definitely belongs in your yard stem tips in *midsummer* has a much less dramatic effect on the overall height. (The perennials will be close to their usual height, but somewhat bushier near the middle to top.) It's worth experimenting with pruning and pinching at different heights and times to figure out which combination works best in your particular conditions.

 HANDS OFF!

Before you go pinching *all* of your perennials, be aware that some definitely do not appreciate being pruned before they bloom. The following perennials will *not* bloom if you pinch or cut them back before flowering. Include all bulbs in this category, too (except for dahlias).

Astilbes *(Astilbe)*

Daylilies *(Hemerocallis)*

Hostas *(Hosta)*

Irises *(Iris)*

Oriental poppy *(Papaver orientale)*

Red hot poker *(Kniphofia)*

GIVE ME SOME SPACE

Another type of pinching—called thinning—can go a long way toward keeping fungal disease, like mildew, from messing up your perfect perennial plantings. Crowded clumps don't allow for good air circulation around the stems, so the foliage stays wet longer, and diseases can get an easy start. But if

---

Try This!

Pinch these perennials and bulbs *before* they bloom for bushier growth:

Anise hyssop *(Agastache foeniculum)*

Asters *(Aster)*

'Autumn Joy' sedum *(Sedum 'Autumn Joy')*

Balloon flower *(Platycodon grandiflorus)*

Bee balms *(Monarda)*

Boltonia *(Boltonia asteroides)*

Chrysanthemum *(Chrysanthemum x morifolium)*

Dahlia *(Dahlia)*

Golden marguerite *(Anthemis tinctoria)*

Joe Pye weed *(Eupatorium purpureum)*

Obedient plant *(Physostegia virginiana)*

Shasta daisy *(Chrysanthemum x superbum)*

Sneezeweed *(Helenium autumnale)*

Summer phlox *(Phlox maculata and P. paniculata)*

you pinch or cut out some of the stems, the rest will have more room to develop and stay healthy.

Late spring or early summer is a great time to try thinning out dense perennial clumps—simply remove a third to a half of the stems in each clump, right at ground level. It may seem drastic, but don't worry—the remaining stems will fill in and bloom better than ever. Good candidates for this technique include the following "mildew magnets": asters, bee balms (*Monarda*), and garden phlox (*Phlox paniculata*).

🪣 DON'T LET 'EM FADE AWAY

Picking off spent flowers not only keeps your garden looking tip-top but it also prevents seeds from forming. This way, you'll prevent unwanted offspring and help conserve the plant's energy. Removing dying flowers promptly can also encourage some perennials to produce a second crop of flowers later in the season.

Even though some plants may not flower a second time, removing faded flowers allows the plant to put its energy into building a strong root system for the following year.

🪣 A PINCH IN TIME

The spent flowers of phloxes, asters, and chrysanthemums often produce seeds that fall to the ground around the parent plants. There they grow into vigorous specimens that end up choking out the choicer varieties you started with. So be sure to pick off the spent flower heads *before* they have a chance to reproduce!

🪣 SUPER SHEARING SECRET

Good grooming not only makes your garden look better, but it can also encourage your plants to bloom again! Cut these

Dutch crocus
Crocus vernus

Nothing says "Welcome, Spring!" like these cheerful little bulbs

OFF WITH THEIR HEADS!

Cut off the tops of spent tulips, daffodils, and hyacinths so they don't form seedheads. But don't cut the foliage down until it's brown and dry—green foliage stores nutrients that are needed for next year's growth.

perennials back by half to two-thirds when most of their first crop of flowers fade, and you'll probably be rewarded with another flush of flowers in a few short weeks:

Catmints (*Nepeta*)

Cinquefoil (*Potentilla*)

Coreopsis (*Coreopsis*)

Delphiniums (*Delphinium*)

Frikart's aster (*Aster* x *frikartii*)

Golden marguerite (*Anthemis tinctoria*)

Jupiter's beard (*Centranthus ruber*)

Perennial flax (*Linum perenne*)

Phlox (*Phlox*)

Rose campion (*Lychnis coronaria*)

Spike speedwell (*Veronica spicata*)

Violet sage (*Salvia nemorosa*)

TOOL TIME

Here's a rundown on some of my favorite tools for garden grooming:

Pruning shears: Handheld shears are good for snipping off individual flowers and stems. Use one hand to hold the stems while you cut with the other.

Hedge or grass shears: These long-bladed clippers make quick work of cutting off many small flowers or of cutting back perennials for size control before they bloom.

String trimmer: For even faster results, this power tool makes cutting down carpets of low-growing perennials (like pinks and bugleweeds) a snap!

 MARVELOUS MUMS

How come the mums in your garden aren't as full and bushy as they were the year you bought them? Because they need frequent pinching to keep their full-bodied form. Nip the tips of the growing stems twice—once when the stems are 6 to 8 inches tall, and again about four weeks later. This'll keep your mums from growing too tall, plus encourage more blooms.

THE KINDEST CUT

Ever notice that some perennials look just super when they're in bloom, and just awful shortly afterward? They sprawl all over the place, or their foliage looks tired and ratty. Don't despair—just use this simple trick to get them looking good again in no time!

Once all the flowers are done, cut these perennials back by half to two-thirds of their height, and they'll quickly produce a new flush of foliage that looks great well into fall: basket-of-gold (*Aurinia saxatilis*), blanket flower (*Gaillardia* x *grandiflora*), cushion spurge (*Euphorbia polychroma*), hardy geraniums, painted daisy (*Tanacetum coccineum*), perennial candytuft (*Iberis sempervirens*), pinks (*Dianthus*), and spider-wort (*Tradescantia* x *andersoniana*).

Cut these perennials back even harder after bloom—to about 2 inches above the ground: bugleweeds (*Ajuga*), dead

PERENNIAL PINCHING PRIMER

Deadheading (which is "gardenese" for removing spent flowers) doesn't take fancy tools or lots of time—just a basic understanding of how a particular perennial produces its flowers. Use this handy chart to help you figure out what to cut—and where!

Where Are the Flowers?	Single Flower on a Single Stem	Single Cluster of Flowers atop a Single Stem	Several Flowers or Flower Clusters on One Stem
Flowering stem comes right up from the ground (few or no leaves on the stem).	When the flower is finished, cut off the flowering stem at the base of the plant (e.g., poppy).	Cut off the main stem at the base when all blooms on that stem are done (e.g., astilbe).	Pinch off individual spent blooms (if desired), then cut off the main stem at the base when all blooms on that stem are done (e.g., iris, daylily).
Flowers and leaves appear on the same stem.	Pinch or cut off the spent flower just above the uppermost leaves on its stem (e.g., cone-flower).	Remove the cluster when all of its blooms are done, pinching or cutting just above the uppermost leaves on its stem (e.g., garden phlox, bee balm).	Remove individual flowers or flower clusters as they fade, pinching or cutting just above the uppermost leaves on that stem (e.g., foxglove, mums); or shear the entire bushy plant back by half when most blooms fade (e.g., catmint).

nettle (*Lamium maculatum*), lady's mantle (*Alchemilla mollis*), lamb's ears (*Stachys byzantina*), moss phlox (*Phlox subulata*), silver mound (*Artemisia schmidtiana*), and snow-in-summer (*Cerastium tomentosum*).

SOS—Save Our Seedheads!

Before snipping off all spent flowers, give a thought to the future—those long, dreary, winter months. A number of perennials have handsome seedheads that can add lots of visual interest to your garden in winter. Plus, their seeds provide food for winter birds! So instead of rushing out and removing them in the fall, wait until late winter or early spring to clean up these long-lasting beauties.

Here's a rundown of some of the best perennials with seedheads worth saving:

Astilbes (*Astilbe*)

'Autumn Joy' sedum (*Sedum* 'Autumn Joy')

Bear's breeches (*Acanthus*)

Blackberry lily (*Belamcanda chinensis*)

Black-eyed Susans (*Rudbeckia*)

False indigos (*Baptisia*)

Feather reed grass (*Calamagrostis* x *acutiflora*)

Fountain grass (*Pennisetum alopecuroides*)

Globe thistle (*Echinops ritro*)

Goatsbeard (*Aruncus dioicus*)

Goldenrods (*Solidago*)

Japanese silver grass (*Miscanthus sinensis*)

Joe Pye weed (*Eupatorium purpureum*)

Purple coneflower (*Echinacea purpurea*)

Russian sages (*Perovskia*)

Sea holly (*Eryngium giganteum*)

Siberian iris (*Iris sibirica*)

Dutch hyacinth
*Hyacinthus
orientalis*

Pretty, perfumed
blooms are
superb for both
indoor and
outdoor growing

Staking Strategies

To keep perennials on the straight and narrow, you sometimes have to give them a little extra support. Staking may not be the most fun job in the garden, but if you follow these simple tips, you'll have a great-looking flower garden without a lot of fuss.

MAKING ¢ents   Here's a money-saving secret: For a never-ending supply of stakes, save the trimmings at shrub-pruning time. Brushy prunings from privet, water sprouts from fruit trees, and other similar materials are perfect for making stakes, and they're free!

🪣 Help 'Em Stand Tall

Want to keep staking chores to a minimum? Follow these step-by-step strategies for helping your perennials and bulbs hold themselves up!

1. Start with a sunny site that's sheltered from strong wind. Plants that aren't getting enough light produce taller stems than usual as they try to stretch for more sun, and strong winds can quickly flatten even normally sturdy stems.

2. Choose compact cultivars.

3. Pick sturdy partners, such as shrubs and sturdier perennials, for floppy plants.

4. Hold off on too much water and fertilizer.

5. Pinch 'em back in early summer to promote more bushy growth.

Dutch iris
Iris Dutch Hybrid

Blue, bronze, yellow, or white spring blossoms; outstanding as cut flowers

🪣 Give Youngsters Some Support

Most folks don't think of supporting their perennials until it's too late. And that, my friends, is a mis-stake! (Sorry—I couldn't help myself!) The best time to stake floppy perennials is in early spring, well *before* they start sprawling. Don't worry—as they grow up, they will eventually cover their stakes, and the supports will hardly be noticeable at all.

THE STAKES ARE HIGH

Single stakes work fine for tall perennials that have a few main stems per plant, such as delphiniums and foxgloves. You can use stakes made from wood, dowels, bamboo, plastic, metal, or wire. You'll often find stakes that are dyed green or covered with green plastic, and I've found black stakes are nearly as invisible as green ones.

When placed in the ground, the stakes should be 6 to 12 inches shorter than the mature height of the plant. Place the stakes behind the stems you want to support, sinking them far enough into the soil to firmly anchor them. They must be able to withstand the wind and rain.

Start securing stems to their stakes when they are about 1 foot tall, then repeat every 12 to 18 inches. Tie stems loosely to the stakes with yarn or strips of panty hose.

CAN IT

Top taller stakes with upside-down, plastic film canisters to protect yourself when working in the garden. You don't want to get scratched or put an eye out when you bend over to admire your beautiful perennial and bulb blooms!

HOOPING IT UP

Try This!

Here's a neat idea—to support your tall plants, use small extension-type curtain rods. As the plants grow, it's easy to adjust the rods up so that they'll always be at just the right height.

For plants that have more than a few stems needing support, you have two options: a stake-and-string combination or a hoop-type support. The first one you make right on the spot—simply insert three to five stakes around the outside of the clump, then make a sort of grid by winding yarn or twine around and among the stakes. Pre-made, hoop-type stakes serve the same purpose, but save you a little time. They are a snap to put up, and you can use them year after year. Either system works great for medium-height, bushy plants like baby's breath (*Gypsophila paniculata*), phlox, and peonies (*Paeonia*).

🪣 LOWER GROWERS NEED HELP, TOO!

Finding a good way to support sprawling, low-growing perennials can be tricky, especially for plants that don't have a lot of leaves to cover the supports. Twiggy prunings from bushy shrubs can be really handy for this—they're natural-looking, and they're free! Insert them stem-side down all around the emerging clumps, then let the perennials grow up around them. Use your pruners to snip off any of the twigs that stick out from the filled-in perennial clump.

Another handy support system is a wire hanging basket turned upside-down and set over the new shoots. These baskets come in a variety of sizes, so you're sure to find one that's a perfect fit for your plants, and they blend in beautifully. Try this trick on catmints (*Nepeta*), balloon flowers (*Platycodon grandiflorus*), 'Autumn Joy' sedum (*Sedum* 'Autumn Joy'), and hardy geraniums.

BE CAGEY

For super hoop stakes, look no further than your vegetable garden! Metal tomato cages can support more than just tomatoes—try them on asters, baby's breath (*Gypsophila paniculata*), peonies (*Paeonia*), and Shasta daisies (*Chrysanthemum* x *superbum*).

Full-sized cages work fine for tall perennials. For shorter plants, cut the hoops in two—snip the vertical wires just above the lower hoop—and you have two different-sized stakes! Spray-paint them black or dark green, if desired, to help them blend in even better.

🪣 PERFECT PEONY PROPS

You can't get any easier than this—simply cut circles of chicken wire about 15 inches in diameter, then drop one over each of your peony plants just as the new shoots show up in spring. As they grow, they'll lift the wire to the perfect height, and they'll cover it with their leaves. You won't see a thing!

🪣 STAKING SECRET FOR PROCRASTINATORS

Despite your best intentions, it's almost inevitable that you'll forget to stake one perennial or another during the spring rush. Fast-forward to midsummer, and you have a sprawling clump of stems that need help *now!* To provide some support without breaking the shoots in the process, take a long piece of yarn or soft twine, and gently wrap it a few times around the plant to gather up the stems. Carefully slip a cage or hoop over the plant, push the cage legs into the soil to secure them, then remove the tie to let the plant resume its full-bodied form inside the cage.

Putting Your Beds to Bed

For those of you who live in the colder regions, proper fall preparation is a key step in getting your perennials and bulbs through the winter in good shape. Read on for tips, tricks, and tonics to help you get it done the fast, fun, and easy Jerry Baker way.

WINTER PREP CHECKLIST

As soon as Jack Frost comes nipping at your nose, it's time to tuck your perennials and bulbs into their beds for the winter ahead. Here's a checklist to help you remember what your plants need from you:

✔ If fall has been dry, give your plants a nice long drink, so they don't go into the winter with parched soil. (Even though their tops aren't growing much, the roots still need a bit of moisture.)

✔ Dig up tender bulbs, such as gladiolus and dahlias, and store them indoors for the winter.

✔ Once frost has killed back the tops, give your garden a

Dwarf canna
Canna hybrid

Great foliage and bright flowers for summer garden color; perfect for pots

thorough cleaning. Cut back dead leaves and stems, and remove the debris. Make sure you weed thoroughly, too.

✔ Gather up stakes, clean them, and store them indoors. The same goes for your garden tools!

✔ Once the ground freezes, mulch beds with chopped leaves, composted manure, salt hay, or pine needles.

 SOME LIKE IT COLD

I know that we bundle up at the drop of the thermometer, but to get the most from your winter plant coverings, you should only apply them *after* the ground freezes. Why wait so long? Because your real enemy is not the falling temperatures; it's the fluctuations of heat and cold that you need to control. You actually want to protect plants *to keep them cold* during those midwinter thaws that cause the ground to heave, which results in root damage.

Unprotected plants that are heaved out of the soil can die from exposure, or they may just dry out. Likewise, unseasonable warm spells can cause dormant buds on unprotected plants to start growing, only to have the next freeze kill them. But if you mulch soon after the ground freezes, you keep the ground colder, lessening the chance of heaving during a warmer spell.

 HIBERNATION SNACK

Give your perennial beds a winter snack by applying 25 pounds of garden gypsum, 5 pounds of bonemeal, and 10 pounds of garden fertilizer (4-2-4 or

---

Mixers & Elixirs

FLOWERBED BONANZA

After fall cleanup, spray all of your perennial beds with this mixture:

1 can of beer
1 can of regular cola (not diet)
½ cup of dishwashing liquid
½ cup of tobacco tea*

Mix all of the ingredients together in a bucket, then apply liberally with your 20 gallon hose-end sprayer.

*To make the tea, take three fingers' worth of chewing tobacco from the package, place it in the toe of a nylon stocking, and place the stocking in a gallon of hot water. Let the tobacco steep until the water is dark brown.

5-10-5) for every 100 square feet. Then cover the entire
area with a blanket of grass clippings and shredded leaves.

🪣 BURN, BURY, OR COMPOST?

We all know how important it is to clean up
our flower gardens at the end of the growing season, but how we should dispose of
the plant remains is an ongoing debate.
Should you burn them, bury them, or add
them to your compost pile?

   Some folks compost everything, while others are afraid
to compost anything at all, saying they're afraid they'll end
up spreading pests, pathogens, and seeds all through their
garden. I fall somewhere between the two—I burn material
that is definitely diseased or insect-ridden (as well as woody
stalks that are almost certain to harbor borers), and try to
compost everything else that looks reasonably safe.

Try This!

To help your sum-
mer-flowering
bulbs survive the winter,
dust them with medicated baby
powder before storing them in
old onion sacks.

Caring for Containers

**Petunias and geraniums aren't the only plants you can
use to fill your flowerpots! Sure, annuals are great for
containers, but many perennials and bulbs can fill the
bill just as well—or even better! Here are some tips to
help you get the best out of your potted perennials.**

🪣 CONTAINER SMARTS

Any container you use for other flowers can work just fine
for perennials, too. Drainage holes are a must, of course!
Clay pots are a classic choice, but they lose water quickly

Elephant's ears
Colocasia esculenta

If you like your
bulbs big,
you'll love this
one's huge leaves

English primrose
Primula vulgaris

A cottage-garden charmer with fragrant yellow blooms in spring

through their porous sides, so you'll need to pay extra-close attention when watering them. Light-colored containers are ideal for sun-baked sites, because they absorb less heat than dark pots.

WEIGH YOUR OPTIONS

Large containers are great for providing perennials and bulbs with lots of root room, but they can also get mighty heavy when they're packed full of plants. To help cut down on some of the weight, first fill the bottom of large pots with empty soda cans set on end, *then* add the potting soil. Now you're ready to get your plants growing without breaking your back!

On the other hand, there are times when you want to *add* bulk to lightweight or top-heavy containers to keep them from getting blown over. In this case, fill the bottom one-third to one-half of the pot with compost or sand, and maybe even a few rocks, before adding the potting soil.

CALL IN THE RESERVES

Even the best-kept flowerbeds have their share of disasters during the growing season. To combat this, be prepared—keep extra plants on hand for replacements. Potted perennials are great for this! You can enjoy them on your deck or patio, then move them to the garden later in the season to fill in any gaps that develop.

SOMETHING'S FISHY

Here's a great green-thumb tip: When you change the water in your fishbowl or freshwater aquarium, save the old water and feed it to your potted plants. The fish have already added the best natural fertilizer money can buy!

Another nutrient-rich source of water is what's left in the pot after you cook vegetables. Let it cool, then give each of your container plants a good, long drink of veggie water.

HELP PERENNIALS KEEP THEIR COOL

Hot spells can play havoc with container plants, heating up their roots and drying them out in no time at all. To help your potted perennials and bulbs beat the heat, set them, pot and all, inside a larger container, then fill the space in between with peat moss. This extra insulation will help reduce heat stress and keep your flowers in top form.

 COPING WITH CLAY

Perennials look great growing in clay pots, but these porous containers can be a real pain to keep moist. You can cut down on your watering chores by lining the pots with newspaper, to within about 2 inches of the rim, before you add the potting soil.

If you are going to be away for a few days, try wrapping the outsides of your clay pots with aluminum foil. It looks a little funny, but it'll really help to hold in the moisture.

Mixers & Elixirs

PERFECT POTTING MIX

If you've got a lot of perennials to pot, you'll need plenty of potting soil. So instead of constantly running out (and running to the store), mix up a batch of this simple blend and keep it handy:

1 part topsoil
1 part peat moss
1 part vermiculite
1 part compost

Mix all of the ingredients together and use for potting up all kinds of perennials and bulbs.

GET YOUR POTTED PLANTS PLASTERED!

Perennials can stay in one pot for several years, but over time, their soil can get pretty tired! To liven things up again, add a can of beer or a shot of bourbon, scotch, vodka, or gin to a gallon of room-temperature water. Add 1 ounce of dishwashing liquid, and let this mixture sit for half a day or so. Then add it to your favorite plant food, and water your potted plants with this boozy treat.

TROUBLE-FREE POTS AND PLANTERS

Keeping containers watered is probably the most time-consuming part of caring for pots and planters. What's the answer? Mulch! The same secret that minimizes garden

Mixers & Elixirs

ULTRALIGHT POTTING SOIL

To keep your really big pots and planters from being back-breakers, fill them with this ultralight potting soil mix:

4 parts perlite, moistened
4 parts compost
1 part potting soil
½ part cow manure

Mix all of the ingredients together, then use the mixture to fill your planting containers. This mix dries out very quickly, particularly in the hot summer sun, so be sure to keep an eye on your containers and water them as needed.

watering works great for containers, too. After planting, top your pots with 1 to 2 inches of shredded bark, chopped leaves, or other good-looking organic mulch to keep the soil from drying out so fast.

COMBINE AND CONQUER

Containers are a super way to show off your plants, but the extra attention they need can be a problem if you have many pots scattered here and there throughout your yard. To stream-line your container-care chores, try grouping all of your potted perennials in one highly visible spot—ideally, near a water source. That way, it'll be easy to take care of all the grooming, water-ing, and feeding at one time, and you won't have to haul hoses all over your yard to water the scattered pots and planters.

BIRD-PROOF YOUR HANGING BASKETS

Our fine feathered friends often mistake outdoor hanging baskets for ready-made condos—complete with its own gar-den! If birds are making nests in your hanging baskets, don't despair. Take a section of chicken wire, cover the basket with it, then gently pull the plants through it. That should stop the birds from feathering their nests with your flowers!

TRENCH-ANT TIPS FOR CONTAINERS

Potted annuals and perennials need pretty much the same kind of care—but the real difference comes at the end of the growing season. With annuals, you simply pull them out and toss them onto your compost pile. But with perennials, you'll need to give some thought to getting them through the winter in good shape.

In mild-winter areas, it may be enough to bring your containers up close to the house or against the wall of a garage or other outbuilding. In cooler areas, dig a trench in your vegetable garden and sink the pots into the soil, up to their rims. For extra protection, cover the sunken pots with a foot or so of leaves, then lay chicken wire over the top to hold down the leaves and keep the critters out.

European
wild ginger
Asarum europaeum

Glossy evergreen
foliage makes a
great groundcover
in shady areas

Mixers & Elixirs

POTTED PLANT PICNIC

Here's a meal your flower-filled containers are sure to appreciate:

2 tbsp. of brewed black coffee
2 tbsp. of whiskey
1 tsp. of fish emulsion
½ tsp. of unflavored gelatin
½ tsp. of baby shampoo
½ tsp. of ammonia
1 gal. of water

Mix all of the ingredients together and water your potted perennials and bulbs with it on a weekly basis.

MAKING MORE PLANTS

Perennials and bulbs light up our landscapes with beautiful blooms and lovely leaves for months and months each year. What else could you possibly ask for? How about having *more* of them—*without* paying one red cent! Here are my secrets to expanding your plantings by making new plants from the perennials and bulbs you already have. With a little grow-how, you won't believe how easy it is!

Seed-Starting Secrets

Growing perennials from seed takes a little patience, but the results are worth it. If you've ever grown annuals or vegetables from seed, then you already have the basic know-how to start perennial seeds. And if you haven't tried seeds before—well, what are you waiting for? For the price of a few seeds—just a couple of bucks, at most—you can get dozens and dozens of great-looking new plants!

HOMEGROWN GARDEN SEEDS

Two convenient sources of seeds are the seed racks at your local garden center and the enticing pages of those mail-order seed catalogs that arrive in early to midwinter. But before you rush out and spend your hard-earned money, consider that you may have a ready source of seeds right in your own garden!

Collecting seeds from your favorite perennials and bulbs is a fun and rewarding summer and fall project. You can use them to start more plants for your own garden, or trade them with other gardeners to get seeds of new plants you want to try. Just follow these simple steps:

1. Watch the plants you want to collect seeds from. As soon as the flowers start to fade, inspect them every day or two. Some, like columbines and poppies, produce their seeds inside pods; on others, including daisies and yarrows, the seeds themselves are visible.

2. When the seedpods or seedheads begin to turn brown, cut them off and let them drop into paper bags (one type of seed per bag). You want the seeds to be dry when you harvest them, but don't wait too long, or they may drop to the ground or blow away before you have a chance to gather them. And make sure you label each bag!

3. Leave the bags open and set them in a warm, dry place for a week or two, so the seeds can finish ripening. (If the

Feather
reed grass
Calamagrostis x
acutiflora

Narrowly upright
ornamental grass;
excellent as an
accent or in masses

BEST BETS FOR BEGINNING SEED-STARTERS

Just getting started with seed-sowing? Then give these super-easy perennials a try! Sow them indoors in early spring or outdoors in late spring or early summer.

Black-eyed Susans (*Rudbeckia*)

Blanket flower (*Gaillardia* x *grandiflora*)

Hollyhock (*Alcea rosea*)

Jupiter's beard (*Centranthus ruber*)

Lance-leaved coreopsis (*Coreopsis lanceolata*)

Lupines (*Lupinus*)

Mountain bluet (*Centaurea montana*)

Rose campion (*Lychnis coronaria*)

Shasta daisy (*Chrysanthemum* x *superbum*)

Yarrows (*Achillea*)

seeds or seedheads are still on the greenish side, spreading them out on an old window screen helps speed up the process.)

4. Pour or pick the seeds out of the dried pods, or rub the seeds off the seedheads. Pick out any chaff (bits of dried stems, leaves, and pods), or sift the seeds through a screen to separate them from the chaff.

5. Store the dried, cleaned seeds in a paper envelope labeled with their name and the year. Store in a cool, dry place and use within two years.

🜀 DON'T COUNT ON CLONES

If you save seeds from your own garden, keep in mind that the resulting seedlings probably won't look exactly like the plants you gathered the seeds from. Seeds you collect from a compact, pink-flowered hybrid daylily, for instance, can produce seedlings in a wide variety of heights, colors, and flower forms. If you enjoy variety and like surprises, then this is a good thing! But if you want an exact replica of a particular perennial or bulb, you're better off propagating it by taking cuttings or dividing it.

🜀 SUPER SEED-STARTER

Want to make your own super seed-starting mix? Simply combine equal parts of milled sphagnum peat moss and horticultural-grade vermiculite. Or, if you'd like your mix to drain a bit more quickly, use 2 parts peat moss to 1 part vermiculite and 1 part perlite. A day or two before you plan to plant, sprinkle the mix with water to moisten the peat moss. Don't bother with fertilizer at this point; wait until your seedlings are up before you start feeding them.

SEED-STARTERS' TOOL KIT

Seed-starting doesn't take much special equipment—just a few basic supplies. Here's what you'll want to have on hand:

- Seeds (obviously!)
- Pots (I like to use 3- or 4-inch plastic pots)
- Flats (shallow trays to hold the pots)
- Seed-starting mix (store-bought or homemade)
- Labels (plastic or homemade)
- Water (at room temperature)

You probably already have a supply of suitable pots on hand from previous plant purchases; just scrub out the old soil, and dry them off before reusing them. Otherwise, pick up a few new plastic pots at your garden center. They only cost a few cents, and you can use them over and over again. The same goes for flats— either clean up and reuse some that you already have on hand, or buy a couple of new ones.

READY, SET, SOW!

Late winter to early spring is a good time to sow perennial seeds indoors. Fill the pots with moistened seed-starting

Foamflower
Tiarella cordifolia

Low mounds of heart-shaped leaves with fuzzy white flowers in spring

Mixers & Elixirs

SEEDLING STRENGTHENER

To get your seedlings off to a healthy, disease-free start, mist-spray them every few days with this elixir:

2 cups of manure
1/2 cup of instant tea granules
Warm water

Put the manure and tea in an old nylon stocking, and let it steep in 5 gallons of water for several days. Dilute the mixture with 4 parts of warm water (for example, 4 cups of water for every cup of mix) before using.

Fountain grass
Pennisetum alopecuroides

Clump-forming ornamental grass with arching foliage and fluffy, summer flower spikes

mix to about ¼ inch from the top edge. Tap the base of the pot on the table to settle the mix, then scatter the seeds as evenly as you can across the surface. (The better you can space out the seeds now, the easier transplanting will be later on!) Cover the seeds with a sprinkling of seed-starting mix (see "Super Seed-Starter" on page 110); leave very fine seeds uncovered. Then press down lightly with the backs of your fingers to get good contact between the mix and the soil. Water gently by dropping water onto the surface with a turkey baster, or by setting the pots in a tray of warm water for a few hours, until the surface appears damp.

COVER 'EM UP!

You know those clear plastic, zippered covers that pillows, bedspreads, and sleeping bags are packed in? Well, they make great little greenhouses for baby perennials! Set the sown seed pots in the bags, then place some kind of stake in each corner to hold the plastic away from the emerging seedlings, and zip the bag closed. When the young plants are about an inch tall, gradually unzip the bag to let the fresh air in. After a week, remove the bag entirely, let it dry out, and save it for your next seed-starting session.

SPEEDY SEEDS

You can speed up the sprouting time of seeds by soaking them in a mix of 1 teaspoon of dishwashing liquid, 1 teaspoon of ammonia, and 1 teaspoon of instant tea granules in 1 quart of warm water for 24 hours. Then place the seeds in a piece of old nylon stocking tied up with a twist tie. Let the seeds dry out, remove them from the stocking, and then plant away.

WARM THOUGHTS

Most perennial seeds sprout best when warm (about 70°F). Store-bought seed-starting mats work great, but they can get pretty pricey! You can still get good results without them, though—just set your seed pots on the top of your refrigerator or hot-water heater. Check them every day. As soon as sprouts appear, move the pots to a bright, but still warm spot—either a sunny windowsill or under a fluorescent light.

Seedlings in the Spotlight

Chances are, you'll run out of sunny windowsills long before you run out of seedlings that need light. For a few bucks, though, you can have as much light as you need for your seeds! Buy a 4-foot shop light fixture at your local home center (they're usually less than $15), fit it with two 4-foot, cool-white fluorescent bulbs, and hang it in a convenient spot. Set newly sown seed pots about 2 inches from the lights. As the seedlings grow, gradually raise the lights (or lower the plants) so the lights are about 6 inches above the tops of the young plants.

It's generally best to give your seedlings about 14 hours of light a day, so turn on the lights at breakfast time, and turn them off in the evening. Or better yet, buy an inexpensive timer (usually less than $10) to do the job for you. You won't believe the great results you'll get with this inexpensive, yet easy seed-starting setup!

Try This!

Seedlings growing on windowsills tend to stretch toward the light, so they end up leggy and lopsided. For more even growth, turn the pots every day, or make a reflector from a piece of cardboard covered with aluminum foil. Set the reflector behind the flat, and your seedlings will get plenty of light from all sides.

Give 'Em a Pat

To get seedlings to grow hardier and sturdier, try this trick that professional growers use: Lightly brush your hand across the young plants several times a day.

Don't have time for that? Then set up a small fan at the lowest setting to blow across the tops of your seedlings. Besides promoting denser, bushier growth, the air circulation will go a long way toward discouraging disease problems that want to linger.

Super-Simple Summer Starters

Want to keep seed-starting really low-tech? Then sow your seeds the old-fashioned way—outdoors!

Before planting perennial and bulb seeds outside in

spring, select a good location—one that is at least a little protected from the weather and does not dry out. A cold frame or an unheated hotbed is much better than the open garden this time of year, because you can partially close the cover to prevent drying out. The cover also protects the seeds from being washed away by heavy rains.

Summer is a perfect time to start perennials from seed for blooms next spring. The ground is still warm, so the seeds sprout readily and they still have time to produce good growth before activity ceases with the coming of the cold winter weather.

You have two options when planting the seeds: Either sow them in shallow rows that are a few inches apart, or broadcast them evenly over the entire area. Instead of disturbing the soil to cover the seeds, try sifting a little fine vermiculite over top of them (a $1/8$-inch layer is okay), and press down lightly. Water with a fine mist, and repeat as often as needed to keep the soil evenly moist.

If you planted in an open bed, cover the seedbed with burlap or a sheet of newspaper until you see the young seedlings emerging. Then remove it.

REFRIGERATE THE LEFTOVERS

If you find yourself with leftover perennial seeds after sowing, don't throw them out! You can store them for use next year. Seal them in their original packets, put the packets in small, airtight jars (like baby-food jars) with lids, and then tuck them away in your refrigerator.

Be sure the temperature stays between 36° and 45°F. (Check the temperature with a thermometer, and adjust the fridge setting as needed.)

Foxglove
Digitalis purpurea

Spires of purplish, pink, or white bells; elegant in borders or paired with shrubs

WHAT'S IN A NAME?

After you've sown your seeds, it'll be a while before plants stick their heads up through the soil. By the time they do, you may be scratching your head, wondering what the heck you planted there in the first place! To avoid this confusion, make sure you label all your seed pots and planting beds *immediately* after you plant. Record the plant name and the date of sowing, and you'll avoid a lot of grief later on.

GIVE THEM THE COLD SHOULDER

Most perennial and bulb seeds need warmth and moisture to sprout. There are some exceptions, though, and it's good to be aware of them so you're ready to meet their special needs. Generally, these chill-seeking seeds require cool and moist conditions, just like they'd get outdoors during the winter, before they'll germinate.

The simplest approach is to sow these seeds in pots in late summer or early fall, then leave the pots outside in a sheltered spot over the winter. (If you have a cold frame, that's great; otherwise, set them in a basement window well or against the foundation of your house.) They'll go through the usual freezing and thawing cycles, then sprout in spring when the mild weather returns. If you want faster results, you can speed up the process. Just mix the seed with a small handful of moistened vermiculite, and place it in a sealed plastic bag in your refrigerator for 8 to 12 weeks. Then sow the seed and vermiculite mix indoors, as usual, and set the pots in a warm place for sprouting.

MOVIN' ON UP

When your perennial seedlings have at least four leaves, it's time to transplant them to larger quarters. (If you move them when they have

SOME LIKE IT COOL

Give these perennial and bulb seeds some chillin' time outdoors or in your refrigerator before expecting them to sprout:

Anemones (*Anemone*)

Baneberries (*Actaea*)

Bleeding hearts (*Dicentra*)

Columbines (*Aquilegia*)

False indigos (*Baptisia*)

Foamflowers (*Tiarella*)

Goatsbeard (*Aruncus dioicus*)

Lady's mantle (*Alchemilla mollis*)

Lilies (*Lilium*)

Monkshood (*Aconitum*)

Ornamental onions (*Allium*)

Phlox (*Phlox*)

Primroses (*Primula*)

Sea hollies (*Eryngium*)

Snakeroots (*Cimicifuga*)

Turtleheads (*Chelone*)

Mixers & Elixirs

SEEDLING STARTER TONIC

Give your transplants a break on moving day by serving them a sip of my starter tonic. This will help them recover more quickly from the transplanting shock.

1 tbsp. of fish emulsion
1 tbsp. of ammonia
1 tbsp. of Murphy® Oil Soap
1 tsp. of instant tea granules
1 qt. of warm water

Mix all of the ingredients in the warm water. Pour into a handheld sprayer bottle, and mist the seedlings several times a day until they're back on their feet and growing again.

only two leaves, they may not have the energy to withstand the shock of transplanting.)

I find it easiest to gently slide out the whole potful of seedlings at once (rather than digging them out individually). Starting at the outside of the clump, gently separate the seedlings, handling them by their leaves, not their stems. A pencil makes a handy tool for teasing the roots apart, lifting individual seedlings, and settling the roots in their new pots.

 TOUGH LOVE

You've kept those baby perennials warm and toasty in your home, so don't be cruel at planting time—give them a fighting chance to get used to the great outdoors. Start hardening them off at least a week before you plan to plant them outside.

The first day, set them in a shady, sheltered spot (perhaps on a porch or near a shrub) for an hour or two during the day, then bring them inside again. The next day, leave them out for three or four hours. After that, gradually increase both the time they spend outside and the amount of sunshine they get. By the end of the week, they should be ready to stay outside full-time.

 Don't spend a fortune buying dozens of plastic seedling pots at your local garden center! Instead, go to the grocery store and buy a box of 5-ounce waxed paper bathroom cups (or 8-ounce Styrofoam cups if you have larger seedlings). Poke a few holes in the bottom of each, and they're ready to use.

Be a Cutup!

One of my favorite ways of making new plants from my perennials is by taking stem cuttings. The resulting rooted plants are identical to the plants I collected them from, and they reach flowering size much more quickly than seed-grown perennials. Read on for my terrific tips.

 ## CUTTING REMARKS

If you're not a pro at taking cuttings, don't worry. Just follow these five steps and you'll be successful every time:

1. Take cuttings only from plants that are healthy and mature. Gather them on a cloudy day or early in the morning. Early summer is the perfect time for most perennials.

2. Take cuttings that are about 4 to 6 inches long from semi-mature stems. (Very soft growth will wilt quickly, while tough, almost woody stems will be very slow to root.) As you take the cuttings, loosely pack them in wet paper towels, and put them in a plastic bag. Keep the bag in the shade.

3. Once you're back inside, use a sharp knife to cut each stem about ¼ inch below a node (the joint where a leaf or leaf pair joins the stem). Make a clean, smooth cut so that it heals quickly. Pinch off the lower leaves so the bottom third to half of the cutting stem is bare.

4. To speed rooting, you can dip the bottom of each cutting into a rooting hormone (available at garden centers).

5. Gently insert the bottom third to half of each cutting into damp sand or potting soil. Use the eraser end of a pencil to press the sand or soil firmly around the cutting. Water lightly to help settle the cuttings into the rooting material.

Freesia
Freesia hybrid

Bright and beautiful, sweetly perfumed blooms, ideal for forcing

Grandma Putt's WISDOM

When she took cuttings, Grandma Putt always made it a point to pinch off any flower buds or opened flowers before she inserted the stems into the rooting material. She knew that this simple step speeded up rooting by directing energy toward the new roots, rather than the flowers.

 THE ROOT OF THE MATTER

Your perennial cuttings should start forming roots within three to five weeks, though a few varieties may take a little longer. (Clues to root formation include slight resistance when you tug lightly on the cutting, new shoot growth, or visible roots peeking out of the pot's drainage holes.) Increase their light exposure as soon as the cuttings become strong and sturdy.

Once the cuttings are well rooted, pot them up in small containers, like 2- by 2-inch pots. Use a light, well-drained potting mix. Once the plants are well established in those pots, you can move them into larger pots. Place the pots in a cold frame or other protected spot for the winter, then plant out your new perennials in the spring.

Mixers & Elixirs

REPOTTING BOOSTER TONIC

Once you've repotted your rooted cuttings, give them a dose of this tonic to help them adjust to their new homes:

½ tsp. of all-purpose plant food
½ tsp. of Vitamin B₁ Plant Starter
½ cup of weak tea water*
1 gal. of warm water

Mix all of the ingredients together, and gently pour the tonic through the soil of your repotted plants. Allow it to drain through for 15 minutes or so, then pour off any excess tonic that's in the tray.

*Soak a used tea bag in a gallon of warm water and 1 teaspoon of dishwashing liquid until the water is light brown.

QUICK COVER-UPS

Want to start just a few cuttings? Insert them in a small pot of rooting material as usual, then set a glass jar or a clear plastic soda bottle (with the top or bottom cut off) upside down over them to hold in humidity and prevent wilting. Remove the cover once your cuttings are rooted and producing new growth.

WHIP UP SOME WILLOW WATER

Rooting hormones can dramatically reduce the time it takes your cuttings to produce new roots. You can buy powder or liquid types at your local garden center, or you can make your own—the ingredients are as close by as the nearest willow tree!

Gather a handful of willow twigs, each a few inches long (any kind of willow will work). Soak them in a small jar of water for a few days, then remove them. Soak the bottoms of your perennial cuttings in the willow water overnight, or use the liquid to water just-planted cuttings to get them off to a great start.

DOUBLE THE POTS = HALF THE WORK

Here's a neat way to make a self-watering setup for your cuttings: First, find two clean *clay* pots—one twice the size of the other. Fill the bottom of the bigger pot with potting soil. Place a cork in the drainage hole of the smaller pot, fill it with water, and then set it on the soil in the larger pot. Fill the space between the two pots with more potting soil, place your cuttings in this loose soil, and gently firm it up around them.

Refill the inner pot with water as needed to keep the potting soil moist. When the cuttings have rooted, lift out the smaller pot. Now removing and potting up the cuttings will be a snap!

IT'S NOT THE HEAT—IT'S THE HUMIDITY!

Leafy cuttings need high humidity, so it's smart to put them in some kind of enclosure until they have formed new roots. A tank-type terrarium or aquarium makes a perfect cutting box. The sand should be moist or damp, but not wet or waterlogged.

Although most professional propagators prefer pure sand for rooting cuttings, many home gardeners (me included) mix peat moss in with the sand to help retain more moisture. Either way, use coarse, sharp sand that you have washed thoroughly (rinse until the water stays clean). Perlite and vermiculite are also good to use as rooting materials. Fill your container about 3 inches deep with your cho-

Garden mum
Chrysanthemum x *morifolium*

This fall-flowering favorite grows equally well in the ground or in pots

sen material, then press down firmly with a piece of wood or a clean brick.

Place your cutting box in a spot that is bright, but out of direct midday sun. A north- or west-facing window that has indirect light is best.

🪣 BE ROOTFUL AND MULTIPLY

Believe you me, perennials are habit-forming! Once you start growing them, you'll want more and more. Unfortunately, your budget may put a crimp in your gardening style. But don't despair! That's because once you've established a good clump of your favorite perennial, you can easily make new plants from it, and they won't cost you a penny! One way to multiply your perennial plants is by root cuttings. Here's how:

Plants with slender roots (such as Japanese anemone, blanket flower, and butterfly weed): In late summer or fall, lift the clump out of the ground with a spading fork, and snip off 1- to 2-inch-long pieces of root. Then fill a shallow container with sand or garden soil. Lay the root pieces on their sides, and cover them with an additional 1/2-inch layer of sand or soil. Firm the surface and water carefully. Place the container in a cold frame for the winter. When the cuttings sprout in spring, move the container outdoors until the new plants are large enough to move to their permanent homes.

BEST BETS FOR CUTTINGS

Are you thinking about giving cuttings a try? Here's a rundown of some of the easiest perennials to root from stem cuttings:

Asters (*Aster*)
Bee balms (*Monarda*)
Boltonia (*Boltonia asteroides*)
Catmints (*Nepeta*)
Dahlias (*Dahlia*)
Dead nettle (*Lamium maculatum*)
Golden marguerite (*Anthemis tinctoria*)
Joe Pye weed (*Eupatorium maculatum*)
Leadwort (*Ceratostigma plumbaginoides*)
Mums (*Chrysanthemum x morifolium*)
Obedient plant (*Physostegia virginiana*)
Oxeye sunflower (*Heliopsis helianthoides*)
Perennial candytuft (*Iberis sempervirens*)
Phlox (*Phlox*)
Rock cress (*Arabis caucasica*)
Sages (*Salvia*)
Speedwells (*Veronica*)
Stonecrops (*Sedum*)

Plants with thick roots (such as bleeding heart and Oriental poppy): In late summer or fall, carefully lift the clump out of the soil with a spading fork, and cut off 3- to 4-inch-long root segments. In order to distinguish between the top and bottom, make a straight cut across the top of the root segment and a slanted cut across the bottom. Pot each segment individually, standing it upright in a 5- to 6-inch-diameter clay pot that has been filled with garden soil. Be sure you've inserted the segment with the slanted end down. Set the segment so that the top is about 1 inch below the soil surface. Water carefully. Set the pots in a cold frame for the winter. In spring, when sprouts appear, move the cuttings outdoors to their permanent homes.

🪣 DON'T LOSE YOUR STRIPES!

Be warned: If you take root cuttings from variegated perennials—such as 'Harlequin' and 'Norah Leigh' phlox (*Phlox paniculata* cultivars)—the resulting plants will be all green! It's better to make new plants from these special perennials by cuttings or division.

🪣 LAYERING'S A PIECE OF CAKE

Another easy way to make new plants from your perennials is by using a technique known as layering. It's sort of like taking cuttings, but you leave the shoots attached to the parent plant until they form roots, so you don't have to worry about them wilting. Here's how:

1. In early to midsummer, select a young, flexible shoot near the base of the plant, and gently bend it down so that some part of it behind the shoot tip touches the

BEST BETS FOR LAYERING

These are a few of the easiest perennials to duplicate by layering. But don't let this list stop you— experiment with others, too!

Lavenders (*Lavandula*)
Periwinkles (*Vinca*)
Phlox (*Phlox*, creeping types)
Pinks (*Dianthus*)
Sage (*Salvia officinalis*)
Thymes (*Thymus*)

Garden phlox
Phlox paniculata

Fragrant and colorful flower clusters; outstanding in late-summer beds and borders

BEST BETS FOR ROOT CUTTINGS

Here's a list of the perennials that multiply readily from root cuttings—give them a try!

Baby's breath (*Gypsophila paniculata*)
Bear's breeches (*Acanthus*)
Bergenias (*Bergenia*)
Blanket flowers (*Gaillardia* x *grandiflora*)
Bugloss (*Anchusa*)
Butterfly weed (*Asclepias tuberosa*)
Common bleeding heart (*Dicentra spectabilis*)
Cupid's dart (*Catananche caerulea*)
Drumstick primrose (*Primula denticulata*)
Globe thistles (*Echinops*)
Hardy geraniums (*Geranium*)
Japanese anemones (*Anemone japonica*)
Mulleins (*Verbascum*)
Oriental poppy (*Papaver orientale*)
Phlox (*Phlox*)
Plume poppy (*Macleaya*)
Purple coneflower (*Echinacea purpurea*)
Sea hollies (*Eryngium*)

ground. Pinch off the leaves where the stem meets the ground.

2. Loosen the soil in the area where the stem touches the ground. Dig a small trench about 1 inch deep, bend the stem down into the trench, and cover the bare stem with soil. Make sure you leave at least an inch or two of the shoot tip exposed.

3. Set a rock over the buried stem to help hold it down. Keep the area evenly moist.

4. By fall, the layer should be rooted. Snip the stem off the parent plant, remove the rock, and then dig up and move the rooted layer to wherever you want it to grow.

Multiplying by Dividing

The fastest way by far to multiply your perennials and bulbs is by dividing them. You start with one clump, and with little effort, you can end up with two, three, four, or more new plants to fill your flowerbeds or share with friends!

 MORE THAN YOU BARGAINED FOR

I love perennials because you always get more than you bargained for. Where else can you get all that beauty and grace, plus months of blooms and plants for free, too?

Besides being a super-easy way of duplicating them, dividing perennials and bulbs regularly will help keep your plants in tip-top shape. After a few years, spreading perennials can start creeping into their companions, and even clumping perennials and bulbs can get too crowded. By dividing them every three to five years, you get rid of unproductive old growth and replant the vigorous, young parts. The rejuvenated clumps will bloom better and be much less prone to pests and disease problems—you couldn't ask for more!

Garlic chives
Allium tuberosum

Clusters of white flowers in fall; flavorful foliage

Watch for These Clues

You'll know it's time to divide your perennials and bulbs when you see the following signs:

- The center of the clump is dead.

- The stems are crowded, weak, and floppy.

- The plant produces fewer flowering shoots each year.

- The base of the clump is pushed out of the soil.

- New shoots are crowding out surrounding plants.

TIMING IS EVERYTHING

The best time to divide your plants is when they're *not* actively growing. For most perennials, that means early to midfall. There are a few exceptions, though. Wait until spring to divide fall-flowering perennials (otherwise, you'll cut short their end-of-the-season show). Divide early bloomers right after their flowers fade, so they'll have all

TOOL TIME

Dividing perennials and bulbs doesn't take special equipment—just a few of these basic tools from your shed (and maybe your kitchen!):

Shovel or spading fork: to dig up larger clumps

Sturdy trowel or hand fork: to lift smaller clumps

Razor-sharp spade: for cutting through large, tough clumps

Old kitchen knife (serrated steak knives are great): for cutting apart smaller clumps

Gas plant
Dictamnus albus

Long-lived perennial with aromatic foliage and pink or white early-summer blooms

year to get settled in again. And for bulbs, wait until their top growth has turned yellow to dig and separate them.

GET READY, GET SET...

Preparation is the key to success with divisions. You want the roots to be exposed above ground for as little as possible, so getting everything ready *before* you dig up any perennial will help speed the process, and keep the roots from drying out. Gather the tools you'll need, then decide how many new divisions you hope to make from the clump.

Are you hoping for a few good-sized divisions that you can plant directly back into your garden? I like garden-sized divisions to be about the size of my palm. So for most perennials, that means making only two or three new plants from the original clump. Prepare the new planting sites for these divisions ahead of time. If you'll be setting one of the divisions back in the original spot, also have some compost on hand, so you can enrich the soil before replanting.

Or, would you like to make as many new plants as possible? You can go as small as a single bud or stem per division, as long as each new piece has its own roots. It will take longer to separate a clump into small divisions, but you may get six, 12, or 18 new plants—or even more! These little guys will need some babying, though, so be prepared to pot them up individually and coddle them in a cold frame or sheltered spot for a year or so until they're big enough to hold their own in the garden.

DIVIDE YOUR DIVISIONS

Plan on dividing a few of your perennials each year, rather than digging up all of them at one time. That way, you'll still have a nice-looking garden with plenty of flowers instead of starting from scratch every few years!

🪣 Four Steps to Division Success

Ready to divide and conquer? Here's what to do:

Step 1. Dig up the clump. Use a spade, spading fork, or shovel to cut a circle all the way around the outside of the clump or carpet of plants, about 2 or 3 inches out from the outermost stems. After you go around one time, start going around again along the same circle, inserting the tool more deeply into the soil and pulling the handle toward you to help pry up the clump.

Step 2. Set the cut-out clump on a tarp. If you plan to make many small divisions, dunk the clump in a large bucket of water or use a hose to wash off the soil so you can easily see the roots; otherwise, move on to Step 3.

Step 3. Gently tease or break apart the divisions with your hands, if you can. Tougher divisions call for a sharp knife or a super-sharp spade to cut through the roots. Make sure every new division has at least one bud or stem and some roots.

Step 4. If you want to replace the original plant, work some compost into the planting hole—add more topsoil, too, if need-ed—and set *one* of the divisions in that spot. Move the remaining divisions to other parts of your garden, pot them up, or wrap them in damp newspaper and share them with your friends.

JERRY'S GEMS

If possible, save your dividing for a cool, cloudy day. Otherwise, keep the dug-up clumps and new divisions in the shade as much as possible. If the weather has been dry, give the clumps you plan to divide a long, cool drink about an hour before you dig them up. That way, they'll be all juiced up and less likely to wilt.

Oh, and one more tip—if you're dividing a perennial that has lots of leaves and stems, cut all the top growth back by half before you even dig it up. It will make lifting and dividing the clump *much* easier, and the plant will lose less water in the process.

 NO-DIG DIVISIONS

Do you have a clump you want to divide, but it's too big to dig up? Then divide it right in place! Using a razor-sharp spade, cut right into each perennial clump while it's still in the ground. Cut through the middle, then cut one of the halves into pie-shaped wedges. Carefully dig out the individual wedges and plant them in another spot.

Fill the hole left next to the remaining half with a mix of topsoil and compost. Your plant will appreciate the extra elbow room—especially since you didn't have to disturb its roots all that much in the process!

BULB BASICS

Bulbs will multiply as surely as children will grow. After a few years, you'll probably notice that your daffodils and tulip blooms aren't as big and beautiful as they used to be. Chances are, the bulbs are overcrowded and need dividing. The longer you wait to divide bulbs, the harder the job will be, and the longer it will take the weakened bulbs to reach flowering size again—so plan to divide as soon as you see these signs.

When you dig, try to lift the whole clump at once. Then find a cool, shady place for separating the bulbs. You're going to replant them immediately, but you still don't want them to dry out any more than necessary! Break the bulbs apart with your hands, then replant the largest of the bulbs in the garden. Plant the babies behind them, or put them in a nursery bed for a year or two to grow up, then when you're ready, move them back to the garden.

*I*t's best to dig your bulbs up for dividing at the beginning of their dormant period, as soon as the leaves have died back. The best tool for lifting bulbs is a spading fork. My Grandma Putt always used one that had large tines, so she could get the fork under a clump of bulbs and not through the middle of it. She sure didn't want to go to sleep at night with a bulb shish-kabob on her conscience!

🪣 Do Not Disturb!

I'm not going to give you a list of "best bets for division,"
because there are just too many perennials and bulbs you
can successfully divide! So instead, I'll point out a few that
are better left alone. These long-lived perennials rarely get
overcrowded, so dividing them isn't a must, and it's so easy
to damage their long, deep roots that you may do them
more harm than good by separating them:

Balloon flower (*Platycodon grandiflorus*)

Butterfly weed (*Asclepias tuberosa*)

False indigos (*Baptisia*)

Gas plant (*Dictamnus albus*)

Globe thistles (*Echinops*)

Goatsbeard (*Aruncus dioicus*)

Lupines (*Lupinus*)

Oriental poppy (*Papaver orientale*)

Peonies (*Paeonia*)

Sea hollies (*Eryngium*)

Gladiolus
Gladiolus hybrid

Pretty in the
garden and superb
for bouquets and
arrangements

🪣 Try a Little Tenderness

After replanting your divisions, treat them with a little TLC.
First, water them generously. Then give them an ample
amount of mulch to keep the soil evenly moist, and protect
them from being heaved out of the soil by alternating freezing and thawing during the winter.

CHAPTER 8

PERENNIAL AND BULB PROBLEM SOLVER

You've planned and planted, pinched and
primped—now it's your turn to enjoy the bounty
of beautiful flowers. Don't let a bunch of bugs
or a few funky fungi spoil your party—be prepared
to nip problems "in the bud," and they'll never get
bad enough to blight your beds and borders.

An Ounce of Prevention

Once pests and diseases get a foothold in your perennial gardens, they can seriously damage or even destroy your prized plantings. Fortunately, some regular attention from you and some simple preventive measures can go a long way toward keeping your flowers in top-notch form.

🪣 HEALTHY PLANT CHECKLIST

A healthy garden starts with healthy plants. You sure as heck don't want to bring weak, diseased, or pest-infested plants home from the garden center, so it's smart to check them carefully *before* you buy. Here are some things to look for:

☑ First, consider the overall condition of the place where you're shopping. If there are many dead, wilted, or obviously diseased or buggy plants, walk away! It's not worth taking a chance on a plant that hasn't been well cared for, even if the price is reduced. A potential pest or disease problem is no bargain for any amount of money!

☑ Now, look at the plant's top growth. Are the leaves an even green color (or whatever color they are supposed to be), or are they discolored? Pale leaves may indicate a nutrient deficiency, which you can fix easily. But if the leaves are browned or show distinct streaks or spots, then the plant may have a more serious problem.

☑ Turn the leaves over, and check the stems, too. Pests like to hide in these sheltered spots. Don't buy any plants that have obvious pest problems.

☑ Check the roots, too. If possible, gently slide the plant out of the pot to look for pests and discolored or dead roots. Roots that are heavily matted or are spiraling around

Globe thistle
Echinops ritro

Rounded clusters of silvery blue blooms in summer; good for cutting or drying

START WITH THE SOIL

It's a fact of life—plants growing in well-balanced, humus-rich soil are less likely to be attacked by pests and diseases. The few hours you put into preparing a good planting site will pay off with years of beautiful flowers. What a great investment!

the outside of the soil ball indicate that the plant has been in its pot too long. Such a plant can recover with special care from you, but in the meantime, you'll have a stressed plant that's a magnet for pest and disease problems.

🪣 PUT THEM IN THEIR PLACE

Smart planting can prevent practically 90 percent of all perennial problems. It starts with taking the time to figure out exactly what kind of growing conditions your yard has to offer—sun, full shade, dry soil, or whatever. Then do your research before you buy any perennial or bulb to make sure it can grow in those conditions. A perennial that's stressed out by growing in less-than-ideal conditions is an easy target for pests and pathogens. But when you put the right plant in the right place, it will naturally be more vigorous and problem-resistant, saving you a lot of effort in the long run.

🪣 BACK TO THE BASICS

If you're looking for the most trouble-free garden, it makes sense to stick with tried-and-true, easy-care plants like bleeding hearts (*Dicentra*), daylilies (*Hemerocallis*), and peonies (*Paeonia*), to name just a few. Fill your garden with these dependable, long-lasting perennials, and let them fend for themselves. Then, if you want to grow a few beautiful, but problem-prone plants—such as delphiniums in warm climates—or try one of the latest new rarities on the market, you can concentrate your efforts on them and still not be overwhelmed with garden work.

Mixers & Elixirs

GARDEN CURE-ALL TONIC

At the first sign of insects or disease, mix up a batch of this tonic to set things right:

4 cloves of garlic
1 small onion
1 small jalapeño pepper
Warm water
1 tsp. of Murphy® Oil Soap
1 tsp. of vegetable oil
Warm water

Pulverize the garlic, onion, and pepper in a blender, and let them steep in a quart of warm water for 2 hours. Strain the mixture through cheesecloth, dilute the liquid with three parts of warm water. Add the Murphy's and vegetable oil. Pour into a handheld sprayer and spray perennials and bulbs several times a week.

 KEEP DISEASES AT BAY

When it comes to plant diseases, an ounce of prevention is worth a pound of fungicide. And here's more good news: It doesn't take a lot of time or effort on your part to have a healthy garden. Just follow these secrets to keeping your perennials and bulbs looking their best:

Avoid planting in dank, dark spots. Ample light and air are the keys to strong, healthy growth.

Don't crowd your plants. Leave plenty of "breathing" room around them for good air circulation.

> **Try This!**
>
> Don't plant your bulbs without babying them first! Dust them with medicated baby powder before planting, and the varmints will stay away. This one simple step could save countless bulb lives.

Water your flowerbeds early in the day. That allows the blooms and leaves to dry off before nightfall. Fungal diseases thrive on wet foliage.

Keep your plants clean. Stake those that need support, so they don't flop onto the ground, and use a mulch to prevent soil from splashing up on flowers and foliage.

PERENNIAL SELF-DEFENSE

When reading plant tags or flipping through nursery catalogs, you may run across the phrase "disease-resistant." Perennials with this rating have shown that they're much less likely to suffer from certain disease problems than non-resistant plants growing in the same conditions. That makes them great choices for your garden!

CLEAN UP YOUR ACT

After many years of experience, I can tell you that keeping your perennial beds clean will go a long way toward reducing pest and disease troubles. So, throughout the growing season, remove old flowers as they fade and old leaves as

Glory-of-the-snow
Chionodoxa luciliae

Blue or pink flowers appear as early as late winter; blooms even through light snow they wither and brown. Put all nondiseased foliage on your compost pile.

If your beds become too crowded, divide clumps of perennials and bulbs, and dispose of the extras, or share them with friends and neighbors. In the fall, remove and discard the top growth of delphiniums, peonies, and irises.

Toad-ally Excellent

Toads are a gardener's best friend, so never harm them. In three months, a single toad will devour 10,000 insects, including beetles, worms, snails, caterpillars, wasps, yellow jackets, and ants. So please, cultivate a friendship with your local toads!

BULB SMARTS

Planting hardy bulbs in soggy soil will shorten their lives. They will be poorly developed, their flowers will be smaller, and eventually, the bulbs will rot. Avoid this fate by choosing a well-drained planting site, or build a raised bed for your bulbs.

COMPOST CAUTIOUSLY

Many folks add every scrap of yard waste to their compost pile, in hopes of increasing their future supply of humus. Although it sounds like a good idea at first, going for quantity over quality can spell disaster for your flower garden in the long run.

Overenthusiastic composters can unknowingly fill their piles with numerous insects and a whole host of diseases that carry over from year to year in the form of eggs, grubs, spores, or what have you. Oftentimes, these carriers are on, in, or under some kind of plant growth. Adding this infected

Goldband lily
Lilium auratum

Regal beauty for summer borders, with pure white, gold-striped petals plant material to the compost pile *now* spells big trouble when you use the compost in your garden *next year.*

So, how can you tell what's good to compost, and what should be destroyed? You can't always be sure, unless you're a darned good scientist. But you'll be on the right track if you make it a point to burn or discard any plants and plant parts that you know have been attacked by insects or diseases. Remember—when in doubt, throw it out!

G randma Putt used dried bloodmeal to serve two purposes in her bulb plantings. First, she mixed it into the soil at planting time to protect her bulbs from chipmunks and other varmints. She also sprinkled it on the soil after planting to help repel pesky critters. As a bonus, it supplied a much-needed dose of nitrogen, which helped to keep her bulbs healthy and happy.

 ## BULB ALERT

When shopping for bulbs, avoid any that have mushy gray spots on them. They're not worth carting home at any price, because they're unhealthy and won't recover. But don't worry if the bulb's papery skin is loose—this is completely normal. And don't be concerned about a few nicks—they won't affect the development of otherwise healthy bulbs.

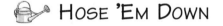 ## HOSE 'EM DOWN

I can't say this often enough—giving your plants a good washing with soapy water before applying liquid fertilizers, weed killers, or pest controls can mean the difference between a garden that's just getting by, and one that is healthy and growing. Why? Because soap removes dust, dirt, and pollution from leaf pores, enabling plants to better take up the good stuff that follows. So before you apply any sprays, give your flower garden a bath with 1 cup of dishwashing liquid applied with your 20 gallon hose-end sprayer, or use my Plant Shampoo (available from www.jerrybaker.com).

 ## SEPARATE, BUT EQUAL

If you plan to apply herbicides (weed control sprays) around your flower garden, I highly recommend buying a separate sprayer specifically for that use. Even with careful cleaning, herbicide residue can contaminate a sprayer. The next time you use that sprayer to apply fertilizers, pesticides, or fungicides, you could do your plants far more harm than good! Clearly label your herbicide sprayer (and insert an orange golf ball to agitate the mix), so that you don't use it by accident to apply any other sprays.

Mixers & Elixirs

ALL-SEASON CLEAN-UP TONIC

Apply this tonic in early evening every two weeks during the growing season to keep pests and diseases at bay:

1 cup of baby shampoo
1 cup of tobacco tea*
1 cup of antiseptic mouthwash
Warm water

Mix all of the ingredients in a 20 gallon hose-end sprayer, filling the balance of the jar with warm water. Liberally apply this mixture to your beds and borders.

*Place three fingers of chewing tobacco in an old nylon stocking and soak in a gallon of hot water until the mixture is dark brown.

ACT FAST!

Many plant diseases—and pests—spread very quickly. So be sure to spring into action at the first sign of trouble. Whether you're applying one of my tonics or a commercial spray, or handpicking diseased leaves and flowers, do it early in the game. This saves you time, effort, and materials—and results in better long-term control.

Don't Dust in the Wind!

Would you rather dust your perennials than spray them? Then apply the dust early in the morning or late in the evening, when the air is still and the dew on the plants will help the dust stick better.

What's Bugging You?

Every garden plays home to a host of bugs, and the vast majority of them are good guys. To keep the few bad apples from spoiling your borders, learn to identify the pests, then take control as soon as you see them.

Golden
hakone grass
Hakonechloa macra
'Aureola'

Arching mounds
of yellow and
green striped
leaves; a winner
for shady spots

JERRY'S PLAN FOR PERENNIAL PESTS

The best way to keep your perennials happy and healthy is also the most fun—simply take plenty of strolls around your garden! If you look over your plants for even a few minutes each day or two, you'll spot any developing pest problems right away. Pick off the pests by hand and drop them into a can of kerosene or a bucket of soapy water, or knock them off with a strong spray of water. If you take care of the problem at an early stage, you won't have to resort to more serious measures down the road.

DUST DOES 'EM IN

Keep thugs away from your flowers by sprinkling a light layer of diatomaceous earth around the base of your plants and on their foliage. This sharp dust/powder scratches soft-bodied insects and slugs, causing them to dehydrate and die.

SYSTEMATIC SPRAYING

Leave no leaf unsprayed! To get rid of pests, you must spray your plants thoroughly—especially under the leaves, where most diseases start and many bugs hide from the light of day.

HELP WANTED

What if you just can't figure out what's bugging your plants? Snip off a damaged shoot and seal it in a plastic bag. If possible, catch one of the bugs you suspect, too. You should be able to find help identifying the guilty party through your local Cooperative Extension Service office (look in the phone book under "Government Offices"). You may also find assistance at a botanical garden or arboretum in your area or even at your local garden center.

WHO DID IT?

So, how do you tell which bugs are bugging your plants? Fortunately, there aren't too many serious perennial pests. To help nail down the likely culprit, check out the descriptions here.

What You See	Possible Perpetrator
Holes in leaves and/or flowers	Japanese beetles or other beetles; caterpillars; slugs or snails (on low-growing plants)
Distorted, sticky leaves, stems, and/or buds; leaves and/or buds that discolor and drop off	Aphids
Powdery black coating on leaves and/or stems	Sooty mold fungus, which is living on sticky "honeydew" released by aphids
Rounded, sunken brown spots on leaves; distorted shoots and buds	Plant bugs
Silvery streaking on leaves; buds that are darkened and fail to open; streaking on flower petals	Thrips
Winding tunnels between upper and lower leaf surfaces	Leaf miners

A Pinch in Time

The simplest and most effective perennial pest control measure is right at your fingertips! Squashing a pest with your fingers—or dropping it into a cup of soapy water or kerosene—will stop the damage immediately. Plus, the pest will have no chance to reproduce, so you'll reduce the chance of future problems.

If you're a bit squeamish, or if you're dealing with plant bugs (which can cause skin irritation), put on gloves before you squash the pests. Or pinch or clip off the infested leaf or shoot and let it drop into a bag, toss it in your freezer for a day or two to kill the pests, then dispose of it.

THIS IS A TEST

Before dousing your perennials with any homemade or commercial concoction, it's smart to test the spray on a few leaves first. Some plants are much more sensitive to sprays than others, and you don't want your perennials to suffer more from the side effects of a spray than from the pests themselves. If you don't notice any discoloration on the leaves within two days of the application, go ahead and spray away!

THIS SOLUTION STINKS!

The strong smell of garlic apparently offends as many bugs as people. To make a pungent pest repellent, cut up six cloves of garlic, and mix with 1 tablespoon of baby shampoo and 1 quart of water. Spray it on your perennials, and the bugs will beat a hasty retreat!

WELCOME, FRIENDS

Not all bugs are bad! Many of them won't have any effect on your plants, and some are actually good guys. These "beneficials" may eat pesky insects directly, or lay their eggs in the bodies of the pests. One way you can attract these helpful critters is to grow a variety of perennials with small, nectar-rich flowers, such as coral bells (*Heuchera*), goldenrods (*Solidago*), pincushion flowers (*Scabiosa*), and yarrows (*Achillea*).

Beneficial bugs also need a water source, so they'll be drawn to your garden if you make them a simple "bug bath." Simply take an old birdbath or other shallow container that can hold water, then place some small

Grape hyacinth
Muscari botryoides

Trouble-free bulb with clustered purple-blue spring blooms

Mixers & Elixirs

ALL-PURPOSE BUG/THUG SPRAY

To kill flower garden insects and diseases in one fell swoop, whip up a batch of this all-purpose spray:

3 tbsp. of baking soda
2 tbsp. of Murphy® Oil Soap
2 tbsp. of canola oil
2 tbsp. of vinegar
2 gal. of warm water

Mix all of the ingredients together, and mist-spray your perennials to the point of run-off. Apply in early spring, just as the bugs and thugs are waking up.

rocks and gravel in the base, and add enough water to almost cover them. The stones will create small islands where the insects can land and drink safely.

KEEP BUGS FROM BUGGING YOU

To keep bugs at bay while you're out working in your flower garden, try these tips:

❧ Avoid using heavily scented cologne, hair spray, hand lotion, or shaving lotion.

❧ Don't wave your arms to ward off an insect. Simply stand still until the pest flies away.

❧ Try an all-natural pest repellent, such as pennyroyal, peppermint, eucalyptus, or citronella.

❧ Cover yourself with tightly knit clothing. Wear a long-sleeved shirt with tight cuffs, and tuck your pant cuffs into your boots or socks.

SUPER-SIMPLE SPRITZER

Keep a bottle of rubbing alcohol on hand in your garden shed. It's a quick and easy way to get rid of all sorts of pests like mealybugs, spider mites, aphids, whiteflies, and gnats. Simply mix $1/2$ cup of rubbing alcohol with a quart of water. Mist-spray any infested plants.

HOLD UP ON CLEANUP

There is such a thing as being *too* tidy in your off-season garden cleanup. Definitely remove all remains of plants that suffered pest or disease problems during the growing season. But leaving a reasonable amount

Grandma Putt's WISDOM

*E*very year, Grandma Putt made sure she grew some hot peppers in her vegetable garden. Ground, dried hot peppers make a very effective spray against ants, spiders, caterpillars, fleas, and many other small insects. Fresh hot peppers work great, too: Chop up some onions and garlic with your peppers, cover the mash with water, and let it stand overnight. The next morning, drain off the liquid and add it to enough water to make a gallon of spray. Grandma Putt's pepper-based brew makes a great all-purpose pest spray for chrysanthemums and other perennials!

of dead stuff (like leaves) lying on the ground around your plants will do your perennials and bulbs good by enriching the soil.

 GET A FIX ON APHIDS

Aphids are pesky little oblong to pear-shaped insects that come in a range of colors. They often hang out in groups on shoot tips and underneath leaves. Aphids suck sap out of a plant's tissues, deforming leaves, shoots, and buds, and causing leaves and buds to fall off. They transmit viruses from plant to plant, too. As they feed, aphids secrete sticky stuff called honeydew, which supports the growth of black sooty mold on leaves and stems.

APHID ANTIDOTE

To keep aphids and other pests off your prized perennials, mix up a batch of this amazingly potent antidote:

1 medium onion, chopped finely
1 tbsp. of dishwashing liquid
Water

In a blender, thoroughly blend the onion in a quart of water. Strain off the clear juice, and mix 2 tablespoons of it per gallon of water with the dishwashing liquid. Pour the liquid into a handheld sprayer, and apply liberally to your flowers at the first sign of aphid trouble.

 SQUISHY SOLUTION

You're most likely to see aphids in spring and early summer, when your perennials are producing lots of soft, juicy new growth. These little buggers aren't picky—they'll feed on a wide range of perennials. Fortunately, it's not too hard to control them. Squish them with your fingers, pinch off and destroy infested parts, or use a commercial or homemade spray, such as my Aphid Antidote (above).

WATER WORKS

One of your best—and safest—bets for controlling aphids is water! Simply turn a forceful spray on the infested plants. You may succeed in knocking off so many aphids that you won't have to use anything more potent. Aphids that are so rudely dislodged generally will not return.

Grecian
windflower
Anemone blanda

Carpets of purple,
pink, or white,
daisylike flowers
in early spring

BEETLE BASICS

Beetles are hard-shelled insects that range in size from $^{1}/_{4}$ to $^{3}/_{4}$ inch in length. Many species are actually good guys, eating other insects, but a few can do serious damage to your perennials. Japanese beetles—with metallic blue-green bodies and bronze-colored wing covers—are one of the most well-known pest beetles. These thugs and their troublesome cousins feed on leaves, buds, and flowers, chewing on the edges or eating holes right through. When a flock of Japanese beetles feast on one plant, they'll practically devour whole leaves, so only the skeleton of leaf veins remains. These pests bother many perennials, but they are particularly fond of hollyhocks (*Alcea rosea*) and their relatives.

Mixers & Elixirs

BEETLE JUICE

This recipe isn't for the squeamish, but nothing beats it for fighting beetles!

½ cup of beetles (dead or alive)
1 tsp. of dishwashing liquid
Water
Cheesecloth

Mix the beetles and 2 cups of water together in an *old* blender. Strain the mix through cheesecloth and mix in the dishwashing liquid. Pour ¼ cup into a 1 gallon handheld sprayer, and fill the rest of the jar with water.

Drench the soil around new plants with this beetle juice to keep beetles from getting started. If they're already on the scene, spray plants from top to bottom, making sure to coat both sides of the leaves. Freeze any extra juice—and be sure to label it clearly!

BEAT THE BEETLES

If you can find the beetles that are attacking your perennials, pick them off by hand and drop them into soapy water or kerosene. Early morning is a good time for beetle-hunting, by the way. That's because cooler temperatures make them more sluggish, so they are easier to catch then.

SAFE AND SOUND

Beneficial beetles can do a banner job controlling a wide variety of garden pests, including slugs, snails, cutworms, and other soil-dwelling creepy-crawlies. These beetles like to hide under stones or leaves during the day and hunt at night, so they appreciate areas that aren't dug or cultivated often. Garden paths made of grass, gravel, or stepping stones also provide safe daytime resting areas for beneficial beetles.

DON'T LET YOUR IRISES GET BORED

Bearded irises are incredibly beautiful, with huge flowers in a true rainbow of colors. But people aren't the only ones who enjoy these exquisite perennials: Iris borers like them, too! How can you tell if your bearded irises are infested with borers? Look for irregular brown lines or tunnels in the leaves, ragged leaf edges, or rhizomes that are soft and foul-smelling—these are all sure signs that borers are around. And that means it's time for you to get a jump on controlling these pests.

BORER BEATERS

Adult iris borers are moths that lay their eggs on bearded iris leaves. Cream-colored larvae emerge from the eggs in spring and feed on leaves and flower stalks, then work their way down into the rhizomes. By late summer, the larvae are pink with brown heads, and about 2 inches long. Besides injuring the rhizomes, these larvae produce damage that provides an entry point for bacterial soft rot.

To control these pests, remove all of the dead leaves from around your irises in the fall to get rid of overwintering eggs. In spring, dust the base of each clump with pyrethrin, or pick young borers off the leaves by hand. When you dig and divide your bearded irises in late summer, remove and destroy any infested rhizomes that you find.

Greigii tulip
Tulipa greigii

Bright red blooms and beautiful blue-green leaves heavily speckled with maroon

TOOL TIME

A long-handled flower duster makes it a snap to apply pest control dusts right at ground level. To make your own, simply punch holes in the base of a coffee can with a nail, then use bolts to attach the side of the can to an old wooden broom or rake handle. You want the bottom of the can to sit about 4 inches above the end of the handle.

When you're ready to dust, put the powder into the can. To apply, simply tap the end of the wooden handle on the ground, and the dust will sift out of the can. It's that easy!

Guernsey lily
Nerine sarniensis

Funnel-shaped
pink flowers in
early fall; bring
indoors for the
winter in areas
with frost

CATERPILLAR CALLING CARDS

Irregular holes in the leaves and buds of your perennials may mean that caterpillars are the culprits. They cause the same kind of damage as beetles, but unlike beetles, caterpillars move slowly and tend to hang around for a while. So if you're trying to tell which thug caused the damage, turn the leaves over, and check the stems for signs of these wormlike pests. Caterpillars come in an amazing array of sizes and colors, and they can be smooth, hairy, or even spiny.

CATCH THAT CATERPILLAR!

Fortunately, caterpillars usually aren't a serious problem for most perennials. And of those that do attack garden perennials, several are the larvae of lovely butterflies (such as monarchs), so you might consider putting up with some chewed leaves in return for the beautiful adults.

If you really want to stop the damage, though, put on some gloves, handpick the caterpillars, and drop them into soapy water or kerosene. Or spray infested plants with my Caterpillar Killer Tonic (at left).

Mixers & Elixirs

CATERPILLAR KILLER TONIC

To keep caterpillars in check and away from your flowers, mix up a batch of this tonic:

½ lb. of wormwood (Artemisia) **leaves**
2 tbsp. of Murphy® Oil Soap
Warm water

Simmer the wormwood leaves in 2 cups of water for 30 minutes or so. Strain out the leaves, then add the remaining liquid and the Murphy's to 2 more cups of warm water. Apply with a 6 gallon hose-end sprayer to the point of run-off. Repeat as necessary until the caterpillars are history!

CUTTING REMARKS

One day you set out a bunch of baby perennials, and the next day, you find all the tops nipped off. Who's the culprit? Probably cutworms! These gray or brown caterpillars curl around young stems and chew through them right at the soil line. To prevent this from happening to your young perennials, place a collar of paper or cardboard around the base of the stems at planting time.

Great Garden Allies

Birds, toads, ladybugs, and garter snakes—they can all help you win the war on bugs. So do what you can to encourage the critters to visit your yard. These bug-hungry allies are worth their weight in gold for cutting down the local pest population! Here's a quick list of attractions to lure these beneficials:

Birds: Feeders and a clean water supply attract our feathered friends. It also helps if you can place your feeders near shrubbery or other protected areas, so that the birds have a place to hide if predators are lurking.

Toads: Make a toad house by simply overturning an old clay flowerpot, and nestling it among plants in a shady spot. Prop it up with a small rock to encourage toads to come in and call it home.

Ladybugs: Plant flowers that are rich in nectar and pollen, such as yarrows (*Achillea*), angelica, and goldenrods (*Solidago*).

Garter snakes: Permanent plantings of evergreen groundcovers, such as Japanese pachysandra (*Pachysandra terminalis*), provide perfect shelter for these pest-eating slitherers.

LEAF MINERS' LAST STAND

If you've ever grown columbines (*Aquilegia*), you've probably noticed funny-looking squiggles inside the leaves—the calling card of leaf miners. These pests are the tiny larvae of inconspicuous black or black and yellow flies. They hatch from eggs laid on the foliage, then tunnel into the leaves and chew winding paths as they feed inside. Besides columbines, other favorite targets for leaf miners include primroses (*Primula*), mums (*Chrysanthemum* x *morifolium*), delphiniums, and Shasta daisies (*C.* x *superbum*).

Leaf miners usually don't cause enough damage to kill a plant, which is a good thing, since it's very difficult to control these pests. Because they're feeding inside the leaves, rather than on top, they're protected from both sprays and natural predators. Simply pick off and destroy (don't compost) infested leaves. Or, if the plant looks really bad, cut off and destroy all the top growth; your plant will quickly sprout fresh, undamaged leaves.

MANY MITES AREN'T RIGHT

Individual spider mites are so small that just a few of these pests can't do much harm. But where there are a few spider mites, more quickly appear! Even in large numbers, it's hard to see these tiny reddish, yellow, or pale green pests, but you might see their fine webs on the underside of damaged leaves. Spider mites are most often a problem in summer, during hot, dry weather. Keeping your perennials well watered and mulched will help minimize the damage they suffer from spider mites. Treat seriously infested plants with a soap-based spray or with my Super Spider Mite Mix (at left).

Mixers & Elixirs

SUPER SPIDER MITE MIX

Send spider mites to an early grave with this suffocating mix:

4 cups of wheat flour
½ cup of buttermilk
5 gal. of water

Mix all of the ingredients together, and apply to your plants with a handheld sprayer. Spray to the point of run-off. This mix will suffocate the little buggers without harming your plants.

MIGHTY MITES

Spiders are good for your garden, because they eat lots of insects. Spider mites, though, are truly troublesome pests. These very tiny, spiderlike pests suck sap out of plant tissues, causing leaves to look like they have small yellow speckles. Seriously infested leaves may turn all yellow or brown, curl up, and drop off, weakening the overall health of the affected plant.

OUT, DARNED SPOT!

Don't spray the "black spots" on delphiniums with a fungicide. These spots aren't a fungus—they're caused by mites. To control them, use rotenone or nicotine sprays, or dust the leaves with powdered sulfur (available at garden centers).

ARE PLANT BUGS BUGGING YOU?

If you see small, round, sunken brown spots on the leaves of your perennials (especially in early summer), plant bugs are probably to blame. The nymphs are wingless, with greenish or red bodies. The adults are ¼ inch long and brown or greenish yellow with four black stripes down their back. Both the nymphs and the adults suck sap out of leaves, causing the brown spots and weakening the plant.

Plant bugs are elusive little critters—they're hard to find, and even harder to catch. Fortunately, most perennials are strong enough to outgrow the damage without any help from you. But if you notice a lot of damage in early summer, try a commercial or homemade soap-based spray.

*M*any old-time gardeners— my Grandma Putt included— swore by a spray made of ground-up bugs and water. To try it for yourself, simply put as many dead insects as you can find in a jar, cover them with water, and allow them to "cook" for a few days. Then mix this buggy solution with 10 parts water, and apply it with an old handheld sprayer or hose-end sprayer (you may not want to use it again for anything else).

No one is sure exactly why this works, but one theory I've heard is that the mixture passes along deadly bug viruses or other pathogens to the target pests.

SNAILS AND SLUGS: GARDEN THUGS

These slimy slitherers need no introduction! Both snails and slugs can appear just about anywhere, in a wide range of sizes and colors—with coiled shells (snails) or without (slugs). These troublesome thugs can chew large irregular holes in leaves or even devour whole leaves. They normally come out only at night to feed, but you may spot them on plants during the day in cool, cloudy, damp weather. You'll also notice their silvery slime trails on the soil, mulch, plants, or paths. They feed on just about any perennial, but they really flock to hostas and delphiniums.

To keep snails and slugs to a minimum, pick up

Haage campion
Lychnis x *haageana*

Glowing orange-red blossoms all summer long atop 18-inch-tall stems

dropped leaves, petals, and other debris. Surround susceptible plants with a scratchy barrier (see "Scratchy Roadblocks" below) to discourage slugs from attacking. If you do spot either slugs or snails on plants, pick them off and drop them into soapy water. If the pests are on the soil or mulch, blasting them with vinegar or sprinkling them with salt can do them in.

Hairy beardtongue

Penstemon hirsutus

Pretty, purple-flowering perennial thrives in hot, dry sites

Mixers & Elixirs

SUPER SLUG SPRAY

For slugs that are too small to handpick, try this super spray:

1½ cups of ammonia
1 tbsp. of Murphy® Oil Soap
1½ cups of water

Mix all of the ingredients in a handheld sprayer bottle, and spray any areas where you see signs of slug activity.

SLUG BUSTER

Get yourself an old handheld spray bottle, and fill it with one-third ammonia and two-thirds cool tap water. Set the spray nozzle on stream, and then any time slugs appear, give 'em a blast. You'll be delighted with the results!

SET A TRAP

Handpicking slugs and snails can help reduce their numbers, but to really make a dent in their populations, try trapping them, too. Set out fruit rinds or cabbage leaves on the soil or mulch around your perennials to provide a daytime hiding place for the pests. Lift the traps every morning, and scrape the collected slugs and snails into a container of soapy water. After a few weeks, you'll notice a definite decrease in your slug and snail population!

SCRATCHY ROADBLOCKS

Slugs have soft, tender bodies, so they don't like to move across irritating or scratchy barriers. Here are some great tips for making barriers out of things you may already have around the house:

✔ Oak leaves are great for mulching pest-prone flowers, because their bitter taste deters slimy slugs and grazing grubs. Plus, they won't pack down like the leaves from softer-wooded trees will, such as maples.

✔ Pine needles can also make a good slug-stopping mulch—some hosta growers swear by them!

✔ Spread wood ashes around your flower garden, where they'll do double duty. First, they'll help lighten the soil, and second, they'll make a great slug roadblock. The slimy slitherers can't glide over the ashes without injuring their skin, so they don't dare cross the border.

✔ Other super-scratchy substances for slug barriers include crushed egg shells, diatomaceous earth (available from mail-order garden suppliers), and grit sold for pet birds (available at pet shops).

THE TROUBLE WITH THRIPS

Buds that don't open; leaves with silvery stripes; petals with off-color streaks or speckles—they're all signs that thrips are at work. Don't expect to see the pests themselves, though; these very tiny yellowish or brownish critters move fast and are just barely big enough to spot without a magnifying glass. They damage plants by sucking out the sap, leaving discolored and deformed growth in their wake. Thrips can attack many perennials and bulbs, but are most troublesome on mums (*Chrysanthemum* x *morifolium*), delphiniums, irises, hollyhocks (*Alcea rosea*), peonies (*Paeonia*), gladiolus, and daylilies (*Hemerocallis*).

It's really tough to control these pests, because they can easily hide under leaves and between flower petals. The best you can do is pick off and destroy infested parts. On daylilies, cut all the damaged leaves to the ground, and let fresh new growth sprout up.

> **Try This!**
>
> To kill thrips that are overwintering on glads and other summer-flowering bulbs, give the bulbs a good long soak before planting. Mix 2½ tablespoons of Lysol® into 1 gallon of warm water, then gently drop the bulbs in. Let them soak for at least 12 hours, then plant them right away (while they are still wet).

SOW BUG SOLUTIONS

Ever notice small gray or brown buglike critters that curl up when you touch them? These $1/4$- to $1/2$-inch-long creatures are commonly called sow bugs or pill bugs, but they aren't really bugs at all—they're more closely related to crayfish. When disturbed, they curl up into round balls so that their jointed, armorlike scales can protect them.

Sow bugs feed mostly on decaying material, not living plants. If there are enough of them, though, they can do serious damage to tender, young perennial seedlings. Trap them by setting out halved cantaloupe hulls, or place used corncobs under pans and flowerpots. Check the traps daily, and tap any collected sow bugs into a bucket of soapy water. You may also catch some slugs this way!

JERRY'S GEMS

Looking for more ways to keep sow bugs from bugging your seedlings? Improving the drainage in your garden will go a long way toward cutting down on these moisture-loving crustaceans. For a more immediate solution, sprinkle diatomaceous earth over the soil where sow bugs are abundant; this scratchy powder will irritate their soft undersides. Reapply after each rain.

SPIT SPOTS

Aaack! Who spit on my perennials? Don't worry, it's not a personal comment on your gardening ability—it's a pest called a spittlebug. These tiny yellowish to greenish nymphs emerge in late spring, then surround themselves with a frothy mass of "spit" to protect themselves while they feed on your plants. Eventually, they mature into small tan, brown, or black insects called froghoppers.

Spittlebugs generally aren't a serious pest in the garden, except for their telltale disgusting masses of spit. I generally just wipe the spit off with a stick, and don't bother with sprays and such.

Get Diseases under Control

Good planning and careful planting will go a long way toward minimizing disease problems in your perennial borders. But if you start seeing spots and rots, don't despair—simply try some of my surefire disease control tips, and your beds will be back on top in no time at all!

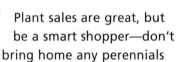 PLAN AHEAD

It's a whole lot easier to prevent disease problems than it is to cure them! So be smart and follow these pointers to help keep your perennials and bulbs looking their very best:

Pick the right planting site. Soggy soil can spell certain death for perennials that need good drainage, and sun-loving plants are much more disease-prone if they get too much shade. When you match your perennials and bulbs to their preferred growing conditions, they'll naturally be more healthy and problem-resistant.

Space 'em out. Crowded perennial clumps are easy targets for disease problems. Lift and divide overgrown clumps every three to five years.

Control insect pests. Bugs can easily spread diseases from plant to plant as they feed. Keep these troublemakers under control, and you'll reduce the chance of diseases getting into your garden.

Water wisely. Wet leaves and stems provide welcoming conditions for many disease-causing organisms. You can't stop the rain, of course, but you *can* avoid wetting the leaves yourself when you water—simply use a soaker hose instead of a sprinkler to get the soil moist without wetting the tops of the plants.

Harebell

Campanula rotundifolia

Dainty beauty with nodding sky-blue bells

MAKING ¢ents Plant sales are great, but be a smart shopper—don't bring home any perennials with off-color spots or streaks in the leaves, or with overall poor growth. And avoid bulbs that have soft spots or that feel very light for their size. Diseased plants will cost you a lot of heartache in the long run, so don't be lured into buying problem-prone plants just because they're bargain-priced.

Heart-leaved aster
Aster cordifolius

Daisylike blue flowers in fall atop 1- to 3-foot-tall stems; great for shade gardens

DIAGNOSING DISEASE PROBLEMS

When a disease does strike, you need to get a handle on what it is before you can choose the right control approach. Just follow these three simple steps:

Step 1. Identify the affected plant. Most perennials and bulbs have only a few common problems, so if you know what kind of plant you're dealing with, you can dramatically narrow down the list of possible suspects.

Step 2. Describe exactly what you see. What does the damage look like? What part of the plant is affected: the leaves, the stems, the buds, or the flowers? Is the damage on just one plant, on more than one of the same plant, or is it on several different plants in the same bed? What has the weather been like—has it been cool and cloudy, hot and dry, or unusually rainy? Make written notes of everything you observe.

Step 3. Try to match the symptoms and the plant to a known disease. If you can't figure out the problem on your own, snip off a damaged shoot, seal it in a plastic bag, and take it to an expert. You can usually get help through your county's Cooperative Extension Service office (look in your phone book under "Government Offices").

To get your seeds off to a disease-free start, lightly sprinkle Jell-O powder on them with a salt shaker. Any flavor will work, but lemon is a super choice, since it will repel some pests. As your young plants grow, feed them more Jell-O. The gelatin helps the plants hold water, and the sugar feeds the good microorganisms in the soil.

SHOP SMART

When you are choosing perennials at the garden center, be sure to look for cultivars that are described as being disease-resistant. Garden phlox (*Phlox paniculata*), for instance, is usually a magnet for powdery mildew. But if you choose a mildew-resistant cultivar like 'David' or 'Shortwood', there's a very good chance that you'll seldom have to worry about this fungal disease affecting your plants.

WHAT'S HAPPENING?

Here's a rundown of some of the most common perennial and bulb problems.

What You See	Common Targets	Possible Cause
Leaves suddenly turn yellow; growth is stunted and deformed	Asters, blanket flowers (*Gaillardia*), Shasta daisies (*Chrysanthemum* x *superbum*); other perennials	Aster yellows
White, gray, or tan fuzzy growth on leaves, stems, buds, and/or flowers	Peonies (*Paeonia*), mums (*Chrysanthemum* x *morifolium*), tulips (*Tulipa*), and lilies (*Lilium*); other perennials and bulbs	Botrytis blight
Seedlings keel over, rot at soil line	Any perennial or bulb seedling	Damping off
Black, brown, or yellow leaf spots of various sizes	Many perennials and bulbs	Leaf spots
Leaves mottled with yellow or light green blotches or streaks	Many perennials and bulbs	Mosaic viruses
White to powdery gray patches on leaves, buds, or stems	Many perennials	Powdery mildew
Plant is weak, then wilts and dies	Any perennial or bulb	Root or crown rot or nematodes
Yellow or orange speckles or streaks on leaves	Hollyhocks (*Alcea rosea*) and related plants; other perennials and some grasses	Rust

🪣 TAKE A PINCH

Whenever you spot a sick-looking leaf on one of your perennials, immediately pinch it off and destroy it. Believe you me, this simple step often stops the dastardly disease dead in its tracks!

🪴 DISEASE LOOK-ALIKES

Sometimes, you might not be dealing with a disease at all. Environmental problems, such as too little water or food, can cause diseaselike symptoms, too. So if the damage you're seeing doesn't match up with any common disease problems, consider these possibilities:

Dead buds, shoots, and/or leaves: Cold damage. Make sure indoor- or greenhouse-grown plants are hardened off before planting them outside. Be sure to protect emerging plants with mulch or overturned buckets or boxes if a late frost threatens.

Iron deficiency: New leaves are all yellow or yellowish with green veins, and old leaves stay green. Apply 1 tablespoon of Liquid Iron or chelated iron per quart of water per plant.

Nitrogen deficiency: Older leaves turn yellow. Apply my Year-Round Refresher Tonic (see page 86).

Pale, spindly growth; variegated plants turn all green: Too much shade. Move the plant to a brighter location.

Wilting and browned leaf edges: Too little water. Turn on the hose *now* to soak the soil, then mulch to keep the soil cool and moist.

Wilting and greenish yellow foliage: Too much water. Avoid watering until the soil dries out a bit.

Hoop-petticoat daffodil
Narcissus bulbocodium

Short, but wide, rich yellow trumpets; something different for the spring garden

Made in the Shade

To prevent transplant shock (see "Simply Shocking," at right), wait for a spell of cloudy weather to do your planting. Water the planting area (and your potted perennials) thoroughly both before and after planting. If you have to plant in hot, sunny weather, give your new perennials some shade for the first few days.

 Don't Overdo It!

A good dose of fertilizer makes perennials look great, so you'd think that an extra shot will make them look super, right? *Wrong!* Too much fertilizer can be just as bad as too little—and it's a lot harder to fix. Instead of applying one big dose of fertilizer, apply the recommended amount in early spring, then see how your plants look a few weeks later. If they still seem spindly or off-color, try to rule out any disease or insect problems. If you can't find any obvious causes, then go ahead and apply a bit more fertilizer (a quarter to half of the suggested dose) to perk them up.

Over and over, you'll hear me recommend watering your perennials and bulbs with soaker hoses rather than sprinklers. Why? Because these water-oozing hoses get the moisture directly to the soil, where the roots can use it. When you spray water into the air, a good part of it is lost to evaporation. The rest wets the leaves, stems, buds, and flowers, leaving a film of water that's like a superhighway for the spread of diseases.

If you absolutely must use a sprinkler for watering, run it *only* early in the morning. That way, your plants will have plenty of time to dry off, and diseases will be far less likely to get started.

Simply Shocking

You just planted a beautiful new perennial and watered it carefully, and the next day, it's all wilted! What happened? Probably a condition called **transplant shock**. It happens when the roots can't take up enough water to support the top growth. Eventually, the flower buds and leaves will drop off, and the whole plant may die.

If you act fast, you should be able to save the plant. First, give it some shade immediately, then make sure the soil is moist. (If the soil already feels damp, though, don't add more water, or you may suffocate the roots and do further damage.) If the plant doesn't perk up within an hour or so, cut all the top growth back by about one-third to reduce water loss through the leaves. Keep the plant shaded from intense sun for a few days, and it should recover.

ASTER ANSWERS

Aster yellows is a viruslike disease that causes foliage to suddenly turn yellow. Growth is stunted and deformed, and affected plants eventually die. Besides asters, several other perennials are likely to be affected, including bellflowers (*Campanula*), blanket flowers (*Gaillardia*), black-eyed Susans (*Rudbeckia*), delphiniums, mums (*Chrysanthemum* x *morifolium*), and Shasta daisies (*C.* x *superbum*).

Aphids and other sucking insects spread this disease as they move from plant to plant, so keeping these pests under control (see pages 138–139) is the key to preventing aster yellows. Remove and destroy any affected plants.

BLIGHTING YOUR HOPES

When botrytis blight strikes, it usually starts as light to dark-colored spots on leaves, stems, buds, and flowers. White, gray, or tan fuzzy growth may appear on the spots in cool, moist weather. Buds shrivel up and drop before they open, and leaves or whole shoots may suddenly fall over. Common targets of this deadly fungal disease include gladiolus, lilies (*Lilium*), mums (*Chrysanthemum* x *morifolium*), peonies (*Paeonia*), and tulips (*Tulipa*).

To prevent bringing botrytis blight home, don't buy any bulbs that show dark, circular, sunken spots. Avoid overwatering, and thin out or divide crowded clumps to improve air

---

Mixers & Elixirs

DISEASE DEFENSE

Wet, rainy weather can mean an outbreak of fungus in your flower garden, especially in late winter and early spring. Keep your perennials and bulbs happy and healthy with this elixir:

1 cup of chamomile tea
1 tsp. of dishwashing liquid
½ tsp. of vegetable oil
½ tsp. of peppermint oil
1 gal. of warm water

Mix all of the ingredients together in a bucket. Mist-spray your plants every week or so before the hot weather (75°F or higher) sets in. This elixir is strong stuff, so test it on a few leaves before completely spraying any plant.

circulation around the leaves and stems. Remove and destroy infected plant parts. And if bulbs come down with this disease, don't replant new bulbs in that spot, or they'll suffer the same fate.

Seedling-Saver

Every time I start seeds, I like to make sure they're getting the best start in life, so I whip up a batch of my Grandma Putt's special seedling-saver solution. It's simple: Just add 4 teaspoons of chamomile tea and 1 teaspoon of dishwashing liquid to 1 quart of boiling water. Let it steep for at least an hour (the longer, the better), then strain and cool. Mist-spray your seedlings with this tonic as soon as their little green heads poke out of the soil, and they'll be off and running!

KNOCK OFF DAMPING OFF

One day, your perennial seedlings are coming along fine—the next, they've shriveled up or fallen over! What's the deal? It's a fungal disease called damping off. This devastating disease can attack any kind of seedlings—from before they emerge from the soil until they are several weeks old. It's especially active where the soil is wet and the air is stagnant. To stop this troublesome fungus in its tracks:

• Use fresh, sterilized, seed-starting mix and clean containers.

• Sow seeds as evenly as possible so the seedlings won't be overcrowded.

• Cover seeds after sowing by sprinkling fine sphagnum moss over them.

• Give emerging seedlings plenty of light to encourage healthy, vigorous growth.

• Improve air circulation by placing a small fan set on "low"

Hosta
Hosta hybrid

Great-looking leaves in a variety of colors and shapes; pretty flowers

to blow just across the tops of the seedlings. Move the fan as needed to move air over all the plants.

• Instead of adding water from the top, set seed pots in a shallow tray of water when they start to get dry. Let them stand for an hour or two to soak up water, then let them drain for an hour before setting them back under the lights.

SPOTTING LEAF SPOTS

A number of fungi and bacteria can cause yellow, brown, or black spots of various sizes on your perennials. Some of the most likely targets include asters, delphiniums, hardy geraniums, irises, mums (*Chrysanthemum* x *morifolium*), phlox, and poppies (*Papaver*).

You can minimize the likelihood of leaf spots with careful watering to avoid wetting the leaves. Divide overcrowded perennial clumps, and set plants widely spaced so that air can move freely around the leaves. Pinch off and destroy spotted leaves, and spray the remaining foliage with my Fungus Fighter Tonic (at left).

Mixers & Elixirs

FUNGUS FIGHTER TONIC

Molasses is great for fighting diseases in your flower garden. So at the first sign of trouble, try this tonic:

1/2 cup of molasses
1/2 cup of powdered milk
1 tsp. of baking soda
1 gal. of warm water

Mix the molasses, powdered milk, and baking soda into a paste. Place the mixture into the toe of an old nylon stocking, and let it steep in the warm water for several hours. Then strain, and use the remaining liquid as a fungus-fighting spray for your flower garden every two weeks throughout the growing season. I guarantee you'll have no more fungus troubles!

IS IT A VIRUS?

Yep—plants can get viruses, too! Their symptoms include leaves that are mottled with a mosaic of yellow or light green blotches or streaks. New growth may be spindly, and the whole plant can be stunted. Just about any perennial or bulb can be affected, but those that seem particularly problem-prone include asters, columbines (*Aquilegia*), delphiniums, and mums (*Chrysanthemum* x *morifolium*). Once a plant is affected, there's nothing you can do but remove it and destroy it. Aphids, and other sap-sucking pests, can spread mosaic viruses as they travel from plant to plant, so controlling these thugs is the best way to prevent damage.

 ## EEEW—MILDEW!

Powdery mildew is probably the most common disease you're likely to see in your perennial garden. Symptoms include white to powdery gray patches on leaves, buds, or stems. Affected plant parts are distorted, and eventually drop off. This fungal disease runs rampant when days are warm and nights are cool and humid—common conditions in late summer and early fall, or sometimes in spring. Some of the most commonly mildewed perennials include asters, bee balms (*Monarda*), black-eyed Susans (*Rudbeckia*), boltonias, delphiniums, lungworts (*Pulmonaria*), mums (*Chrysanthemum* x *morifolium*), and phlox.

 ### Mixers & Elixirs

POWDERY MILDEW CONTROL

4 tbsp. of baking soda
2 tbsp. of Murphy® Oil Soap
1 gal. of warm water

Mix all of the ingredients together. Pour into a handheld mist sprayer, and apply liberally as soon as you see the telltale white spots on your perennials.

 ## MANAGING MILDEW

Powdery mildew makes plants look ugly, but fortunately, it rarely kills them. Here's how to prevent problems:

✔ Grow mildew-resistant cultivars.

✔ Improve air circulation around plant stems by thinning out or dividing crowded clumps.

✔ Avoid wetting the leaves when you water.

✔ Pinch off and destroy affected leaves, then spray the rest of the plant with my Chamomile Mildew Chaser (see page 158).

✔ If the plant looks really bad, cut it down to the ground; fresh new growth will emerge.

Ironweed
Vernonia noveboracensis

Fuzzy purple flowers in fall atop tall stems; perfect for the back of a border

🪣 DON'T LET IT ROT

When the soil is soggy, watch out for root rots! The first sign may be individual leaves turning yellow or brown, or you may not notice anything until entire plants wilt and die. When you dig up infected plants, you'll see that the roots are brown or black.

There's nothing you can do to cure affected plants; you have to remove and destroy them. To prevent future problems, improve the drainage in that area—raised beds work great. Where the soil is still moist, set the crown of each perennial a smidge above the soil surface (maybe $1/4$ to $1/3$ inch above ground level) at planting time. Keep plants spaced out, and divide overgrown clumps, as needed, to prevent overcrowding. Make sure mulches are a few inches away from the base of perennials, and avoid overwatering.

Mixers & Elixirs

CHAMOMILE MILDEW CHASER

Chamomile is an excellent control for powdery mildew, so put it to good use with this elixir. Apply at the first sign of trouble (or as a preventive measure in damp weather) every week throughout the growing season to perennials that are particularly prone to this fungal disease:

4 chamomile tea bags
1 qt. of boiling water
2 tbsp. of Murphy® Oil Soap

Make a good strong batch of tea using the tea bags and boiling water, letting it steep for an hour or so. Let the tea cool, then mix with the Murphy's. Apply with a 6 gallon hose-end sprayer.

🪣 GETTING RUSTY

Rust is an easy disease to diagnose—just look for whitish or yellowish speckles on the upper leaf surface and raised orange spots on the underside. Seriously affected leaves wilt and turn brown, and eventually, the whole plant is weakened. You'll most often see rust when nights are cool and humid (commonly in late summer and early fall, but sometimes in spring). Hollyhocks (*Alcea rosea*) are notorious for rust problems, but many other perennials can show signs, too.

To prevent rust, avoid wetting the leaves when you water, and thin out or divide crowded clumps to get good air circulation around the leaves. Look for rust-resistant species and cultivars, such as fig-leaved hollyhock (*Alcea ficifolia*).

Remove and destroy infected leaves as soon as you spot them, then spray or dust the rest of the plant with sulfur.

NASTY NEMATODES

When is a disease not due to a fungus, bacteria, or a virus? When it's caused by little critters called nematodes. These colorless, microscopic worms usually live in the soil, although some can climb up on plants. Many nematodes are good guys, but some feed on perennial roots or leaves.

JERRY'S GEMS

Say no to nematodes by planting nematode-resistant cultivars, where available. Remove and destroy infested plants, and avoid replanting the same kind of perennials there for three years. In the meantime, work lots of compost into the soil to build up the beneficial microorganisms that will feed on the nematodes.

Aboveground, the only symptom you may see of root-feeding nematodes is stunted or wilted leaves and shoots. When you dig up the plants, though, you'll notice tiny galls all over the roots. Or, if foliar nematodes are at work, you'll see wedge-shaped sections of leaf that turn yellowish brown between the veins. Eventually, these wedges run together, and the whole leaf will dry up and drop. Symptoms usually start at the base of the plant and work upward. Many perennials can be affected, but mums (*Chrysanthemum* x *morifolium*) and phlox are especially susceptible.

GOOD GUYS TO THE RESCUE

It's true that some nematodes can do bad things to your perennials—but not all nematodes are your enemies! In fact, some of them actually help keep the perennial pest types in check. Beneficial nematodes also help to control a number of other common garden pests, including weevils, wireworms, and even other nematodes.

Some garden-supply companies sell nematodes that you can add to your soil. But if you don't want to spend the money, you can encourage the good guys to call your garden home by working lots of rich compost into your flowerbeds before planting.

Italian alkanet
Anchusa azurea

Spikes of brilliant blue blooms for late-spring and early-summer color

Italian arum
Arum italicum

Tropical-looking
leaves appear
in fall; look great
into early summer

Rabbits and Squirrels and Deer—Oh My!

Animal pests are a much more serious problem in the perennial garden than any insect or disease. In just a few minutes, critters can devour entire plants, and they can wipe out an entire flowerbed in just one evening. You may garden for years with no problems, then one year—*bam!* Major damage. Fortunately, you're not likely to have more than one or two animal pests that are common in your area, so you can concentrate your efforts on those few.

WHO'S TO BLAME?

One day, you have a spectacular perennial planting, and the next morning, it looks like someone took a string trimmer to your border. Chances are, animal pests are the culprits. To pick the most effective control, you need to figure out who's doing the damage. Here are some of the most common signs:

What You See	Likely Culprit
Chewed leaves and shoots.	Rabbits, deer, groundhogs (woodchucks)
Flower buds or shoots are nipped off and often left lying by the plants.	Squirrels
Newly planted perennials and bulbs are dug up, left on the surface.	Squirrels, cats, dogs
Wilted top growth; plant falls over; roots are gone; fall-planted bulbs don't emerge in spring.	Voles, pocket gophers

 ## Dusting for Prints

If you're still not sure who's doing the damage, pay special attention to the damaged area over the next few days. Some animal pests may come out to feed during the day, while others come out mainly at night. To catch nocturnal visitors in the act, shine a light out into your garden at various times after dark. Or sprinkle flour over the ground around damaged plants. If you find tracks in the flour the next morning, make a sketch or take a picture of them, then use a field guide to identify the critter that made them.

Rabbit-Proof Fencing

Bunnies are cute and fuzzy, but they're not so sweet when they're chowing down on your perennials and bulbs! And once they start feeding in your garden, it's tough to get them to stop. The best control is to fence them out of your garden, if you can.

Most garden and home-improvement centers sell wire fencing that does a good job. Just make sure the holes are no bigger than 1 inch wide—you'd be amazed at what bunnies can squeeze through! Rabbits can jump pretty high, too, so your fence should be 3 to 4 feet tall, if you use it by itself (2 feet tall, if you're lining a taller decorative fence with the wire). And those pesky rabbits can actually tunnel *under* fences, as well, so make sure that you extend the wire fencing at least 6 inches—and ideally 1 foot—down into the soil.

HARE SCARE

To keep rabbits and other small critters out of your flower garden, wrap bunches of dog or cat hair in old nylon stockings. Hang the bundles in various spots around your beds and borders. The varmints will think that Fido or Fluffy is on duty, and they'll keep their distance.

Bunny Barriers

Is fencing your garden not an option? Then try using barriers around individual plants. The most crucial time for protection is the first few weeks of spring, when your perennials and bulbs are producing sweet and tender new growth. By early summer, the plants are large and a bit tougher, so they're less enticing to rabbits.

For an inexpensive, but effective barrier, cut the bottom out of one of those cheap plastic nursery pots. (You probably have dozens of these stacked in your garage from the perennials you purchased!) Pop one over each emerging perennial, and push the bottom inch or so into the soil to secure it. Leave the barriers in place for a few weeks. When you don't need them any longer, slip them off the plants and stack them together for easy storage until the following spring.

MOLE CONTROL

If you see signs of mole activity near your flowerbeds, try this: Mix together 1/4 cup of castor oil and 1 gallon of warm water in a bucket. Pour the mixture into a sprinkling can, and drench the soil around the edge of each flowerbed. Reapply as needed.

When animal pests made an appearance, my Grandma Putt would send them packing by dusting her perennials and bulb plants with black pepper or garlic powder. She made sure she dusted the soil or mulch around them, too. To keep the heat up, she'd reapply the dusts after every rain. It worked like a charm to keep raccoons, squirrels, rabbits, moles, and groundhogs (also called woodchucks) at bay.

THIS IDEA STINKS!

To rid your yard and garden of moles, open up their tunnels in different locations and drop in freshly cut-up garlic bulbs. Then cover up the holes. The moles will take one whiff, and run in the opposite direction!

CLEANING OUT VOLES

Voles, which are close kin to mice, travel through your yard via mole runs and eat roots in winter, making a mess of your flower gardens (and lawns, young trees, and shrubs, too). Mix diatomaceous earth and Bon Ami cleansing powder with your fall lawn food to pep up the grass and discourage vole damage. Sprinkle the mix in your flowerbeds, too, and around trees and shrubs. You can also sprinkle just plain ol' Bon Ami into bulb-planting holes to keep these nasty little critters away.

CRITTER GITTERS

If rabbits, mice, squirrels, voles, and other chewing critters are treating your perennial garden like their own private salad bar, don't despair—fight back! Here are five of my best critter-deterring tips:

☑ **Call out their archenemy.** Or at least make the pests think you've done that! Get some ferret droppings from a zoo, pet shop, or ferret-owning friend, then sprinkle the stuff in and around the critters' holes. It'll make them scurry in a hurry!

☑ **Sound 'em out.** Gather up six or eight empty glass soda bottles and half-bury them, top ends up, in a line near the critters' hangouts. When the wind passes over, it'll make a scary sound that will send them packing.

☑ **Shine a light in their eyes.** Fill 1 gallon glass bottles with water and set them among your perennials. Sunlight bouncing off the glass startles the animals, especially rabbits, and makes them flee.

☑ **Keep garden-snacking varmints at bay.** Scatter cut-up thorny rose and berry stems over the mulch around your prized perennials and bulbs.

☑ **Give 'em the hair of the dog.** And the human. And the cat! Lay circles of the hair around your plants, and hang mesh bags of it from fences, trellises, and branches. I've found that hairdressers and pet groomers are always happy to supply as much of the stuff as you care to carry off.

BULB BASKETS

Voles, pocket gophers, and other soil-dwelling critters are tough to keep in check. Traps give only partial control, and poisons will pollute your soil, so prevention is the best strategy—plant your bulbs in wire mesh baskets set into the ground. You can also line the sides and bottoms of your bulb beds with half-inch wire mesh. I guarantee this will drive the rodents nuts!

Jack-in-the-pulpit
Arisaema triphyllum

Unusual, hooded, green and purple flowers hidden under handsome, three-parted leaves

Jacob's ladder
*Polemonium
caeruleum*

Summer-blooming
perennial with
deep blue,
grape-scented
blossoms

SPICES SEND PETS PACKING

There's nothing worse than having neighborhood pets tramping through your flowerbeds! Keep dogs and cats away from your precious blooms by dusting crushed, dried red peppers or red pepper (cayenne) powder in and around the beds. And give my Scat Cat Solution (below) and Dog-Gone-It! mixer (at right) a try.

FELINE FOILS

If neighborhood cats call your flowerbeds home, try one or more of these tricks to keep them at bay:

• Grow catnip in an area that's a good distance away from your flowerbeds. Once they discover the catnip, the maurading kitties will forget all about your prized perennials.

• Turn up the heat by sprinkling ground black pepper, hot cayenne pepper, mothball flakes, or dry Borax soap powder in and around the areas you want to keep kitty-free.

• Give 'em a scare by filling large soda bottles half full of water. Put a few long, thin strips of aluminum foil into the bottles and add a bit of bleach to prevent algae from growing inside. Then place the bottles strategically around your flowerbeds. The changing foil reflections will frighten away curious cats.

Mixers & Elixirs

SCAT CAT SOLUTION

Cats can be great pets, but they can also be a real problem if they dig in your garden. Try this spicy solution to keep them away from your prized plantings:

*5 tbsp. of flour
4 tbsp. of powdered mustard
3 tbsp. of cayenne pepper
2 tbsp. of chili powder
2 qts. of warm water*

Mix all of the ingredients in a watering can, and sprinkle the solution around the perimeter of the areas you want to protect.

MAKE A STINK

Cats are very sensitive to odors, so use that to your advantage and mix up a batch of this stinky sauce: Add 1 clove of garlic (crushed), 1 tablespoon of cayenne pepper, and 1 teaspoon of dishwashing liquid to a quart of warm water. Mix well and put into a handheld sprayer. Spray the perimeter of your perennial beds with this pungent potion, and cats should stay away.

🪣 DOGGIE DEFENSE

If dogs are digging in your flower-beds, send them running with these deterrents:

✔ Dip pipe cleaners in tobacco juice and hang them on plants at dog-sniffing height.

✔ Spread moth crystals on the soil underneath flowers and shrubs.

✔ Sprinkle cayenne pepper around their favorite garden spots.

🪣 DOGS TO THE RESCUE!

Even though dogs get a bad rap for digging and doing their buisness in gardens and yards, keep in mind that having a canine or two patrolling your property is one of the best deterrents around. Dogs will chase away deer, ground-hogs, rabbits, and just about any other critter that is eyeing your flowerbeds.

   Now, I'm not suggesting that you run out and adopt a dog or two if you don't already own them. I'm just saying that if you do have dogs, give them every opportunity to roam around, instead of confining them to just one area of the yard. This way, they'll be sure to put a stop to those marauding varmints. And when your dogs do capture a garden thief, be sure to reward them for their hard work so they'll keep at it.

Mixers & Elixirs

DOG-GONE-IT!

Man's best friend can be your flower garden's worst enemy. To keep dogs away from their favorite digging areas, liberally apply this mix to the soil:

2 cloves of garlic
2 small onions
1 jalapeño pepper
1 tbsp. of cayenne pepper
1 tbsp. of hot sauce
1 tbsp. of chili powder
1 qt. of warm water

Chop the garlic, onions, and pepper finely, then combine with the remaining ingredients. Let the mix sit for 24 hours, then sprinkle it on any areas where digging dogs are a problem.

🪣 DEER DETERRENTS

Deer are probably the toughest animal pests to control. Once they develop a taste for your garden, they're likely to come back again and again. So *before* your perennial border becomes the next all-you-can-eat salad bar for the local herd, try any or all of these repellents:

🍃 Sprinkle bloodmeal or human hair trimmings on and around plants. Renew after each rain.

🍃 Hang bars of strongly scented deodorant soap at deer nose level on stakes set around garden areas.

🍃 Spray with my Deer Buster Egg Tonic (at left).

Mixers & Elixirs

DEER BUSTER EGG TONIC

2 eggs
2 cloves of garlic
2 tbsp. of hot sauce
2 tbsp. of cayenne pepper
2 cups of water

Put all of the ingredients in a blender and purée. Allow the mixture to sit for two days, then pour or spray it all over and around the plants you need to protect.

🪣 STINK 'EM OUT

Here are two more ways to wage the never-ending battle against deer. They sure ain't pretty, but they work!

• Sprinkle baby powder or athlete's foot powder on old T-shirts, and hang them up near your flowerbeds or scatter them among the plants.

• Find the stinkiest stuff you can—old shoes (especially rotting sneakers!), sweaty old unwashed T-shirts, stinky socks… you get the idea. Place these pungent products in amongst your perennial beds and deer will run the other way.

🪣 FENCE 'EM OUT

The only surefire way to keep deer out of your garden is to fence them out of your property. Don't count on just any little fence, though—it needs to be about 8 feet tall to be truly effective. A solid fence isn't a must; it can be as simple as heavy-duty, black plastic netting. Besides being relatively inexpensive—especially compared to buying new perennials each year—after a while, this type of barrier blends into the surrounding foliage, so you'll hardly even know it's there.

Double Dare Ya!

Foil hungry deer with a row of double fencing. Install another row of fencing parallel to your current fencing, with about 3 feet between them. Since deer can jump fairly high, but not over a long distance, this should do the trick and keep them out.

DEER STEER CLEAR OF THESE

If deer are hungry enough, they'll eat just about anything! But, in general, they don't like to eat plants with fuzzy or strongly scented leaves. They tend to stay away from these plants, so if you've got deer problems, give them a try:

- ✓ Globe thistles *(Echinops)*
- ✓ Lenten roses *(Helleborus)*
- ✓ Lily-of-the-valley *(Convallaria majalis)*
- ✓ Wormwoods *(Artemisia)*
- ✓ Yuccas *(Yucca)*

Japanese iris
Iris ensata

Huge blooms (up to 8 inches across!) in a range of colors; likes wet soil in spring

PERENNIAL POSSIBILITIES

CHAPTER 9

PERENNIALS 101

Ready to join the millions of gardeners who
have discovered the fun of growing their own
perennials? In this chapter, you'll learn the
basics of what a perennial is and what these
high-class plants can add to your garden.

What's the Story?

You hear a lot of folks these days talking about their new perennial border or the latest and greatest perennial they just picked up at the local garden center. Bookstores are chock-full of books about perennials, and gardening magazines are packed with pictures of fabulous perennial plantings. So what exactly *are* perennials, and why are they so great? Read on, my friends, and find out!

☀ KNOW THE BASICS

Generally speaking, a **perennial** is a plant that returns year after year, even after setting seed. (**Annuals**, in contrast, sprout from seed, grow leaves, bloom, and then set seed all within one growing season.) This definition includes both plants that we normally think of as perennials—like peonies—as well as all kinds of shrubs, trees, roses, and many vines. To separate the two groups, some experts use the term **herbaceous perennial** for those plants with top growth that dies back to the ground in winter, and **woody perennial** for those that sprout from a woody-stemmed top growth each year.

☀ BIENNIALS BLEND IN

Two plant groups that are easy to confuse are perennials and **biennials**. Technically, biennials live only two years—the first year, they sprout and

PERENNIAL ANNUALS

Some annuals are so dependable at self-sowing that they act almost like perennials. These easy keepers make great fillers for new perennial gardens, until the real perennials can fill in and cover the soil. Sow or set out transplants once, let them set seed, and new plants will sprout up each spring! Try any one of these:

Bells-of-Ireland
(*Moluccella laevis*)

California poppy
(*Eschscholzia californica*)

Corn poppy (*Papaver rhoeas*)

Cosmos (*Cosmos bipinnatus*)

Larkspur (*Consolida ajacis*)

Love-in-a-mist
(*Nigella damascena*)

Shoo-fly plant
(*Nicandra physalodes*)

Spider flower
(*Cleome hasslerana*)

Sweet alyssum
(*Lobularia maritima*)

produce leafy growth, then the next year, they flower, set seed, and (usually) die. Common biennials include such classics as common foxgloves (*Digitalis purpurea*), forget-me-nots (*Myosotis*), Canterbury bells (*Campanula medium*), dame's rocket (*Hesperis matronalis*), money plant or honesty (*Lunaria annua*), and rose campion (*Lychnis coronaria*). Hollyhocks (*Alcea rosea*) fall somewhere in between—some plants will come back for a few years, but most flower generously in their second year, and then die.

Even though they are short-lived, biennials definitely belong in the perennial garden. If you're vigilant about snipping off the fading flowers, the plants will often return for another year or more of bloom. Or you can let them ripen and drop their seed, and you'll have plenty of new plants every year without any extra work!

☀ LOVE ME TENDER

One more term you're likely to run across sooner or later is **tender perennial**. Used alone, "tender" generally means a plant that is hurt by chilly temperatures. A tender perennial acts like a regular perennial where temperatures are mild all year, but dies off where the winters are too cold for it. Some tender perennials can't take temperatures below 40°F, while others can tolerate enough cold to overwinter outdoors as far north as Zone 6 (or even colder areas).

ANNUAL PERENNIALS

Many tender perennials are so beautiful and grow so quickly that gardeners in any climate can enjoy them as annuals. Simply start new plants from seed each spring, or buy transplants. Or you can overwinter your favorites indoors by taking cuttings in late summer, and growing them on a sunny windowsill until spring!

Brazilian vervain (*Verbena bonariensis*)

Coleus (*Coleus blumei*)

Dusty miller (*Senecio cineraria*)

Four-o'clock (*Mirabilis jalapa*)

Garden verbena (*Verbena x hybrida*)

Impatiens (*Impatiens*)

Mealycup sage (*Salvia farinacea*)

Petunias (*Petunia x hybrida*)

Snapdragons (*Antirrhinum majus*)

Star flower (*Pentas lanceolata*)

Sweet potato vine (*Ipomoea batatas*)

Wax begonia (*Begonia semperflorens*)

✿ FAST-FLOWERING PERENNIALS

Most perennials take at least two years to reach flowering size, but these speedy selections can bloom the same year you sow them—just like annuals—then live on to flower again in the future. To help ensure first-year flowers, give these fast-maturing perennials an early start by sowing their seeds indoors in late winter, then setting out transplants after the last spring frost:

Anise hyssop (*Agastache foeniculum*)

Balloon flower (*Platycodon grandiflorus*)

Carpathian harebell (*Campanula carpatica*)

Crimson pincushion flower (*Knautia macedonica*)

Fern-leaved yarrow (*Achillea millefolium*)

'Foxy' foxglove (*Digitalis purpurea* 'Foxy')

'Goldsturm' black-eyed Susan (*Rudbeckia fulgida* 'Goldsturm')

Jupiter's beard (*Centranthus ruber*)

'Lady' lavender (*Lavandula angustifolia* 'Lady')

'Southern Charm' mullein (*Verbascum* 'Southern Charm')

Tree lavatera (*Lavatera thuringiaca*)

Tree mallow (*Malva sylvestris*)

Japanese lily
Lilium speciosum

Fabulously fragrant, late-blooming lily with wavy white petals striped with pink

Making a Perfect Match

The hardest part of growing perennials is deciding which ones to try! They are so versatile, and there are so many to choose from—where do you start? Here are some tips to help you make the most of these perfect plants.

Japanese
primrose
Primula japonica

Tiered clusters of
red, pink, or white
flowers in early
summer; ideal
for wet areas

✳ A PERENNIAL FOR EVERY PLACE

Sure, perennials are perfect choices for traditional flower-beds and borders—but that's just the beginning! Here are some other places where perennials can add easy-care color:

Container plantings. Perk up your pots and planters with a variety of perennials displaying beautiful flowers and foliage.

Decks and patios. Perennials are perfect for adding color and fragrance to outdoor areas where you like to dine, entertain, or just relax.

Foundation plantings. Jazz up those boring evergreens with plantings of long-blooming perennials.

Gates and doorways. Add a welcoming touch to your yard and home by greeting your visitors with cheerful, free-flowering perennials.

Paths and walkways. Turn a boring access route into a pleasant place to stroll. And don't forget to stop and smell the flowers!

Slopes. Perennials are more than pretty—they're practical, too. Many perennials are perfectly suited to life on the slopes, adding months of interest, while eliminating soil erosion.

Swimming pools. The heat and reflected light from pools can be tough on some plants, but carefully chosen perennials will give you lots of color without a lot of maintenance. Tall-growing perennials can also provide a welcome bit of privacy!

Under trees and shrubs. Forget all that hand-trimming around the trees and shrubs in your landscape. Plant perennial groundcovers there, and spend your time doing something fun!

Garden plans are great road maps, but don't keep the blinders on as you're wandering down the perennial garden path. Go ahead and take a few detours every now and again; you'll be glad you did. Choose a flower on a whim, and try a small planting. If it does well for you this year, add more next year.

☀ MULTIPLES FOR PERSONALITY

Perennials look great mixed with each other, or combined with different plants, including bulbs, annuals, shrubs, and trees. To add a dramatic accent to your landscape, consider a mass planting of one kind of perennial, such as a sweep of daylilies (*Hemerocallis*) or a "hedge" of peonies (*Paeonia*). When the whole group comes into bloom—*WOW!*

☀ FOCUS YOUR ATTENTION

Another way to make perennial design easier is to pick plants based on their bloom time. A bed of spring-flowering perennials, for example, can be a welcome sight outside of a family room window after you've been cooped up inside all winter. Or, if you do a lot of outdoor entertaining on your deck or patio, then a border packed with summer-flowering perennials is a great addition.

When you combine a bunch of perennials that flower at the same time, you're guaranteed a spectacular show during that season. Just remember that it won't look like much at other times of the year. Single-season beds work best in spots where you can enjoy them in their glory and then turn your attention elsewhere; they're not a good choice for a very visible or high-traffic area, such as a front-door garden.

Try This!

With so many wonderful perennials to choose from, where do you start? My secret is to come up with some kind of "theme" for each bed, then choose from perennials that fit into that category. Sometimes, it's a color or colors, like only white flowers, or blue and yellow flowers, or all pastel colors. Or you can combine perennials based on their special features or uses, such as herbs, cut flowers, fragrance, or butterfly-attracting. Having a theme in mind really helps you narrow down your plant choices, and makes creating a beautiful garden a snap!

☀ AN ANNUAL EVENT

Since most perennials are at their best in spring, early summer, or fall, you won't have much late-summer color in your perennial plantings unless you bring in some annual reinforcements. So plant annuals in the gaps in your beds and borders, and they'll look super from spring to frost!

✻ MATCH THE MOOD

Colors can have a noticeable effect on your mood—so use that to your advantage! If you're usually enjoying your garden after a stressful day at the office, then choose perennials in soothing colors, such as pastel pink, pale blue, and pale yellow. For a more stimulating effect—perhaps something to pep you up while you're washing dishes and staring out the kitchen window—go for a mixture of bright red, orange, and yellow. And there's nothing like a shady garden full of frosty, white flowers to make you feel cooler on a sultry summer day.

WHAT'S IN A NAME?

Botanical names can look intimidating at first, but once you know a few basic definitions, you can learn a lot about a plant by its name. For example, a perennial with *odorata* in its name has fragrant flowers or leaves. Here are some other terms you're likely to run across:

alba: white

argentea: silvery

aurea: golden

autumnale: relating to fall

azurea: sky blue

caerulea: deep blue

cardinalis: scarlet

chinensis: from China

dentata: toothed

elata: tall

fistulosa: hollow

flava: yellow

flore-pleno: with double flowers

fulgens: shiny

humilis: low-growing

incana: grayish

laciniata: deeply cut

laevigata: smooth

maculata: spotted

minima: smallest

nana: dwarf

niger: black

japonica: from Japan

odorata: scented

pallida: pale

praecox: very early (in spring)

pubescens: fuzzy

pumila: dwarf

rosea: rosy pink

rugosa: wrinkled

sanguinea: blood red

sinensis: from China

speciosa (or *spectabilis*): showy

striata: striped

stricta: upright

tomentosa: very woolly

variegatus: multicolored

veris (or *vernalis* or *vernus*): relating to spring

virginalis: white

zebrina: striped

❂ KNOW YOUR PLANT LINGO

What's with all those fancy Latin names, anyway? Wouldn't it be easier to call plants by their regular names? Well, that works for a few really common perennials, like peonies. But what about those that have several common names? Gayfeather and blazing star, for instance, are two different names for the same plant. It's hard to communicate with others gardeners who may know one common name, while you know another. But if you used the botanical name—*Liatris*—you'd all know what you were talking about!

❂ BEYOND BLOOMS

When you think of perennials, the first thing that comes to mind is flowers, of course. But beautiful blooms are just the start! Perennials have a lot more to offer: lovely leaves, showy fruits and seedpods, or fabulous fall color. Work some of these into your beds and borders, and you'll add weeks or even months of extra excitement! Here are a few ideas to get you started:

Beautiful fruits: Baneberry (*Actaea*), blackberry lily (*Belamcanda chinensis*), Italian arum (*Arum italicum* 'Pictum'), and stinking iris (*Iris foetidissima*).

Fantastic foliage: Heucheras, hostas, lamium (*Lamium maculatum*), lamb's ears (*Stachys byzantina*), lungworts (*Pulmonaria*), wormwoods (*Artemisia*), and zebra grass (*Miscanthus sinensis* 'Zebrinus').

Flashy fall color: Arkansas blue star (*Amsonia hubrectii*), balloon flower (*Platycodon grandiflorus*), bloody cranesbill (*Geranium sanguineum*), and flame grass (*Miscanthus* 'Purpurascens').

Showy seedheads: Gas plant (*Dictamnus albus*), globe thistles (*Echinops*), purple coneflowers (*Echinacea*), sea hollies (*Eryngium*), showy stonecrop (*Sedum spectabile*), and Siberian iris (*Iris sibirica*).

Lavender
Lavandula angustifolia

Purple flower spikes over silvery leaves; aromatic and great for cutting or drying

CHAPTER 10

EVERY SEASON, EVERY REASON

No matter what you want from your garden—pretty flowers, fabulous fragrance, bird and butterfly habitat, or a bounty of blooms for cutting—perennials can do it all. And best of all, these versatile plants can give you something to look at nearly every day of the year, no matter where you live. Ready to take the plunge into perennials? Then read on!

Superb Spring Flowers

After a long, dreary winter, true gardeners are just itching to get out and start playing in the dirt, aren't we? So be sure to add lots of early-flowering perennials to your beds and borders, and you'll have plenty of gorgeous blooms to welcome the return of warmer weather.

Lenten rose
Helleborus x *hybridus*

Red, pink, or white flowers in early spring with evergreen foliage; thrives in shade

EARLY BLOOMS GET THE BEES

Spring-blooming perennials tend to be low-growing. Why? Because making tall stems takes lots of energy, and so does making flowers. Few plants can store enough energy in their roots to shoot upward *and* produce blooms in just a few weeks. So, spring perennials concentrate their efforts on making flowers, instead of sturdy stems.

One disadvantage of flowering so early is that the blooms are much more susceptible to damage by harsh weather conditions. But for many of these brave perennials, the risk is worth it. Because there aren't many flowers blooming in spring, early-flowering perennials have a much easier time attracting pollinators, such as bees. (Later in the season, there are so many flowers around that pollinators have many more plants to choose from.) Pretty clever way to generate some buzz, eh?

SPRING INTO FALL

Summer vacations are great, but while you're away from home, who's enjoying all those beautiful summer flowers you worked so hard for? If you're always away for part of the summer, then focus your gardening efforts on the seasons you *are* home. Pairing spring-blooming and fall-flowering perennials in the same bed gives you a great show at the beginning

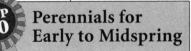

TOP 10 **Perennials for Early to Midspring**

Basket-of-gold
 (*Aurinia saxatilis*)
Bergenias (*Bergenia*)
Creeping phlox
 (*Phlox stolonifera*)
Crested iris (*Iris cristata*)
Cushion spurge
 (*Euphorbia polychroma*)
Lenten rose
 (*Helleborus* x *hybridus*)
Moss pink (*Phlox subulata*)
Rock cress (*Arabis caucasica*)
Siberian bugloss
 (*Brunnera macrophylla*)
Woodland phlox
 (*Phlox divaricata*)

and end of the growing season. As a plus, the tall stems of late-blooming plants will provide welcome summer shade for the more delicate spring wildflowers.

☀ LUNGWORTS GALORE

Okay—their name isn't very pretty, but you can't beat the beauty of the plants themselves! Lungworts (*Pulmonaria*) are ideal for gardens that are sunny in spring and shady for the rest of the year. You can enjoy their dainty, bell-shaped blue, pink, or white flowers in March and April, then admire their showy, silver-streaked or spotted leaves through the rest of the growing season. Here are some of the best cultivars—look for them at your local garden center:

'Berries and Cream'—pink flowers; silver leaves with ruffled green edges.

'Excalibur'—pink flowers; long leaves that are bright silver with a narrow green edge.

'Mrs. Moon'—pink buds open to blue flowers; silver-gray, spotted leaves.

'Roy Davidson'—pale pink buds open to baby blue flowers; narrow, deep green leaves with distinct silver spots.

'Sissinghurst White'—white flowers; silver-gray spotted leaves.

'Spilled Milk'—pink flowers; wide silvery leaves with green streaks.

Grandma Putt's WISDOM

*W*hen she set out her annual transplants each spring, Grandma Putt always potted up a few of the extras. Once the early perennials were done blooming, she'd cut them back, then plant those potted annuals in the space left behind. No wonder her gardens looked great all season long!

☀ LOVELY LEAVES FOR EARLY INTEREST

When you're picking pretty flowers for your spring gardens, don't overlook the allure of leaves. Perennials with showy foliage make super companions for pretty flowers. One of my favorites for spring foliage is variegated bulbous oat grass (*Arrhenatherum elatius* var. *bulbosum* 'Variegatum')—a really long name for a great little grass! This charmer makes cute-as-a-button clumps of green-and-white-striped leaves. Try it paired with white pansies (*Viola* x *wittrockiana*) for an elegant white-on-white combo, or with a rich blue polyanthus primrose (*Primula* x *polyantha*) for an exciting contrast.

Other perennials with good-looking spring foliage include golden creeping Jenny (*Lysimachia nummularia* 'Aurea'), purple-leaved heucheras (*Heuchera*), gardener's garters (*Phalaris arundinacea* 'Picta'), and wild gingers (*Asarum*).

JERRY'S GEMS

It's a smart idea to label spring-blooming perennials that go dormant soon after flowering, such as bloodroots (*Sanguinaria canadensis*) and Virginia bluebells (*Mertensia virginica*). Once their leaves die down, it's easy to dig into them by accident if there's no marker to remind you that they're there!

✿ PHLOX FACTS

Many folks think of phlox as being only for summer gardens, but if you don't grow some of these early-blooming kinds, too, you're missing the boat!

❧ **Creeping phlox** (*Phlox stolonifera*): The carpets of deep green, rounded leaves make a great groundcover in shady areas. Loose clusters of pink, lavender-blue, or white flowers flutter atop 4- to 6-inch-tall stems in spring. 'Bruce's White' has pure white blooms; 'Pink Ridge' produces purplish pink flowers. Needs partial to full shade; humus-rich, evenly moist soil. Zones 3 to 8.

❧ **Moss phlox** (*P. subulata*): Evergreen, 2- to 6-inch-tall, spreading mats of short, evergreen, needlelike leaves that look great all year long. In spring, the leaves are completely covered by masses of white, pink, or purplish flowers. Some cultivars even have striped blooms, like pink and white 'Candy Stripe'. Needs full sun, well-drained soil. Zones 2 to 9.

❧ **Woodland phlox** (*P. divaricata*): Spreading clumps of semi-evergreen leaves are simply spectacular in spring, when they're topped with clusters of lavender or white blooms on

Lily-of-the-valley
Convallaria majalis

Dense, quick-growing groundcover; arching sprays of perfumed, white spring blooms

8- to 12-inch-tall stems. Plus, the flowers are wonderfully fragrant! Needs partial shade; humus-rich, well-drained soil. Zones 3 to 9.

✿ GRAB YOUR PARTNERS

Looking for ideas to get you started with spring perennial pairings? Here are some classic combinations to get your creative juices flowing!

• White-flowered Lenten rose (*Helleborus* x *hybridus*) with white snowdrops (*Galanthus nivalis*).

• Yellow leopard's bane (*Doronicum*) with bright blue Siberian bugloss (*Brunnera macrophylla*).

• Greenish yellow cushion spurge (*Euphorbia polychroma*) with purple-blue English bluebells (*Hyacinthoides nonscripta*).

• White-flowered, variegated Japanese Solomon's seal (*Polygonatum odoratum* var. *thunbergii* 'Variegatum') underplanted with white- or pink-flowered lamium (*Lamium maculatum*).

✿ PLAN AHEAD

Don't count on spring bloomers to look good much after May—at least for a while. After flowering, many early-rising perennials tend to look tired and tattered, and they may even die back to the ground. Trim off any yellowing foliage, and the plants

---

Perfect Perennials

FOR MID- TO LATE SPRING

These pretty perennials are perfect for bridging the gap between early risers and the spectacular, early-summer show-offs:

Bleeding hearts (*Dicentra*): Pink flowers. Light to full shade. Zones 3 to 9.

Columbines (*Aquilegia*): Red, yellow, pink, blue, purple, white, or bicolor flowers. Partial shade. Zones 3 to 9.

Foamflower (*Tiarella cordifolia*): White flowers. Partial to full shade. Zones 3 to 8.

Moss phlox (*Phlox subulata*): White, pink, red, or blue flowers. Full sun. Zones 2 to 9.

Perennial candytuft (*Iberis sempervirens*): White flowers. Full sun. Zones 3 to 9.

Violets (*Viola*): Purple, pink, or white flowers. Partial shade. Zones 4 to 8.

will often sprout fresh new foliage. But if they don't, don't worry—they'll be back again next year!

In the meantime, though, you'll be left with gaps in your beds and borders. To minimize this wasted space, pair early perennials with later-rising companions that will bush out to fill the space that's left. Plants like asters, balloon flowers (*Platycodon grandiflorus*), and hostas are just a few great choices.

✱ THE PRIMROSE PATH

What would spring be without primroses (*Primula*)? These perky little perennials are among the first to brave the often-uncertain weather of early spring. You may even find them blooming under the last of the melting snow!

Primroses are pretty easy to grow, as long as you give them a spot with humus-rich soil that doesn't dry out during the year. They can take full sun in cool climates, but appreciate partial shade in hot-summer areas. Polyanthus primrose (*Primula* x *polyantha*) grows 6 to 12 inches tall and blooms in a rainbow of colors, often with a contrasting "eye" in the center of the bloom. The yellow-flowered ones are often fragrant. Zones 3 to 9.

Live-forever
Sedum purpureum

Dense clumps of fleshy leaves; upright stems topped with pinkish flower clusters

Summertime Classics

As the temperatures rise, so do the perennials! Many of the most well-known perennials come into their glory in June to welcome the summer season, then more emerge to keep the excitement level up right through the dog days. I tell you, it's a glorious time to be a gardener!

Mixers & Elixirs

SIMPLE SOAP-AND-OIL SPRAY

Are pests bugging your summer perennials? Try this tonic:

1 tbsp. of dishwashing liquid
1 cup of vegetable oil
1 cup of water

Mix together the dishwashing liquid and vegetable oil. Add 1 to 2 teaspoons of the mixture to the water in a handheld sprayer. Shake to mix, then spray on plants to control aphids, whiteflies, and spider mites.

Lungwort
Pulmonaria saccharata

Pink and blue spring flowers over silver-spotted leaves; superb for shade

✳ TAKE TWO PLANTS

If I had to name my favorite time in the perennial garden, I'd definitely say early summer. There are just so many lovely flowers to choose from, it's impossible to make a bad combination! Here are some time-tested, tried-and-true partnerships to get you thinking about the endless possibilities:

✔ Orange Oriental poppies (like *Papaver orientale*) below the purple spires of 'Black Knight' delphinium (*Delphinium* 'Black Knight').

✔ Pink roses (such as 'Mary Rose' or 'The Fairy') rising out of clouds of a blue-flowered catmint (*Nepeta*) or 'Johnson's Blue' hardy geranium (*Geranium* 'Johnson's Blue').

✔ Purplish pink foxgloves (*Digitalis purpurea*) marching behind the frothy, yellow-green mounds of lady's mantle (*Alchemilla mollis*).

✔ White 'Festiva Maxima' peony (*Paeonia* 'Festiva Maxima') against the rich blue blooms of 'Caesar's Brother' Siberian iris (*Iris sibirica* 'Caesar's Brother').

✳ COOL IT DOWN

It's a fact—strong summer sun can really bleach out paler-colored blooms. So if you still want to enjoy pastel-flowered perennials during the sultry summer weather, you'll need to give them a bit of shade.

White flowers are also great for decorating summer-shady spots. Besides brightening up dark areas, there's nothing like wintry white blooms to make you feel cool, even on a scorching summer day.

✴ RING IN SUMMER WITH BELLFLOWERS

The early-summer perennial border simply wouldn't be the same without beautiful bellflowers (*Campanula*). Their cupped or bell-shaped blooms have a limited color range (either purplish blue or white), but they come in a wide range of sizes—from low-growing carpeters to tall towers of eye-level blooms. Give bellflowers a spot in full sun (or partial shade in warm-summer areas), with evenly moist, but not soggy, soil. Here are a few of the best to get you started:

☑ **Carpathian harebell** (*C. carpatica*): Rounded, 6- to 12-inch-tall mounds with upturned blue or white cupped blooms from early summer into fall (with a midsummer trim). Easy to grow from seed, and often blooms the first year. Zones 3 to 8.

☑ **Clustered bellflower** (*C. glomerata*): Upright, 1- to 2-foot-tall, leafy stems topped with rounded clusters of deep purple-blue or white flowers from early to midsummer. Zones 3 to 8.

☑ **Peach-leaved bellflower** (*C. persicifolia*): One- to 3-foot-tall stems bearing bells in white or shades of blue from early to midsummer over low, spreading mounds of narrow, evergreen leaves. Zones 3 to 8.

TOP 10 **Perennials for Early to Midsummer**

Astilbes (*Astilbe*)

Bellflowers (*Campanula*)

Blue false indigo
(*Baptisia australis*)

Catmints (*Nepeta*)

Delphiniums (*Delphinium*)

Hardy geraniums (*Geranium*)

Oriental poppy
(*Papaver orientale*)

Peonies (*Paeonia*)

Shasta daisy
(*Chrysanthemum* x *superbum*)

Siberian iris (*Iris sibirica*)

✴ SUMMER SIZZLE TO THE MAX

Spring is a time for "cool" colors: soft yellows, pastel pinks, and baby blues. But by midsummer, we're ready for a bit more zip—and boy, oh boy, perennials are just what the doctor ordered!

Fill your beds and borders with a variety of perennials that fall in the "hot" color range—red, orange, and gold—along with some royal purple and bright blue to add a bit of zest. Some of the best perennials for perking up mid- and late-summer plantings include radiant red bee balm (like *Monarda* 'Jacob Cline'), vibrant, golden black-eyed Susans (*Rudbeckia*), and the amazing orange-tipped spikes of torch lilies (*Kniphofia*).

Mixers & Elixirs

ALL-PURPOSE PERENNIAL FERTILIZER

1 part bloodmeal
3 parts bonemeal
3 parts greensand or wood ashes

Mix the ingredients together. Apply 3 to 5 pounds per 100 square feet before planting and work it into the soil, or scatter 2 tablespoons around each clump, and scratch it into the soil surface.

❋ ENCHANTED EVENINGS

Bring the magic home to your summer garden with magic evening primrose (*Oenothera glazioviana*, also known as *O. erythrosepala*). At dusk, reddish buds unfurl quickly—in just a few seconds!—to reveal large, fragrant, pale yellow flowers. They bloom from mid- to late summer atop 3- to 4-foot-tall stems. This species is actually a biennial, but it comes back from self-sown seed, so you don't need to replant it. It's a favorite with young people—and the young-at-heart! It thrives in full sun in average, well-drained soil. Zones 5 to 9.

Lupine
Lupinus hybrid

Showy spikes of red, pink, blue, yellow, or white blooms in early summer

The Manure Cure

Late summer is a super time to lay in a supply of farm animal manure for next spring's perennials. But fresh manure needs to be cured. Here's how I make mine cool, weed-free, and almost odor-free!

1. Spread out a big tarpaulin, and dump the manure on top. Fold up the tarp's edges around the manure.

2. Lay another tarp across the top, and add a few rocks, so that it stays put.

3. Cut a few small slits in the tarp, for ventilation.

4. Let it sit for six months or so and—presto!—you've got the best lunch your flowers could ask for.

❋ LOOPY OVER LUPINES

Lupines' distinctive spiky blooms are a traditional favorite for the June perennial garden. They come in a veritable rainbow of colors—some even have two colors in each pealike flower. The only downside is that lupines hate hot weather, so they're tough to grow in Southern gardens. But if you live in an area where summers are just comfortably warm (Zone 6 and north), then you should definitely give these pretty perennials a try.

Lupines are surprisingly easy to start—just soak the seeds in water overnight before sowing them indoors in pots or outside in spring. Transplant the seedlings to the spot where you want them to bloom while they are still a few inches tall; don't wait too long, though, because older plants have deep roots and really don't like to be moved.

Your lupines will thrive in humus-rich soil that doesn't totally dry out during the growing season. If you give them full sun or light shade, and an adequte amount of water, you'll have an amazingly beautiful show next summer!

❋ AUGUST FILLERS

August is often a tough time in the perennial garden—the early-summer bloomers are done, and the fall-flowering species aren't open yet. But it's still possible to have a flower-filled planting with this little trick—simply fill the

---

Perfect Perennials

FOR MID- TO LATE SUMMER

Here's a half-dozen beautiful bloomers for the dog days of summer:

Black-eyed Susans (*Rudbeckia*): Orange-yellow flowers. Full sun. Zones 3 to 9.

Butterfly weeds (*Asclepias*): Orange, yellow, pink, or white flowers. Full sun. Zones 3 to 9.

Coreopsis (*Coreopsis*): Yellow, golden, or pink flowers. Full sun. Zones 3 to 9.

Daylilies (*Hemerocallis*): Yellow, orange, red, purplish, cream, or bicolor flowers. Full sun to light shade. Zones 3 to 10.

Phlox (*Phlox maculata* and *P. paniculata*): White, pink, red, orange, or purple flowers. Full sun to partial shade. Zones 3 to 8.

Purple coneflower (*Echinacea purpurea*): Rosy pink or white flowers. Full sun to light shade. Zones 3 to 9.

"holes" with annuals! Seeds will sprout quickly in the warm soil, and can reach flowering size in just a few weeks. Midsummer cuttings from already established annuals also make great fillers. If all else fails, buy a few pots of ornamental kale or cabbage to tide you over until fall.

Perennial Favorites for Fall

As summer's heat and humidity give way to the cool, crisp weather of fall, the perennial garden puts on a glorious show of bright blooms on big plants. So put on a cozy flannel shirt, grab a mug of warm apple cider, and get out there and enjoy it!

❋ FALL = TALL

Fall-blooming perennials have had plenty of time to soak up the sun, so they tend to be tall growers. That makes them great choices for the back of a border, or for the center of a bed that's surrounded by lawn. These lofty lovelies can even make terrific temporary hedges to provide summer and fall screening—a great idea around a swimming pool or patio, where you want warm-season privacy without the expense and effort of a permanent hedge.

❋ CLASSY ASTERS

Asters are a classic choice for fall flower gardens, and with good reason. Thanks to the efforts of dedicated plant breeders and nurserymen, these colorful perennials have gone from being scrawny, roadside weeds to personality-packed garden plants.

Madonna lily
Lilium candidum

Pure white, trumpet-shaped blooms on tall stems; lovely for summer beds and borders

There are hundreds of aster species, but the two most popular for fall perennial gardens are New England aster (*Aster novae-angliae*) and New York aster (*A. novi-belgii*). Both grow best in full sun and humus-rich, well-drained soil in Zones 4 to 8. If you want your aster plants to be bushy rather than tall, select naturally compact cultivars, or pinch off the tip of each shoot in midspring and again in early to midsummer. Divide clumps every two or three years to keep them healthy and vigorous.

✺ FANTASTIC FALL FOLIAGE

Lots of folks enjoy driving around the countryside in fall to admire the colorful leaves of deciduous trees and shrubs. But you can bring the best of autumn's bright hues right into your own backyard, simply by planting perennials with foliage that changes color in fall.

For some reason, gardening books and catalogs rarely mention when a perennial has colorful fall foliage, so you'll just have to keep your eyes open as you pay autumn visits to other gardens in your area. Some of my favorites are the reddish leaf colors of bloody cranesbill (*Geranium sanguineum*) and leadwort (*Ceratostigma plumbaginoides*). For yellow fall foliage, plant bluestars (*Amsonia*), balloon flowers (*Platycodon grandiflorus*), and hostas. Grasses are often glorious in fall, too: Enjoy the cranberry red leaves of Japanese blood grass (*Imperata cylindrica* 'Red Baron'), and the bright orange and red hues of flame grass (*Miscanthus* 'Purpurascens') and switch grass (*Panicum virgatum*).

✺ GO FOR THE GOLDENRODS

Goldenrods (*Solidago*) have long gilded fall meadows and roadsides with golden fall blooms, but sadly, you don't see them in many gardens. That's because these pretty plants

---

TOP 10 **Perennials for Fall**

Asters (*Aster*)

'Autumn Joy' sedum (*Sedum* 'Autumn Joy')

Boltonia (*Boltonia asteroides*)

Goldenrods (*Solidago*)

Japanese anemone (*Anemone* x *hybrida*)

Monkshood (*Aconitum carmichaelii*)

Mums (*Chrysanthemum* x *morifolium*)

Plumbago (*Ceratostigma plumbaginoides*)

Sneezeweed (*Helenium autumnale*)

Turtleheads (*Chelone*)

Try This!

Begonias are gorgeous garden plants, but the slightest hint of frost sends most of them to an early grave. But guess what—there's actually a *perennial* begonia! This fall-blooming beauty produces 1- to 2-foot-tall clumps of light green leaves topped by arching clusters of pale pink flowers. Hardy begonia (*Begonia grandis*) thrives in partial to full shade and evenly moist (but not soggy), humus-rich soil in Zones 6 to 9.

have gotten a bum rap for causing fall hayfever. The real culprit is the dull green flowers of ragweeds (*Ambrosia*)—they bloom at the same time as goldenrods, but nobody notices their boring blooms.

So, now that you know it's safe to enjoy goldenrods in your sunny garden, go wild! Some fun selections you may find at your local garden center include 'Fireworks' (3 to 5 feet tall) and 'Golden Fleece' (1 to 2 feet tall).

Perennials in the Off-Season

Fall frosts don't have to signal the end of your gardening fun! True, there's not much happening in the flower department during the coldest months of the year. But if you include perennials with evergreen foliage and long-lasting seedheads, you'll still have something nice to look at while you're waiting for spring to return.

GREAT GRASSES

If you really want your garden to look great in winter, ornamental grasses are a must! The grasses that bloom early in the summer tend to put on most of their leafy growth in the cooler months, so their foliage is at its best in fall, winter, and spring. Some cool-season grasses that look great in the off-season include blue fescue (*Festuca glauca*), blue oat grass (*Helictotrichon sempervirens*), and variegated bulbous oat grass (*Arrhenatherum elatius* var. *bulbosum*).

Besides offering showy, fall foliage colors, late-summer and fall-flowering grasses tend to hold their stems and seedheads at least partway into winter. Some super warm-season grasses for winter interest include Japanese silver grass (*Miscanthus sinensis*), ravenna grass (*Erianthus ravennae*), and switch grass (*Panicum virgatum*).

✷ LOVELY LEAVES

Mention the word "evergreen," and what comes to mind? Pine trees? Arborvitae? Spruces? Sure, evergreen *trees* are great for adding winter interest to a garden, but so are evergreen *perennials*. They're just a little shorter—that's all!

The usual evergreen perennials have—not surprisingly—green leaves, but they come in other colors, too. For more excitement, toss in some with evergray leaves, like lamb's ears (*Stachys byzantina*). And don't forget the everpurples—such as 'Plum Pudding' heuchera (*Heuchera* 'Plum Pudding')—and the everyellows—like golden oregano (*Origanum vulgare* 'Aureum'). There are even everstriped perennials, including 'Variegata' and 'Goldband' Japanese sedges (*Carex morrowii*), to name just a few.

✷ DASHING THROUGH THE SNOW

If you live where winter snow is a sure thing, there's not much point in planning your garden around winter-interest plants. But look on the bright side: Snow provides a perfect insulating blanket for perennials, so you don't have to worry much about winter mulching.

But here's another great thing about snow: It makes a super tool for garden planning! Thinking about putting in a new flowerbed or enlarging an existing one? Put on your boots, and shuffle along the outline of the new bed

Maiden grass
Miscanthus sinensis

Tall clumps of arching grayish green leaves topped with silvery seedheads in fall

TOP 5

Perennials with Evergreen Leaves

Lilyturfs (*Liriope*)

Moss phlox (*Phlox subulata*)

Pachysandra (*Pachysandra*)

Perennial candytuft (*Iberis sempervirens*)

Yuccas (*Yucca*)

or border, then step back and see how it looks. Don't like it? Sweep or shovel snow into your tracks, or wait until the next snowfall, then try again. You could even pile up snow to experiment with the effect of different-sized perennials. What a great way to get your kids to help out in the garden!

❁ A COLD DAY IN THE HELLEBORE PATCH

My favorite hellebores are the Lenten roses (*Helleborus* x *hybridus*, also sold as *H. orientalis*), because they bloom in a variety of colors. Christmas rose (*H. niger*) blooms a few weeks earlier—usually starting in late February—with white flowers. Both are hardy in Zones 4 to 9.

I can't figure out why more people don't grow these *amazing* perennials. They have handsome evergreen foliage all year long, and pretty flowers in late winter to early spring. They can take anything from full sun to full shade (partial shade is best), and average, well-drained soil is fine. These versatile plants are perfect for tough spots under trees and shrubs, where the soil is simply too dry in summer for more delicate perennials to survive. Best of all, hellebores (*Helleborus*) shrug off pests and diseases—even deer don't eat them! Established clumps can live for years without any maintenance at all. And if you want more of them, simply transplant some of the seedlings that appear around the base of the clumps each spring.

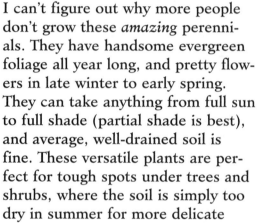

Maiden pink
Dianthus deltoides

Low-growing with pink, rose, or white flowers; beautiful at the front of a bed or border

Fabulous Fragrances

To me, a flower garden without fragrant plants is like a day without sunshine. So, help your gardens be all they can be by tucking in a few great-smelling perennials—your nose will thank you!

☀ THE NOSE KNOWS

To get the most from fragrant perennials, plant them near areas where you spend lots of time, such as near a garden bench or outside your bedroom window. Scents are often most powerful in the evening, when the air is still, so they're nice around decks, patios, or porches where you sit on summer evenings. Perennials with fragrant leaves are perfect for planting along paths, because they'll release their scent when you step on or brush by them.

☀ PRETTY IN PINKS

Pinks (*Dianthus*) are one group of perennials that have long been prized for their great, spicy fragrance. They're called "pinks" mainly because their petal tips often look like they've been clipped with pinking shears. But the name also refers to their color range: mostly shades of pink, but also red or white. Pinks like full sun, but appreciate a bit of midday shade where summers are hot; average, well-drained soil is fine.

There are many species and hybrids, but not all are created equal in the fragrance department. Here are three of my favorites (all hardy in Zones 3 to 9):

Allwood pink (*D.* x *allwoodii*): Gray-green leaves in dense clumps with pink, red, or white flowers on 12- to 18-inch-tall stems in late spring and early summer. Many

Perfect Perennials

FOR SCENTED FLOWERS

Here are eight great perfumed perennials to fill your yard with fabulous fragrance!

August lily (*Hosta plantaginea*): Sweetly fragrant white trumpets in late summer.

Dame's rocket (*Hesperis matronalis*): Night-scented, purplish pink blooms in early summer.

Lemon lily (*Hemerocallis lilioasphodelus*): Lemon-scented, yellow trumpets in late spring.

Lily-of-the-valley (*Convallaria majalis*): Fragrant white bells in late spring.

Peonies (*Paeonia*): Richly perfumed, pink, red, or white blooms in late spring to early summer.

Pinks (*Dianthus*): Clove-scented, pink blooms in late spring to early summer.

Rock cress (*Arabis caucasica*): Honey-scented, white flowers in spring.

Swamp milkweed (*Asclepias incarnata*): Vanilla-scented, pink or white flowers in summer.

fragrance lovers rave about the scent of 'Rainbow Loveliness', in particular.

Cheddar pink (*D. gratianopolitanus*): Dense mats of gray-green leaves topped with pink, red, or white flowers on 6- to 12-inch-tall stems in late spring to early summer. 'Bath's Pink' has single, soft pink blooms.

Cottage pink (*D. plumarius*): Mounds of blue-green leaves with small clusters of pink, red, or white flowers on 1- to 2-foot-tall stems from spring to early summer.

❋ LAVENDER IN BLUE AND GREEN

Of course, no collection of fragrant perennials would be complete without lavender! The most obvious feature of these 1- to 2-foot-tall mini-shrubs is their dense spikes of small, scented summer flowers—usually in shades of purple-blue, but sometimes white or pink. The gray-green to silvery leaves and stems are aromatic, too.

The kind you're most likely to find for sale is English lavender (*Lavandula angustifolia*). Hardy in Zones 5 to 9, it likes full sun and average, well-drained soil. If you want lots of lavender in a hurry, sow seed of the kind called 'Lady' in early spring—you will have flowers the very first summer!

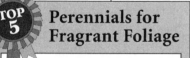

Perennials for Fragrant Foliage

Anise hyssop (*Agastache foeniculum*)

Bee balms (*Monarda*)

Lavenders (*Lavandula*)

Sages (*Salvia*)

Thymes (*Thymus*)

❋ MAKING SENSE OF SCENTS

Fragrance is definitely a subjective issue. Part of our reaction to fragrance is physical—some people can detect most or all of the chemical compounds that cause various scents, while others can smell only some. But there's also an emotional element—you may like a particular fragrance because you have pleasant memories of the first time or place you smelled it.

So what does all this have to do with your perennial garden? Just this—if you want to grow perennials for fragrance, don't buy plants just because someone else says they smell nice. Go to the nursery yourself, and take a test sniff before you buy!

Best Bets for Birds and Butterflies

Beautiful gardens provide more than gorgeous flowers to look at—they make great places for birds, butterflies, and other creatures to live. To attract more of Mother Nature's beauties, make sure you provide for their three basic needs: food, water, and shelter. Read on for a whole slew of tips on drawing them to *your* backyard.

❀ PUT AWAY YOUR SPRAYER

If you want to attract the widest range of wildlife to your perennial garden, you might need to make a few changes in your gardening style. First, you should avoid using chemical pesticides in your garden. Birds need lots of insects to eat, so getting rid of all the bugs will send the birds looking elsewhere for food. Also, eating pesticide-laced insects can make birds sick—especially hummingbirds. Plus, some caterpillars are the larvae of beautiful butterflies, so killing them all will reduce the number of butterflies in your garden later on. If plant damage really gets out of hand, then use a safe, homemade spray (like one of my pest control tonics; see "Flower Fixers, Magical Mixers & Excellent Elixirs" starting on page 344), and spray it *only* on the seriously infested perennials.

The other change you need to make is to put up with a

Maltese cross
Lychnis chalcedonica

Fire-engine-red flower clusters atop 2- to 3-foot-tall stems

little less tidiness in your perennial garden. Leave some dropped leaves and other plant litter on the ground for birds to root through in search of insects. And letting some seedheads stand into winter provides food for seed-eating birds, and also supplies shelter for butterfly larvae.

✸ CREATE AN AVIAN HAVEN

Sometimes, gardens are literally for the birds! To have a garden full of feathered friends, make sure you supply:

Food: Trees, berried shrubs, seed-producing perennials, and plenty of feeding stations.

Water: A birdbath, small pool, pond, stream, or other source of water for drinking and bathing.

Cover: Shrubs, vines, and trees to protect your birds from marauders and give them a safe place to make their nests.

✸ BIRD MAGNETS!

Perennials that produce lots of seeds are *perfect* for birds. So are those with many tiny flowers that attract lots of insects—your fine feathered friends will flock to this ready-made, all-you-can-eat buffet! Here's a quick overview of three beautiful and bird-attracting perennials:

 Anise hyssop (*Agastache foeniculum*): Dense spikes of tiny purple flowers on 2- to 3-foot-tall plants from midsummer to frost. Both the leaves and flowers smell like root beer! The flowers attract hummingbirds, while sparrows and finches love the seeds. Full sun; average, well-drained soil. Zones 5 to 9.

Gayfeathers (*Liatris*): Also called blazing stars, these 2- to 5-foot-tall perennials produce fuzzy spikes of rosy pur-

MAKING ¢ents

Don't spend a fortune buying a fancy birdbath for your feathered friends! Just turn a large clay pot upside down in your perennial garden (don't cover up any plants!), and put a clay saucer on top of it. Place a few brightly colored marbles in the bottom of the saucer—they'll attract the birds. Then just add water. Believe you me—the birds will flock to your flower garden!

ple or white flowers from midsummer to early fall. Goldfinches and other birds love the seeds. Gayfeathers are also butterfly magnets! Full sun; average, well-drained soil. Zones 3 to 9.

🐦 **Mulleins** (*Verbascum*): Three- to 6-foot-tall spikes of yellow, white, pink, or purple flowers in summer over low rosettes of green or fuzzy gray leaves. Many small birds enjoy the seeds, and they'll also feed on the insects and larvae that try to overwinter on the flower stalks. Full sun; average, well-drained soil. Zones 3 to 8.

✿ SOAK IT TO 'EM

Roll out the red carpet and invite birds over to your yard—for a bath. You don't have a bird-bath? Well, get one! It can be as fancy as a store-bought marble fountain or as simple as an old clay saucer set on a milk crate. Set the bath a few feet away from a bush or tree, so the birds have a good place to hide if they spot a predator. Keep it full of water, but not *too* full—experts suggest there be no more than 3 inches for the birds to splash in. Change the water every few days to keep it fresh, and clean the basin itself often by scrubbing it with a paste of baking soda and water (rinse well to remove all traces of the baking soda before refilling).

TOP 10
Perennials for Attracting Birds

Asters (*Aster*)

Black-eyed Susans (*Rudbeckia*)

Columbines (*Aquilegia*)

Coreopsis (*Coreopsis*)

Eupatoriums (*Eupatorium*)

Gayfeathers (*Liatris*)

Globe thistles (*Echinops*)

Goldenrods (*Solidago*)

Perennial sunflowers (*Helianthus*)

Purple coneflower (*Echinacea purpurea*)

Meadow anemone
Anemone canadensis

Bright white spring blooms over lacy green leaves

Great Grasses for Wildlife

Perennial grasses provide food and shelter for birds, butterflies, and other critters. Here are some must-haves: big bluestem (*Andropogon gerardii*), Indian grass (*Sorghastrum nutans*), little bluestem (*Schizachyrium scoparium*), sideoats grama grass (*Bouteloua curtipendula*), switch grass (*Panicum virgatum*), tufted hairgrass (*Deschampsia cespitosa*), and wild oats (*Chasmanthium latifolium*).

❋ HANG AROUND FOR HUMMINGBIRDS

To entice hummingbirds to your yard, hang long strands of orange yarn on trees and shrubs near your hummingbird feeder. For a more permanent attraction, plant perennials, shrubs, and trees that produce orange or red flowers or berries.

As for the feeder itself, don't waste your money on a fancy one—a cheap feeder with bright, red plastic tips will work just fine. Or get one of those little water bottles sold for gerbils and hamsters, and tie a red ribbon around the end.

Mixers & Elixirs

HUMMINGBIRD TONIC

If you know there are hummingbirds in your area and you want to set up a feeder, try this mixture to lure them into your yard:

1 part granulated sugar
4 parts water

Heat the mixture to a boil, and stir until all the sugar has dissolved. Let the mixture cool before putting it in your feeder.

Once hummers start coming, decrease the solution to about 1 part sugar to 8 parts water. No, this isn't the old bait-and-switch tactic—there's a good reason for diluting the solution. Hummingbirds can sometimes suffer a fatal liver disorder if they get too much sugar.

❋ SWEET TREAT

Even if you have plenty of hummingbird-attracting flowers in your garden, it's still a good idea to hang up a hummingbird feeder. That way, you'll catch the first hummingbirds of the season, which may show up before the perennials they like best start to bloom. Plus, the hummers will be assured of a food source, even if dreary weather keeps the flowers from opening.

Fill your chosen feeder with purchased nectar mix, or make up a batch of my Hummingbird Tonic (above). Store any leftover mix in the refrigerator. Every other day, dump any unused liquid out of the feeder, rinse out with boiling water, and refill with fresh mix. This regular cleaning is critical to keep harmful fungus from building up in the feeder, so don't neglect to do it. (I put red *H*'s on my calendar to remind me.)

✺ TOTALLY TUBULAR

Topping the list of hummingbirds' favorite flowers are the beardtongues (*Penstemon*). Sometimes simply called penstemons, these perennials produce slender spikes of tubular flowers in summer in just about every color but yellow. To have good luck with beardtongues, it's important to pick types that are adapted to your climate: Those from the West will suffer in the more humid East, and vice versa. They all like full sun to light shade and adapt to average, well-drained soil. Two of my favorites (both hardy in Zones 3 to 8) are:

Keep in mind that the sugar water you put out for hummingbirds may bring on more than just your feathered friends. Hummingbird feeders can attract ants, bees, and other sweet-loving insects, as well. But hey, don't say I didn't warn you!

✔ Dwarf hairy beardtongue (*P. hirsutus* 'Pygmaeus'): Red-tinged green leaves, light purplish pink flowers. Height to 6 inches.

✔ 'Husker Red' beardtongue (*P. digitalis* 'Husker Red'): Maroon foliage and stems, pinkish white flowers. Height to 4 feet.

✺ A SPOONFUL OF SUGAR

If you live in the West or Southwest, sugar water will make you popular year-round with hummingbirds. In colder climates, use sugar water only during the warm months, serving it in hummingbird feeders or in a glass cup hung in a tree.

Missouri evening primrose
Oenothera macrocarpa

Reddish buds open in evening into fragrant, lemon-yellow, bowl-shaped blooms

Hold Off on the Honey

When feeding hummingbirds, stick to sugar-based mixtures; never substitute honey for the sugar. According to the experts, honey supports the growth of microorganisms that can be fatal to the little hummers.

❋ BRING ON THE BUTTERFLIES

Who doesn't enjoy the sight of butterflies fluttering around their yard and garden? Here's what you need to provide to entice these beauties to your yard:

• **Food plants:** Baby butterflies need lots of food, so grow leafy plants for the caterpillars to eat. Good choices are fennel (*Foeniculum vulgare*), milkweeds (*Asclepias*), parsley (*Petroselinum crispum*), and passionflowers (*Passiflora*).

• **Nectar plants:** Butterflies find nectar flowers by their colors. They're attracted to "hot" colors, like yellow, orange, red, and purple. They also need flowers that provide some sort of platform for them to perch on while they probe for nectar, so avoid planting very frilly, double blooms. Butterflies are generally around from spring into fall in most parts of the country, so plant perennials for a succession of blooms throughout the growing season.

• **Water:** Butterflies can't drink from open water, so wet sand, earth, and/or mud are their best water sources. To make a butterfly bath, sink a pail into the ground, fill it with mud, and place a few sticks on top for the butterflies to perch on.

• **Shelter:** It's hard for butterflies to fly and feed in open sites exposed to strong winds, so choose a sheltered spot for your butterfly garden. But make sure it's sunny—butterflies need plenty of sunlight to warm their wing muscles enough to fly.

Perfect Perennials

FOR BUTTERFLIES

Bring a bounty of winged beauties to your yard with these long-blooming, sun-loving perennials—they're butterfly magnets!

Anise hyssop (*Agastache foeniculum*): Spikes of purple-blue or white flowers. Zones 5 to 10.

Asters (*Aster*): Fuzzy purple, pink, or white blooms. Zones 3 to 8.

Coreopsis (*Coreopsis*): Yellow, golden, or pink daisylike flowers. Zones 3 to 9.

Gayfeathers (*Liatris*): Fuzzy-looking, purplish pink flower spikes. Zones 3 to 9.

Milkweeds (*Asclepias*): Heads of orange, yellow, pink, or white flowers. Zones 3 to 9.

Phlox (*Phlox*): Clusters of flat flowers in a wide range of colors. Zones 3 to 8.

Stonecrops (*Sedum*): Dense heads of red, pink, white, or yellow blooms. Zones 4 to 9.

Yarrow (*Achillea*): Flat-topped flower heads in many bright and pastel colors. Zones 3 to 9.

✻ GOT MILKWEEDS?

My vote for the top perennials for butterfly gardens are the milkweeds (*Asclepias*). They are favorites with Monarch butterflies, but they attract many others, too, including skippers, swallowtails, and fritillaries. Their leaves provide food for larvae, and the small, but abundant blooms are a super source of nectar for adults.

Cutting Remarks

Flowers are great in the garden, but they're even better when you bring them indoors to brighten your home! With a little planning, your perennial garden can provide an endless supply of beautiful blooms for formal arrangements, casual bouquets, wreaths, and even potpourri.

✻ PLAN AHEAD FOR ABUNDANT BLOOMS

If you simply like to snip a few flowers every now and then, your regular perennial plantings should provide all the blooms you need. But if you like big bouquets, or you like to have lots of flowers to share with friends, consider planting a patch of perennials specifically for cutting.

A cutting garden isn't planned to look pretty—it's primary function is to provide a season-long supply of your favorite flowers. Consider putting your cutting garden in a corner of your vegetable garden or in another sunny, well-drained spot that isn't highly visible. Concentrate on perennials that flower in your favorite colors, but be sure to include other colors, too, for some variety in your arrangements.

Moss phlox
Phlox subulata

Ground-hugging carpets of evergreen foliage smothered with flowers in spring; superb for slopes

❋ CUTTING-GARDEN CLASSICS

When you find something that works, you stick with it! My Grandma Putt grew lots of different flowers, but there were some that she especially liked for cutting. These old stand-bys made the grade because they were easy to grow, provided lots of blooms, and lasted a long time. Here are three of Grandma's favorites (and mine, too):

• **Baby's breath** (*Gypsophila paniculata*): The airy clouds of tiny white, early-summer blooms are a classic companion for florists' roses, but the bushy, 2- to 4-foot-tall plants are easy to grow at home, as well. Full sun and humus-rich, evenly moist, but well-drained soil. Zones 3 to 9.

• **Obedient plant** (*Physostegia virginiana*): Upright 3- to 4-foot-tall stems topped with spikes of rosy pink flowers from midsummer to early fall. The individual flowers have unique hinged bases, so you can turn them from side to side, and they'll stay where you put them! Full sun to partial shade; average soil that doesn't totally dry out in summer. Zones 3 to 9.

• **Summer phlox** (*Phlox paniculata* and *P. maculata*): Showy heads of sweetly scented flowers in just about every color but yellow. Two- to 4-foot-tall plants bloom in mid- to late summer and sometimes even into fall. Look for mildew-resistant cultivars like 'David' (white) and 'Shortwood' (pink). Zones 3 to 8.

Perfect Perennials

FOR FRESH-CUT FLOWERS

When you're ready to bring the best of your garden indoors, here are my top picks for long-lasting blooms:

Astilbe (*Astilbe*): Pick when fully open.

Bleeding hearts (*Dicentra*): Pick when four or five flowers on the stem show good color.

Delphiniums (*Delphinium*): Cut when half of the spike shows good color.

Irises (*Iris*): Cut when the first bud is nearly open.

Mums (*Chrysanthemum* x *morifolium*): Cut when flowers are fully open.

Purple coneflowers (*Echinacea purpurea*): Pick just as the petals are expanding.

Spike gayfeather (*Liatris spicata*): Cut when the top flowers in the spike are open.

Yarrows (*Achillea*): Pick when half of the flowers in the head are open.

❀ GROW SOME YARROW

No cutting garden is complete without yarrows (*Achillea*). They come in a wide range of colors (except blues and purples), they bloom for several months in the garden, they have sturdy stems, and they last for well over a week as fresh-cut flowers. Give yarrows a spot in full sun with average, well-drained to dryish soil. Divide plants every two or three years to keep them healthy and free-flowering. 'Coronation Gold' is a cutting-garden classic, with large, flat clusters of golden flowers on strong 2- to 4-foot-tall stems. Newer hybrids come in different colors—try light pink 'Appleblossom', rusty orange 'Terra Cotta', or deep red 'Summerwine'. All of these yarrows are hardy in Zones 3 to 9.

When choosing perennials for your cutting garden, avoid low-growing or dwarf varieties. These compact cuties are great for minimizing staking in the regular garden, but for cutting, you want the longest stems possible!

Container Choices

Growing perennials in pots is a great way to show them off. You can get up close to admire their beautiful colors and fragrances without having to get down on your knees—plus, soil preparation and planting is a breeze! So even if you don't have the space, time, or energy for an in-ground garden, you can still enjoy growing a wide variety of pretty plants. Read on to find out how easy it is!

❀ UNRESTRAINED CONTAINERS

Potted perennials are perfect for brightening up doorways, decks, patios, and porches. But besides adding beauty to

Mullein
Verbascum thapsus

Towering spikes of bright yellow blooms over rosettes of fuzzy, grayish foliage

your home, growing perennials in pots has a number of practical benefits. Let's say you found a great bargain on a plant, but it's too small to put in the garden—stick it in a nice-looking pot, and let it grow for a few months, until it's big enough to hold its own against other perennials. Or maybe you couldn't resist that beautiful perennial at the garden center, but when you get home, you realize you have no open space in the garden. Plant it in a pot until you have time to find a permanent home for it in a bed or border.

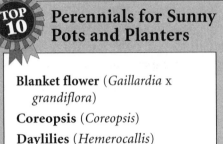

Perennials for Sunny Pots and Planters

Blanket flower (*Gaillardia* x *grandiflora*)

Coreopsis (*Coreopsis*)

Daylilies (*Hemerocallis*)

Hen and chicks (*Sempervivum tectorum*)

Heucheras (*Heuchera*)

Lamb's ear (*Stachys byzantina*)

Lavenders (*Lavandula*)

Pincushion flowers (*Scabiosa*)

'Pink Panda' strawberry (*Fragaria* 'Pink Panda')

Stonecrops (*Sedum*)

KEEP 'EM IN BOUNDS

Pots are a great place for growing perennials that spread quickly by creeping roots. The container will keep the roots in bounds, so you can enjoy the plant without worrying about whether it will take over your whole garden. And if your garden soil tends to be on the soggy side, pots provide excellent drainage for perennials that don't like wet feet.

SMART CONTAINER CHOICES

If you're planning a garden of potted perennials, I highly recommend using plastic containers. Now, don't turn your nose up at that suggestion—I'm not talking about the cheap-looking white, dark green, or black plastic pots that you buy your plants in at nurseries and garden centers. I mean the really attractive ones that look just like clay or molded concrete, but are far more practical. They won't break, they clean up more easily, they're a snap to store, and they retain moisture longer on hot surfaces than clay pots do. Moss and mold don't build up on them in the shade, and they're ideal for holding large plants—when it comes time to move them, you won't break your back! What more could you ask for?

✳ PICK PINCUSHION FLOWERS

One of my all-time favorite perennials for containers—and beds and borders, as well—is the pincushion flower (*Scabiosa*). These perky little perennials start blooming in early summer, and they'll keep going well into fall—especially if you pick off the dead flowers every now and then. Their flower heads look just like little pincushions, with a domed center of tiny florets surrounded by a ruff of slightly larger petals.

Look for 'Butterfly Blue', with lavender-blue blooms, and 'Pink Mist', with pale pink flowers. Both grow 1 to 2 feet tall. Give them full sun and regular watering and fertilizing for best bloom. They're quite cold-tolerant (Zones 3 to 9 normally), so potted specimens won't need special winter care in most climates.

Naked ladies
Amaryllis belladonna

Leaves die back by midsummer; trumpet-shaped pink flowers appear several weeks later

✳ SWEET MARGUERITE

Here's a perennial that can even beat some annuals for pure flower power! Golden marguerite (*Anthemis tinctoria*) fills both container and garden plantings with dense, 2-foot-tall mounds of aromatic, deep green leaves topped with golden domed daisies from early summer into fall. Pinching off the dead flowers every few days will help keep the plants looking their best. Give golden marguerite full sun. It prefers dry soil, so it won't mind if you occasionally forget to water it. In the ground, it's hardy in Zones 3 to 9, so it should get through the winter as a container plant in most areas, with just a little protection.

Mixers & Elixirs

CONTAINER PLANT TONIC

2 tbsp. of whiskey
1 tbsp. of all-purpose 15-30-15 fertilizer
½ tsp. of unflavored gelatin
½ tsp. of dishwashing liquid
¼ tsp. of instant tea granules
Water

Put the whiskey, fertilizer, gelatin, dishwashing liquid, and tea in a clean 1 gallon milk jug, and fill it up with water. Mix, then mark the jug "Container Plant Tonic." Add ½ cup of this mix to every gallon of water you use to water your potted perennials.

❊ FEED EARLY, FEED OFTEN

Perennials growing in pots and planters need watering much more often than garden plants—maybe even daily during hot, dry weather. All this watering quickly leaches nutrients out of the soil, so you'll also need to fertilize regularly to keep potted plants looking their best. It's a good idea to use a diluted liquid fertilizer, like my Container Plant Tonic (on page 205), each time you water.

❊ POTTING POINTERS

Here are my best container-related pointers to help you get the most from your potted perennial garden:

☑ Make sure your pot has adequate drainage. There should be at least three holes, each about 1/2 inch across.

☑ Line the base of the pot with newspaper before adding soil. It will keep the soil from washing out of the pot when you add water or fertilizer.

☑ Use light-colored containers in hot climates. Dark pots absorb too much heat and can damage the roots.

☑ Set containers on bricks or blocks so that excess water will drain out freely.

☑ If you choose clay pots, pay special attention to watering. Clay is porous, so the soil in clay pots will dry out much more quickly than the soil in plastic pots.

Perfect Perennials

FOR SHADY CONTAINERS

Spruce up tough, shady spots with pots of pretty perennials like these!

Astilbes (*Astilbe*): Red, pink, white, or salmon flower plumes.

Bugleweeds (*Ajuga*): Glossy green, purple, or variegated leaves.

Fringed bleeding heart (*Dicentra eximia*): Pink, red, or white flowers.

Golden hakone grass (*Hakonechloa macra* 'Aureola'): Green-striped yellow leaves.

Hostas (*Hosta*): Green, blue, yellow, or variegated leaves; purple or white flowers.

Japanese painted fern (*Athyrium goeringianum* 'Pictum'): Silvery gray fronds with dark maroon stems.

Lamiums (*Lamium maculatum*): Silver-and-green leaves; pink or white flowers.

Lungworts (*Pulmonaria*): Pink or blue flowers; silver-spotted green leaves.

❀ Don't Overdo It

When planting a perennial in a container, leave a 2-inch space between the top of the soil and the top of the container. That will give you enough room to spread an inch or so of mulch over the soil, and still allow you to add water without it running over the top of the pot.

❀ Winter Container Care

Most perennials need some amount of cold weather each year to grow properly, so it's usually best to leave them outside in their pots. In areas with moderately cold winters (roughly Zones 6 and south), your container perennials should do fine if you just gather them together in some sheltered spot, such as up against the foundation of your house. In colder areas, you might also want to surround each pot with a tied-on layer of bubble wrap, or pile mulch or straw between and around the pots, for extra insulation.

Mixers & Elixirs

PERFECT POTTING SOIL

Here's how to make the perfect blend of potting soil for all your container-grown perennials:

1 part sharp sand
1 part clay loam
1 part compost, peat moss,
  or potting soil

Per cubic foot of soil mixture, add:

1½ cups of Epsom salts
¾ cup of coffee grounds (rinsed)
12 eggshells (dried and crushed to
  a powder)

Blend all of the ingredients together, and use the mixture to make your perennials feel comfy and cozy in their new home.

Watch Out!

The vast majority of perennials are great garden plants, but as with any group, there are a few bad apples that can spoil the bunch. In this section, I'll tell you about a few perennials to watch out for, and how to make sure they don't ruin your gardening fun.

❈ THESE GIVE ME THE CREEPS!

My vote for the most obvious problem perennials are those that spread by creeping roots or stems. At best, these mean just a little extra work for you. Left unchecked, though, they can gradually crowd out less vigorous companions and take over whole beds! Don't worry—just take at least one of the precautionary steps below, and you can still enjoy these wide-roaming perennials.

> Fortunately, keeping self-sowing perennials from spreading all over is a snap—simply pinch or snip off the fading flowers before any seeds form. Or, if you like to leave the seedheads for your feathered friends, then make sure you add a fresh 1- to 2-inch-deep layer of mulch over the whole garden in early spring. This will smother any remaining seeds and discourage them from sprouting.

❧ Dig up and divide the plants every year or two. Replant one piece, and give away or discard the rest.

❧ Surround the patch with some sort of root barrier, such as a strip of metal roof flashing. Make sure the barrier extends several inches down into the soil, and leave an inch or two above ground level, too. Or cut the bottom out of an old bucket, sink the bucket into the soil almost up to the rim, add soil, and set the plant inside.

❧ Plant creepers in some sort of naturally enclosed area, such as a strip of ground that's surrounded by paving on all sides.

❧ Grow them in pretty pots or planters on a deck or patio, and enjoy their beauty with no fear of their getting out of control.

New England
aster
Aster novae-angliae

Clustered flowers
in pink, purple,
blue, or white

❈ SELF-SOWERS CAN TAKE OVER

Another group of perennials to keep your eye on are the ones that produce lots of seeds. Of course, the seeds themselves aren't the problem—in fact, perennials that produce plenty of seeds are a super source of winter food for wild birds. The problem is the seeds that *don't* get eaten, and instead, sprout up into new plants—probably where you don't want them!

✺ SAY NO TO LOOSESTRIFE

Please, please, please—don't plant purple loosestrife (*Lythrum salicaria*) in your perennial garden. It's undeniably pretty, with bright, purplish pink flower spikes in summer. Unfortunately, this imported perennial has now seeded into many thousands of acres of wetlands, crowding out the native plants, and drastically altering the natural habitats of many forms of wildlife. In fact, several states now make it illegal to grow this troublesome plant. So do your part, and steer clear of this thug!

✺ PERENNIAL POISONS

If you frequently share your garden with kids and/or pets, be aware that some common perennials—including foxgloves (*Digitalis*)—are actually poisonous. Usually, they cause a reaction only when eaten (not simply when touched), so making sure nobody snacks on your plants will prevent any problems. For more information on poisonous plants, contact your local Cooperative Extension Service office (check under "Government Offices" in your phone book) or go to the FDA Poisonous Plants Database at http://vm.cfsan.fda.gov/~djw/plantnam.html.

THINK TWICE!

Some of the prettiest perennials can quickly take over your flowerbeds, if you don't watch out. Here are some of the worst offenders:

Bugleweeds
   (*Ajuga*)
Chameleon plant
   (*Houttuynia cordata* 'Variegata')
Goldmoss stonecrop (*Sedum acre*)
Knotweeds
   (*Polygonum*)
Loosestrifes
   (*Lysimachia*)
Plume poppies
   (*Macleaya*)
Showy evening primrose
   (*Oenothera speciosa*)
Silver sage
   (*Artemisia ludoviciana*)
Variegated bishop's weed
   (*Aegopodium podagraria* 'Variegata')
Yellow archangel
   (*Lamiastrum galeobdolon*)

CHAPTER 11

PROBLEM-SOLVING WITH PERENNIALS

Perennials aren't just pretty faces—they're
practical problem solvers, too! Whatever landscaping
challenge you have to handle—whether it's shady
spots, sun-baked sites, soggy soil, or dry slopes—
carefully picked perennials can handle them all!

Made for Shade

C'mon, shade gardeners—don't give up! Sure, you have a big challenge to cope with, but with a little grow-how, you can have a beautiful garden, too. Read on, for my best tips for making the most of shade.

❋ THE MANY SHADES OF SHADE

Before we begin, I want you to remember that not all shade is created equal. There's the dense, all-day, every-day shade, cast by a building or evergreen tree, and there's the spring-sunny, summer-shady conditions under a deciduous tree. A site might get a few hours of direct sun for part of the day, or dappled sunlight all day, or a whole day of bright light, but no direct sun at all.

In general, a partial-shade plant needs between three and six hours of sun a day, while a shade-loving plant can get by with three hours, or less. Start by planting the perennials you think will like the kind of shade you have, but be prepared to experiment with lots of different plants, to see which work best for you.

❋ LOOK TO THE LEAVES

Flowers aren't the only things you can use to light up a shady space. Look for perennials with colorful or variegated foliage, too. Hostas, for example, come in an exciting array of leaf colors—every shade of green, plus yellow, blue, green with white stripes, green with gold stripes, blue with yellow stripes, and so on. Lamium (*Lamium maculatum*)—also called dead nettle—is another true beauty, with silver-and-green leaves that simply sparkle in shade.

Obedient plant
*Physostegia
virginiana*

Spikes of pink or
white blooms in
late summer;
spreads quickly in
moist, rich soil

ON A ROLL

Does your garden area have too much shade to get anything to grow? Here's an idea—put your garden on wheels! Make a movable bed out of an old toy wagon. Drill drainage holes in the bottom, add a thin layer of gravel, top it with soil, and plant lots of shade-loving flowers and foliage. When the plants start looking a little spindly due to the lack of light, just wheel them into a brighter spot for a few days, then roll them back into the shade. It's that simple!

✳ Let's Be Fronds

What would a shade garden be without ferns? These lacy lovelies are a perfect complement to the big, bold leaves of those other shade-garden standbys—hostas. There are hundreds of beautiful ferns to choose from, in a wide range of heights and habits. In general, though, they'll do fine in partial to full shade and compost-enriched soil. Most ferns like evenly moist soil, but they can tolerate some dryness, too—especially once they've had a few years to get their roots settled in. Here are a few of my ferny favorites:

❧ **Christmas fern** (*Polystichum acrostichoides*): Clumps of 12- to 18-inch-tall, evergreen, deep green fronds. Tough as nails! Zones 4 to 9.

❧ **Cinnamon fern** (*Osmunda cinnamomea*): Four- to 5-foot-tall, vase-shaped clumps of deep green, deciduous fronds around cinnamon brown, spore-bearing spikes. Zones 3 to 10.

❧ **Japanese painted fern** (*Athyrium nipponicum* 'Pictum'): Clumps of 12- to 18-inch-tall, green, deciduous fronds that are strikingly shaded with silver and burgundy. Zones 4 to 9.

❧ **Lady fern** (*A. filix-femina*): Spreading, 2- to 3-foot-tall mounds of finely cut, light green, deciduous fronds. Zones 3 to 8.

❧ **Male fern** (*Dryopteris filix-mas*): Dense, 2- to 4-foot-tall clumps of lacy, dark green fronds that are evergreen in most areas. Zones 2 to 9.

TOP 10

Perennials for Shade

Astilbes (*Astilbe*)

Bleeding hearts (*Dicentra*)

Foamflowers (*Tiarella cordifolia*)

Hellebores (*Helleborus*)

Heucheras (*Heuchera*)

Hostas (*Hosta*)

Lamium (*Lamium maculatum*)

Lungworts (*Pulmonaria*)

Monkshoods (*Aconitum*)

Woodland phlox (*Phlox divaricata*)

✳ Shady Characters

Many perennials that work well in summer-shady gardens are the same stunning wildflowers that grace woodlands in April and May—including bloodroot (*Sanguinaria canadensis*) and Virginia bluebells (*Mertensia virginica*). These delicate beauties put on a spectacular show while they can get the sun, then go dormant, or produce pretty leaves that thrive in the dappled shade cast by taller trees and shrubs. Combine them with other shade-loving foliage plants, like ferns and hostas, and your shady garden will look great from late winter to late fall!

✳ PILE IT ON!

Trying to dig planting holes in the root-filled soil under trees can be a real pain-in-the-you-know-what! To make your life easier, spread a layer of newspaper about four sheets thick over the area, then spread 4 to 6 inches of good topsoil over the papers. Planting in that loose soil will be a breeze! By the time the newspapers break down and the tree roots work their way up into the new soil, your perennials will be well established and prepared to compete with the tree for water and nutrients.

Brighten up your shady spots by planting lots of light-colored flowers there. Whites, pale yellows, and pinks are perfect for bringing light into any gloomy garden!

✳ ASTILBE LOVING YOU...

Shade gardeners rejoice—here's a fabulous flowering perennial that's just perfect for you! Astilbes—also called false spireas—are pretty enough to earn a place in your garden by their leaves alone, but when they bloom, *WOW!* Their fluffy plumes are packed with hundreds of tiny blooms that open white, cream, pink, purple, salmon, or red. They begin flowering in June, and last through much of the summer, then gracefully age to shades of beige to reddish brown by fall. As a plus, their seedheads can look great well into winter. Talk about multi-season interest!

   Besides coming in a range of colors, astilbes are available in a range of heights—from 10-inch-tall 'Sprite' (bronze-green leaves and pink flowers), to 4-foot-tall 'Superba' (with rosy purple flowers). I haven't yet met an astilbe I didn't like, so I suggest you see what your local garden center has to offer, then choose by the color and height

Oriental lily
Lilium Oriental Hybrid

Late-summer bloomer in various shades of pink, red, and white; beautiful bulb for borders

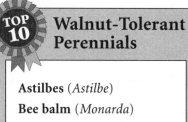

TOP 10 Walnut-Tolerant Perennials

Astilbes (*Astilbe*)

Bee balm (*Monarda*)

Bugleweeds (*Ajuga*)

Heucheras (*Heuchera*)

Hostas (*Hosta*)

Jacob's ladders (*Polemonium*)

Lungworts (*Pulmonaria*)

Solomon's seals (*Polygonatum*)

Sweet woodruff (*Galium odoratum*)

Wild gingers (*Asarum*)

Oriental poppy
Papaver orientale

Huge, bowl-shaped blooms light up the early-summer garden, then die back to the ground

you want. Give your astilbes partial shade, and work plenty of compost into the soil before planting. Be prepared to water well during dry spells for best flowering.

✴ PLANTING UNDER WALNUTS

Gardening under the shade of black walnut (*Juglans nigra*) trees can be especially difficult, because these trees produce a substance called juglone that discourages many other plants from growing near them. Fortunately, not all perennials are equally sensitive to this stuff. So, if you have trouble growing a good-looking garden under black walnuts, experiment with varieties that are walnut-tolerant (see "Top 10 Walnut-Tolerant Perennials, at left). Also, pick up dropped nuts and leaves to minimize the amount of juglone that leaches into the soil. If you still have trouble, try building raised beds under the trees, and filling them with fresh topsoil before planting.

✴ BIG OR SMALL? YOU MAKE THE CALL

To make a small shade garden look bigger, plant dark- or blue-leaved perennials and shrubs around the edge, where they'll blend in with the shadows. Keep the brighter greens and light-colored flowers up close, so they'll really pop out.

If you'd rather make a larger shady space look more intimate, reverse the process—whites and light colors will draw your eye to the boundaries of the garden, and make the edges seem closer than they really are.

✴ MADE FOR THE SHADE

Shady spots with moist soil offer lots of options, but when you're dealing with dry shade, you've got a major challenge on your hands. But even these difficult areas can be beautiful, if you fill them with tough perennials that are well suited to the conditions. Some great plants for dry shade include barrenworts (*Epimedium*), lady's mantle (*Alchemilla mollis*), Robb's wood spurge (*Euphorbia robbiae*), and variegated fragrant Solomon's seal (*Polygonatum odoratum* 'Variegatum'). Water regularly for the first year or two, to get them off to a good start. Then give them a generous mulch of compost or chopped leaves, and let them do their thing!

Some Like It Hot

Gardening in hot climates is another kettle of fish altogether. Most gardening books completely ignore the plight of you Southern gardeners, probably because the growing conditions you have to cope with are so different from those in most parts of the United States. But I've collected some great tips that should help make your yard the best-looking property in the neighborhood!

❋ A SHADY SOLUTION

Smart Deep South gardeners know they can't believe everything they read about what particular perennials need—specifically, the amount of sun they can take. Plants that prefer full sun in most parts of the country may need partial shade, or even full shade, in hot, humid climates. So, unless you're sure that a newly purchased perennial is suited to growing in the sun in your area, try it in some shade first!

If your taste in flower color runs on the soft side, keep those pastels in your shadier spots. Otherwise, intense sun will quickly bleach out their delicate hues, and may even burn their tender petals. Bright sunshine calls for bright colors: radiant reds, passionate purples, glowing oranges, and gleaming golds.

✳ SOME SAGE ADVICE

Colorful and fragrant, sages (*Salvia*) are perfect for spicing up sultry Southern gardens. They thrive in sun (or in some shade, where it's really hot) and in average, well-drained garden soil. There are dozens of spectacular species and hybrids in a range of heights and a rainbow of colors—I suggest that you try any and all you can get your mitts on!

One species I really like is Gregg sage (*S. greggii*). This hummingbird favorite grows 1 to 2 feet tall, with bright, green leaves and small, but abundant blooms in shades of red, pink, purple, peach, yellow, and white from late summer to frost. It's hardy outside in Zones 7 to 10; elsewhere, it's great as an annual.

Even the best-planned sunny Southern borders may not be able to take the heat during the worst of the summer. So to keep the show going, be sure to include plenty of plants with good-looking leaves!

✳ SAY NO TO STAKING

When you garden in a hot climate, you quickly learn that plants tend to grow taller than they do in cooler areas. While their stems may be taller, they're also less sturdy, so you may be stuck with a lot of staking, if you want your perennials to hold their heads up high. Here's a great tip to cut down on that boring, time-consuming chore—choose cultivars that are described as being dwarf or compact.

✳ BLANKET YOUR GARDEN WITH COLOR

Looking for knock-your-socks-off color for a hot, sunny site? You can't beat blanket flower (*Gaillardia* x *grandiflora*). Each showy bloom is made up of a broad, rusty red button, surrounded by fringed petals that are usually orange near the center and gold toward the tips.

Typical blanket flowers grow 2 to 3 feet tall, but there are two popular dwarf cultivars: 8-inch-tall 'Baby Cole' and 1-foot-tall 'Goblin'. Give blanket flowers a sunny site with fairly dry soil in Zones 4 to 9, divide them every two to three years—to keep them vigorous—and you'll have non-stop color from early summer well into fall.

❋ DO ALL YOUR PLANTING IN AUTUMN

Knowing just one, simple secret can mean the difference between a delight and a disaster when you're starting a new perennial garden in the South. What's the secret? Plant your perennials in fall—*never* in spring! That way, they'll have plenty of time to put down new roots through the winter, and they'll be all set to do their thing in spring without any extra pampering from you.

Soggy-Soil Standbys

Are you tired of navigating around puddles in your yard after a rain? Then turn those soggy spots into lush and lovely landscape features by filling them with moisture-loving perennials!

❋ DAMP-SITE SOLUTIONS

Just as there are different kinds of shade, there are different kinds of wet-soil sites, too. In both conditions, the key to success is experimenting with lots of perennials, to see which are best adapted to your particular conditions. But if you've tried many different perennials, and are still having problems getting anything going, consider testing your soil's pH. If your soil turns out to be acidic (under 6.0 on the pH scale), add dolomite lime to bring the pH up to a more normal level.

Ostrich fern
Matteuccia struthiopteris

Tall, vase-shaped clumps of lacy leaves; spreads to form dense colonies

Oxeye
*Heliopsis
helianthoides*

Sun-loving
perennial covered
with bright
yellow daisies all
summer long

Perfect Perennials

FOR MOIST SOIL

These dependable perennials are some of the best bets for consistently moist soil. (Standing water for a few hours after a rain is okay, but not for extended periods.)

Astilbes (*Astilbe*): Showy flower plumes in white, pink, red, or salmon. Zones 4 to 8.

Bee balm (*Monarda didyma*): Shaggy heads of red, pink, white, or purple blooms. Zones 4 to 8.

Goatsbeard (*Aruncus dioicus*): Creamy white flower plumes on shrub-sized plants. Zones 3 to 7.

Japanese iris (*Iris ensata*): Large, showy blooms in shades of purple, blue, pink, and white. Zones 4 to 9.

Japanese primrose (*Primula japonica*): Spikes of tiered blooms in shades of red, pink, and white. Zones 5 to 8.

Joe Pye weeds (*Eupatorium*): Fuzzy clusters of rosy pink or white flowers. Zones 3 to 8.

Swamp milkweed (*Asclepias incarnata*): Pink or white flower clusters. Zones 3 to 8.

☀ LOOSEN THINGS UP

If you're trying to garden around a newly built home, it's likely that the soil's been compacted by all those heavy construction vehicles. Hacking out planting holes in that packed-down stuff is hard enough, but when the first rain comes along, your newly planted perennials will probably pop right out of their holes and float away!

When compacted soil's causing a drainage problem, you're much better off trying to prepare a whole new bed, rather than digging many individual planting holes. To make the job go a bit more easily, use a heavy-duty rotary tiller to loosen the soil as deeply as possible, then spread a 2- to 3-

inch layer of compost or other organic matter on the soil, and till again. Another option is to build raised beds and fill them with 6 inches or more of good topsoil. Either way, you'll end up with a moist, but well-drained site that's perfect for a wide variety of beautiful perennials!

❀ ON THE BOARDWALK

Walking on wet soil isn't just uncomfortable for you—it's bad for your plants, too. Wet soil packs down easily, squeezing more air out of the soil and making it hard for even moisture-loving perennials to thrive. If you need access through a garden area that's often wet, build a mini-boardwalk path out of rot-resistant wood. You'll have a safe, dry path, and your perennials will be a whole lot happier!

❀ TOPS FOR SOGGY SPOTS

There are dozens of gorgeous perennials perfectly suited to wet-soil sites. Here are three of my all-time favorites; of course, don't limit yourself to just these three—there's plenty more where they came from!

• **Ligularias** (*Ligularia*): Four- to 5-foot-tall stems topped with clusters of orange-yellow daisies or spikes of bright yellow blooms in late summer. Partial shade. Zones 4 to 8.

• **Lobelias** (*Lobelia*): Cardinal flower (*L. cardinalis*) has rich red blooms; great blue lobelia (*L. siphilitica*) has blue flowers. Both bloom in dense spikes atop leafy, 2- to 4-foot stems in late summer into fall. Partial shade. Zones 3 to 8.

• **Rodgersias** (*Rodgersia*): Looking like astilbes on steroids, these bold beauties produce huge, creamy plumes atop tall 4- to 6-foot stems in mid- to late summer. Partial shade. Zones 5 to 8.

TOOL TIME

Planting perennials in soggy sites can get you pretty muddy, so be prepared by setting up a simple cleanup station. Mount the blade end of a broken hoe near your hose spigot, and you've got yourself a handy holder for a bar of soap!

Perennials for Parched Patches

If you've got dry soil, your plants will quickly let you know it. They'll be short and stubby—or they may not grow at all—and they'll wilt dramatically whenever rainfall is lacking. Fortunately, you don't have to spend your summers with a hose permanently attached to your hand, and you don't have to settle for cactus, either. Read on to learn how even dry-soil sites can provide you with a bounty of beautiful flowers.

❀ SIX STEPS TO DRY-SOIL SUCCESS

Ready to turn that desert you call a yard into a flower-filled oasis? Simply follow these six easy steps:

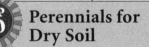

Perennials for Dry Soil

Black-eyed Susans (*Rudbeckia*)

Blanket flower (*Gaillardia* x *grandiflora*)

Butterfly weed (*Asclepias tuberosa*)

Coreopsis (*Coreopsis*)

Moss phlox (*Phlox subulata*)

Russian sage (*Perovskia atriplicifolia*)

Sundrops (*Oenothera fruticosa*)

Wormwoods (*Artemisia*)

Yarrows (*Achillea*)

Yuccas (*Yucca*)

Step 1. Pick perennials that are naturally adapted to growing in dry soil—and there are plenty of them!

Step 2. Work lots of organic matter into the planting area. Two inches of compost, dug or tilled into the top 6 to 8 inches of ground, will help the soil hold on to whatever moisture it gets from rainfall or irrigation.

Step 3. Plant and move perennials only in the fall, when temperatures are moderate and rainfall is more dependable.

Step 4. After planting, snake a soaker hose around the clumps, so it comes within a few inches of each one. If needed, use wire pins made from old clothes hangers to hold the hose in place.

Step 5. Mulch with 2 to 3 inches of organic material (chopped leaves, pine straw, or whatever's handy) to cover the soaker hose and prevent moisture loss from the soil due to evaporation. Reapply, as needed, each spring and fall to keep the soil covered.

Step 6. For the first year after planting, water regularly—even drought-tolerant perennials will need some time to get their roots established. After that, you can remove the soaker hose, and use it to get another bed or border started.

❊ A CROP OF STONECROPS

Dry-soil sites were made for the sun-loving stonecrops (*Sedum*). There are dozens and dozens available—from ground-hugging carpeters to full-figured clumpers, in a range of flower and foliage colors, and with spring, summer, or fall blooms—so there's sure to be at least one that's perfect for your needs. Here are three super stonecrops to get you started:

✔ **'Autumn Joy' sedum** (*S. 'Autumn Joy'*): This handsome hybrid produces bushy, 2-foot by 2-foot clumps of fleshy, light green leaves and stems. The mounds are topped with clusters of buds that open pale pink in late summer, gradually aging to rusty brown by late fall and lasting well into winter. Zones 4 to 9.

✔ **Dragon's blood** (*S. spurium 'Dragon's Blood'*): Creeping, 3-inch-tall mats of red-flushed, evergreen leaves with deep, rose-pink flowers in midsummer. Zones 3 to 9.

✔ **Kamschatka stonecrop** (*S. kamtschaticum*): Four-inch-tall carpets of bright green, semi-evergreen leaves dotted with clusters of yellow flowers in early summer. Zones 3 to 9.

Oxeye daisy
Chrysanthemum vulgare

Pretty white daisies, wonderful for wildflower gardens

My Grandma Putt sure knew what she was doing when she put sturdy oak barrels out to collect the rain. Of course, back then, rainwater was used for just about everything—from drinking and cooking to bathing and watering the garden.

But there's no good reason you can't collect rainwater today for your perennials and other plants. You can choose from any number of containers in all shapes, sizes, and colors that'll slip easily under a downspout. Attach a simple spigot near the bottom of the container, and you've got a ready source of water for your garden!

❀ LOOK AT THE LEAVES

With a little know-how, you can guess if a perennial might be drought-tolerant. Simply look at the leaves for any of these clues: fuzz or dense hairs; a silvery or blue color; thick, juicy foliage; a very narrow, needlelike shape; thorns or prickles.

Painted daisy
*Tanacetum
coccineum*

Lush, lacy leaves
topped with
pink daisies
in early summer;
top-notch
cut flower

Planting Along Paths

What could be more welcoming than a flower-lined walkway leading right to your door? With perennials, you can have pretty pathside plantings that are a joy to look at, and easy to take care of, too!

❀ PERFECT PATHWAY PERENNIALS

When I'm considering a perennial for planting along a path or walkway, I make sure it meets all three of these criteria:

JERRY'S GEMS

Pathway plantings packed with colorful flowers will attract lots of attention from passersby—but also from bees. If kids, pets, or bee-phobic adults often use your paths, consider sticking with perennials that mostly produce foliage, rather than flowers.

☑ **Low-growing.** Keep pathside plantings no more than 18 inches tall—the lower the better.

☑ **Looks good all season.** A perennial that blooms for three months or more is a plus. A shorter flowering period is okay, too, as long as the leaves are nice to look at the rest of the time. Evergreen foliage is a plus!

☑ **Not sprawling.** It's nice to have the plants overlap the path edges a little, but you don't want ones that are going to reach out into the path, and trip up your guests.

✹ PATH PLANNING POINTERS

Not all walkways are created equal. Make sure main access routes to your house—such as the path to the front door—are at least 5 feet wide, so two people can walk comfortably side by side. The footing should also be comfortably firm and level, such as concrete, brick, or some other stable surface.

For smaller paths within your yard—like the routes you use to reach your flower garden or the kids' play area—3 feet is usually sufficient. Bricks and pavers are appropriate here, too, but gravel can work as well. Save stepping stones or bark mulch for seldom-used paths; 18 inches is a good width for these minor walkways.

✹ WHAT'S YOUR STYLE?

For a formal effect, line paths and walkways with just one kind of perennial—all 'Golden Tiara' hosta, for example. This uniformity creates a clear outline that makes it easier for visitors to follow the path quickly. Plantings of mixed perennials are nice for more casual paths, where you want people to slow down and admire individual flowers.

✹ LIVING ON THE EDGE

When you're deciding which perennials to plant along your paths, don't forget to look at the leaves, too. Here are two classic edging plants that offer both colorful flowers and great-looking leaves:

Bugleweeds (*Ajuga*): Green, bronze, or multicolored, leafy rosettes send out runners in all directions to create

Try This!

Turn a boring walkway into a magical pathway by making your own mosaic stepping stones! Here's how:

Step 1. Build a wood frame about 1 foot square using scrap pieces of 1" x 3" lumber.

Step 2. Spread a plastic trash bag on a flat surface, and set the frame on top of it.

Step 3. Gather colorful stones, marbles, old keys, pieces of broken china—whatever you can find around the house—and arrange them in a pleasing pattern next to the frame.

Step 4. Carefully fill the frame with cement, then move the pieces onto the cement to re-create the pattern.

Step 5. Press each piece gently, but firmly, to settle it into the cement, then let dry for 24 to 48 hours.

Step 6. Move your creation into your garden, and be prepared for lots of compliments!

ground-hugging carpets. In late spring, 4- to 6-inch-tall stems bear spikes of purple-blue, pink, or white blooms. Full sun to full shade, but partial shade is best; well-drained, evenly moist soil. Zones 3 to 9.

Lady's mantle (*Alchemilla mollis*): The tidy clumps of velvety, gray-green leaves are about 1 foot tall and wide, with clouds of dainty, greenish yellow flowers on stems up to 18 inches tall in early summer. Cut back hard after flowering, for fresh new leaves. Sun to partial shade; average soil. Zones 3 to 8.

Best Bets for Slopes

Slopes can be a real maintenance hassle. Left uncovered, they're prone to erosion, so you're stuck with an ugly-looking bank, and a mess of soil at the base. Grass makes a good cover for preventing erosion, but then you have to try to mow it—a difficult and dangerous proposition, at best. What's the answer? Perennials! They offer a problem-solving *and* low-maintenance solution that looks great, too.

☀ MAKING THE GRADE

If you already have grass growing on your slope, don't bother trying to remove it. You'll just make a lot of work for yourself, and then you'll have to worry about the bare soil washing away. One option is to spray the turf with herbicide, then wait a week or so. Alternately, cover the grass with sheets of clear plastic for several weeks during the hottest part of the summer to kill it. Either way, plant right through the dead turf, then mulch to cover the browned grass. It's easy!

Paperwhites
Narcissus tazetta

Powerfully perfumed white flowers; a favorite for growing indoors in winter

Perfect Perennials

FOR SLOPES

Cloak a sunny, dry slope with any of these tough-as-nails perennials, and kiss that problem site good-bye!

Basket-of-gold (*Aurinia saxatilis*): Clusters of bright yellow blooms in spring. Zones 4 to 8.

Catmints (*Nepeta*): Spikes of purplish or blue blooms from early summer into fall. Zones 3 to 8.

Dalmatian bellflower (*Campanula portenschlagiana*): Upturned purple bells from late spring through early summer. Zones 4 to 8.

Daylilies (*Hemerocallis*): Trumpet-shaped blooms in a wide range of colors. Zones 3 to 10.

Fountain grass (*Pennisetum alopecuroides*): Fuzzy greenish or purplish black spikes from midsummer into winter. Zones 5 to 9.

Hardy ice plant (*Delosperma*): Bright purple or yellow, daisylike blooms through the summer. Zones 6 to 9.

Kamschatka sedum (*Sedum kamtschaticum*): Flat clusters of bright yellow flowers in late summer. Zones 4 to 9.

Moss phlox (*Phlox subulata*): Masses of pink, blue, or white flowers in mid- to late spring. Zones 2 to 9.

Showy evening primrose (*Oenothera speciosa*): Cup-shaped, pink flowers from early summer to fall. Zones 5 to 8.

Woolly yarrow (*Achillea tomentosa*): Flat-topped clusters of yellow flowers from early summer to fall. Zones 3 to 7.

Peony
Paeonia lactiflora

Classic border beauty with fragrant white, pink, or red blooms

❀ SILVER IS SUPER FOR SLOPES

It seems like silver-leaved plants are perfect for sunny slopes. I guess that's because they are well suited to the dry conditions that sloping sites usually offer. My two best suggestions for silver-leaved slope huggers are:

🌰 **Lamb's ears** (*Stachys byzantina*): Spreading clumps of fuzzy, silvery leaves about 8 inches tall. Spikes of tiny purple-pink flowers appear in early summer to fall. Zones 4 to 8.

Snow-in-summer (*Cerastium tomentosum*): Fast-spreading, 6-inch-tall mats of small, woolly, silver-gray leaves, sprinkled with clusters of small, white flowers in early summer. Zones 2 to 7.

Want to tackle a slope soon, but don't have a big plant-buying budget? Try a two-step approach. First, cut down any existing vegetation, then cover the slope with a layer of wet newspaper (about 10 sheets thick), and top it with a 2-inch layer of wood chips or bark mulch. Then buy a few plants of the groundcover you want to use, and propagate them by cuttings or division. Once you have all the perennials you need, simply scoop aside the mulch, set in the plants, and pull the mulch back around them. It's that simple!

☀ A Bright Idea

Want to spruce up your slope even more? Then add some spring bulbs! Planting crocuses, dwarf tulips, and other small bulbs on a slope lifts them closer to eye level for easy enjoyment. The emerging leaves of the perennial groundcover keep soil from splashing up on the bulb flowers. And by the time the bulb leaves begin to go dormant, the perennial's new growth is tall enough to cover the bulbs' yellowing leaves.

☀ Stepping Up

For just a little sweat equity, you can turn that troublesome slope into a super-looking, stepped garden! Simply build low walls across the slope every foot or so—cut logs, held in place by rebar pegs, look great on shady slopes, while rocks or chunks of broken concrete create a nice rock-garden effect on sunny ones. Add some soil behind each wall to create flat planting areas along the slope. Set in your plants, give them a good watering and mulching, then stand back and enjoy your great-looking perennial garden!

CHAPTER 12

PERENNIAL ALL-STARS

There are a few perennials that are so
beautiful, dependable, and easy-to-care-for
that every perennial gardener needs to have at
least some of them in their yard. Read on to
learn more about these surefire selections!

Dazzling Daylilies

If you're looking for easy-care summer color, look no further than daylilies (*Hemorocallis*)! These dependable perennials come in an amazing range of heights, flower forms, and colors. While they prefer full sun, they can take light shade, and they'll adapt to just about any soil that's not constantly soggy or desert-dry. What more could you ask for?

✺ FLOWER FACTS

Daylilies get their name from the fact that each flower stays open for only one day. The blooms of some daylilies open in the morning and close by evening; others open in the evening, and close up by noon. Each bloom stalk (called a **scape**) can produce 40 or more buds that open in succession, so a single clump can bloom for a month or more. **Reblooming** daylilies send up new scapes after their first flush of blooms, so they flower for several months.

✺ SMART SHOPPING

With many thousands of named daylilies to choose from, how can you possibly decide which ones to grow? I suggest starting with the cultivars that are available at your local nursery, because these selections are likely to be reasonably priced and well suited to your area. Shop when the plants are in bloom, then choose the flower forms and colors that appeal to you.

Each year, many new daylily hybrids are released, and

MAKING ¢ents Sometimes hybrid daylilies produce miniature plants, called **proliferations,** on their normally leafless flower stems. ('Fairy Tale Pink', 'Prairie Blue Eyes', and 'Siloam Red Toy' are three that tend to produce these growths often; there are others, too.) Cut off these little plants right where they join the stem, stick the base of each one in some moist potting soil, and then treat them like cuttings. By fall, they'll have produced roots, and you'll have brand-new plants that are identical to the daylilies they came from—for free!

these tend to come with high price tags. If you see one you really like, wait a few years to see if it stands the test of time; by then, the price will be lower, too.

✹ DAYLILY LINGO

To get the best from your daylilies, it's important to choose cultivars that are suited to your climate. Here are some terms that can help you out:

Herbaceous: Also called dormant daylilies, herbaceous daylilies die back to the ground at the end of the growing season. These are the best choice for cold-winter areas.

When shopping for daylilies, you'll often run across the terms "diploid" and "tetraploid." Diploid means that the plant has two sets of chromosomes, which is normal. A tetraploid daylily has four sets—twice the usual amount; as a result, these plants are usually bigger and more vigorous than diploids, with larger flowers and thicker petals that often have frilly or ruffled edges.

Semi-evergreen: These daylilies may keep their leaves through the winter or die back to the ground, depending on the climate. They need some cold-winter temperatures to stay healthy, but don't like very cold temperatures.

Evergreen: These daylilies hold on to their green leaves all year 'round. They're a good choice for mild climates, where they'll keep on producing new leaves, even in winter.

✹ DISCOVER DAYLILIES—FOR FRAGRANCE

As if all the fabulous flower colors weren't enough reason to grow daylilies, here's another—some are also fragrant! The perfume comes from a few species that have been used to create the hybrids: in particular, *Hemerocallis citrina* and *H. lilioasphodelus* (often known as lemon lily). Both of these species have yellow flowers that are open in the evening, so many of the hybrids that share these traits are also fragrant.

　　Remember—scent can vary widely, depending on the

Peruvian lily
Alstroemeria hybrid

Striped and spotted, multicolored blooms; long-lasting as a cut flower

climate and growing conditions. A few hybrids that fragrance enthusiasts swear by include 'Kathy Rood', 'Ruffled Apricot', 'So Lovely', and 'Tetrina's Daughter'. But for best results, I suggest that you sniff for yourself in nurseries and display gardens to see which scents you find most pleasing.

Delightful Daisies

Call me old-fashioned, but to me, a garden without daisies is like a summer without sunshine! The yellow-centered, white-petaled kinds are probably the first ones that come to mind, but there are many, many more in all sizes and colors. If you're a daisy lover like I am, you can enjoy these beautiful blooms from early spring well into fall.

Plume poppy
Macleaya cordata

Towering stems topped with coppery plumes in summer; spreads quickly in loose soil

❀ CRAZY FOR DAISIES

The classic white she-loves-me, she-loves-me-not daisy that adorns roadsides and meadows in early summer is commonly called oxeye daisy (*Chrysanthemum vulgare*). This little cutie can be a thug in the garden, though, because it creeps all over the place.

A better choice is any of the hybrid Shasta daisies (*C. x superbum*). They're like oxeye daisies on steroids—with stronger stems and larger, longer-lasting blooms from early summer to early fall—but are much slower to spread. Most are 3 to 4 feet tall, but if you need something shorter, try 8-inch-tall 'Little Miss Muffet' or 1-foot-tall 'Snow Lady'. Shastas thrive in Zones 4 to 8, in full sun and well-drained soil with a little extra compost worked in. Snip off spent flowers to encourage rebloom.

☀ MORE POWER FROM CONEFLOWERS

If you like the daisy look, but want more color, consider planting coneflowers. These easy-care, summer-blooming perennials produce distinctive, large flowers with distinctive dark, raised centers.

🌿 Orange coneflowers: (*Rudbeckia*), also commonly called black-eyed Susans, typically have orange-yellow petals. 'Goldsturm' is probably the most widely grown cultivar, with 3- to 4-inch-wide blooms that grow on 24- to 30-inch-tall plants.

🌿 Purple coneflowers: (*Echinacea*), aren't purple at all, but actually more of a rosy pink. They're a special favorite with many butterflies. 'Magnus' has particularly large blooms—up to 6 inches across!

Spent blooms of daisy-like flowers often produce viable seeds that fall to the ground among the parent plants. The seeds germinate and grow there, and pretty soon, they end up choking out the choicer, parent varieties. So be sure to pick off the seedheads before they have a chance to drop their seeds—or be prepared to pull out unwanted seedlings each spring.

Both coneflowers are hardy in Zones 3 to 9. Give them full sun and well-drained soil. Pinch off the spent flowers to promote repeat bloom, or leave the seedheads—goldfinches just love them!

☀ SPRING FLING

Daisies are most often associated with summer gardens, but you can get your daisy fix much earlier if you plant leopard's banes (*Doronicum*). These summer-bright perennials bloom in early to midspring, with sunny yellow petals surrounding a golden center button atop 1- to 2-foot-tall stems.

Leopard's banes grow in Zones 3 to 8. In cooler climates, they like full sun; where summers are hot, they prefer partial shade. Give them moist, but well-drained soil, work in an extra shovelful of compost at planting time, and

Mixers & Elixirs

HOMEGROWN DAISY SPRAY

If you grow painted daisies (*Tanacetum coccineum*)—also called pyrethrum daisies—you have the makings for this great homemade pest spray.

⅛ cup of 70% isopropyl alcohol
1 cup of packed, fresh painted daisy flower heads

Pour the alcohol over the flower heads, and let sit overnight. Strain out the flowers, then store the extract in a labeled and sealed container. When you need it, mix the extract with three quarts of water to make a spray that controls a wide range of garden pests.

your leopard's banes will reward you with their cheerful yellow daisies each and every spring.

✻ PRETTY IN PINK

If you're delighted by daisies and are partial to pink flowers, I've got just the perennials for you! Any or all of these are sure to please in a sunny, well-drained spot:

• **'Clara Curtis' chrysanthemum** (*C. zawadskii* var. *latilobum* 'Clara Curtis'): Yellow-centered daisies with bright pink petals from midsummer to early fall, on 2- to 3-foot-tall clumps. Zones 3 to 9.

• **Painted daisy** (*Tanacetum coccineum*): Loose clumps of ferny green leaves topped with red, rose, or pink daisies in early summer. Zones 3 to 7.

• **'Pink Jewel' daisy fleabane** (*Erigeron* 'Pink Jewel'): Semi-double, pink daisies appear through the summer atop 30-inch-tall stems. Zones 3 to 8.

A Host of Hostas

Here's a great group of perennials that are literally made for the shade! You won't choose these no-fuss plants for their flowers—their main claim to fame is their great-looking leaves.

❀ HOSTAS, HOSTAS EVERYWHERE

Hostas come in such a wide range of heights and habits, there's sure to be one for just about any spot in your yard. Here are a few ideas on how to use these versatile perennials:

Edgings: Low-growing hostas make tidy, easy-care edgings for beds and borders.

Fillers: Tuck midsize hostas among flowering plants for foliage interest.

Backgrounds: The biggest hostas make great backdrops for colorful flowers.

Specimens: A single hosta clump can make an eye-catching garden accent.

❀ NOT JUST FOR SHADE

What if you love hostas, but don't have much shade for them? Well, if you have a wet spot in your yard, or if you don't mind watering, you're in luck! A fair number of hostas can tolerate full sun (at least in Northern gardens), as long as their soil is always moist.

To find hostas for a sunny garden, check catalog descriptions or nursery tags for the terms "sun-resistant" or "sun-tolerant." If a particular hosta has fragrant flowers, that's also a good clue that the plant is likely to tolerate sun. Hostas with gold foliage tend to look brighter in sun, while those with blue leaves often appear more greenish. Some hostas that usually grow well in sunny sites with adequate moisture include 'August Moon', 'Fragrant Bouquet', 'Francee', *H. fortunei albomarginata*, *H. plantaginea*, 'Invincible', 'Royal Standard', 'Sum and Substance', 'Sun Power', and 'Wide Brim'.

Prairie
coneflower
Ratibida pinnata

Rich yellow petals surrounding a raised center cone; thrives in sunny sites

*G*randma Putt knew her hostas liked lots of water, so she always planted them near her downspouts. With this extra supply of moisture from each rain, Grandma's hostas always grew bigger, better, and faster than anyone else's in the neighborhood!

Prairie phlox
Phlox pilosa

Flat pinkish to
purplish flowers in
clusters atop 1- to
2-foot-tall stems in
late spring

❋ HUGE HOSTAS

Looking for a really big hosta? Here are some super choices
for you. It may take them three to five years to reach their
mature size, but these big boys (and girls) will eventually
top out at 3 to 5 feet in height! Set your sights on 'Big
Mama', 'Blue Angel', 'Blue Mammoth', 'Blue Umbrellas',
'Krossa Regal', *H. montana* 'Aureomarginata', *H.
plantaginea*, 'Northern Exposure', 'Royal Standard', and
'Sum and Substance'.

❋ SWEET AND PETITE

In the market for something smaller? Dwarf hostas can perk
up even the tiniest spots in your garden. Tuck these com-
pact cuties into small beds and borders, try them along
paths and walkways, or enjoy them in pots and planters—
they'll grow no more than 10 inches tall. Look for 'Bitsy
Gold', 'Bitsy Green', 'Blue
Moon', 'Cheatin' Heart', 'Dew
Drop', 'Dorset Blue', 'Green
Eyes', 'Hope', 'Island Charm',
'Just So', 'Kabitan',
'Masquerade', 'Medusa',
'Pandora's Box', and 'Stiletto'.

Here's a handy guide to help
you figure out how big your
hostas might get, and how far
apart to plant them:

☑ **Dwarf hostas** usually mature at 8 to 10
inches tall. Plant them 8 to 10 inches apart.

☑ **Small hostas** generally grow 10 to 15
inches tall. Space them 10 to 15 inches apart.

☑ **Medium hostas** range from 15 to 24
inches tall. Set them 18 to 24 inches apart.

☑ **Large hostas** are over 2 feet tall when
mature. Plant them 2 to 3 feet apart.

❋ MAKING SCENTS

Hostas can do more than just
look leafy—they can fill your
garden with fragrance, too!
These sweetly scented beauties
tend to do better with a bit
more sun than most hostas;
heavy shade can discourage
flowering, and fewer flowers mean less fragrance. Most fragrant hostas have white flowers, and their perfume is most
intense in the evening, so they're great when planted around

a deck or patio, where you relax after a hard day at work.

Some of the best hostas for good perfume include 'Aphrodite', 'Fragrant Blue', 'Fragrant Bouquet', 'Fried Bananas', 'Fried Green Tomatoes', 'Guacamole', 'Honeybells', 'Hoosier Harmony', *H. plantaginea,* 'Invincible', 'Iron Gate Delight', 'Royal Standard', 'So Sweet', 'Sugar and Cream', and 'Venus'.

❋ GET THE BLUES

Blue-leaved hostas are an eye-catching addition to any perennial garden. You might be surprised to find out that these beauties actually have green leaves—it's the waxy, white coating on their foliage that makes them appear blue. A hard rain—or a finger rubbing the leaf—can knock off this coating, but young leaves will soon produce a new covering. By mid- to late summer, the mature leaves are no longer growing vigorously, so they tend to look more greenish as the season goes on.

Compared to typical green-leaved hostas, those with blue foliage tend to be less heat-tolerant, so they appreciate slightly shadier sites. Some of my favorites in the blue group include 'Abiqua Drinking Gourd', 'Blue Moon', 'Krossa Regal', and 'Halcyon'—but there are many others, too!

Slug-Resistant Hostas

'Abiqua Drinking Gourd'

'Aurora Borealis'

'Big Daddy'

'Blue Moon'

'Frances Williams'

'Halcyon'

'Krossa Regal'

'Love Pat'

'Midas Touch'

'Sum and Substance'

Send Slugs Packing

Hostas do have one weakness—they're like candy to slugs! Sure, there are lots of tricks you can use to control these slimy pests before they make Swiss cheese out of your hosta leaves (see pages 145–147). But if you know slugs are a problem in your garden, the smartest thing you can do is plant hostas that are naturally slug-resistant (see "Top 10 Slug-Resistant Hostas" above).

✻ Go for the Gold

If you want to bring some sunshine into your shady garden, you need to grow golden-leaved hostas. These bright beauties look like pools of light against the dark green foliage of so many shade plants. 'Chartreuse Wiggles', 'Gold Edger', 'Midas Touch', 'Sum and Substance', 'Sun Power', and 'Zounds' are a few of my favorite golden hostas.

One word of warning, though: Golden hostas can be a bit of a puzzle to site properly. The more light they get, the brighter their leaves will be. But if temperatures get really hot, golden hostas growing in too much sun can turn brown. A spot with a bit of midday sun and bright, but indirect light for the rest of the day is usually ideal for them.

Mixers & Elixirs

Quassia Slug Spray

4 oz. of quassia chips (bark of the quassia tree; available at health food stores)
1 gal. of water

Crush, grind, or chop the chips, then add them to the water in a bucket. Let steep for 12 to 24 hours. Strain through cheesecloth, then spray the remaining liquid on slug-prone plants, such as hostas. This spray also helps control aphids, but will not hurt good guys like lady beetles and honeybees.

✻ See for Yourself

If there's anything tricky about growing hostas, it's remembering to give them enough room to mature. When you look at the potted hostas for sale at your local garden center, they'll all look about the same size, but they won't stay that way! Some will get just slightly taller, while others can easily triple in height, and all of them will gradually get wider. I strongly suggest visiting perennial display gardens in your area to see how big different hostas can get before you buy and plant them!

✻ Very Varied Variegation

If there were a prize for the perennials with the widest variety of leaf colors, hostas would win, hands down! Besides green, gold, and blue, they come in a kaleidoscope of combinations: green with white (as in 'Francee'), green with gold ('Golden Tiara'), gold with blue ('Frances Williams'), gold with white ('St. Elmo's Fire'), and so on. The multicolor patterns may appear as contrasting edgings, bold center stripes, or irregular splotches. The possibilities are endless!

The less green a leaf has, the less chlorophyll it has, so variegated hostas need a bit more sun than their plain green cousins. A spot with morning shade and afternoon sun should do the trick.

Purple coneflower
Echinacea purpurea

Favorite for summer color, with masses of rosy pink daisies; attracts birds and butterflies

Easy Irises

I scream, you scream, we all scream—for iris! It's hard to believe that such easy-to-grow plants can produce such exquisite flowers. I think of them as the orchids of the perennial garden! You most often see irises in early-summer gardens, but with a little planning, you can enjoy these beauties through a good part of the year.

☀ SHORT AND SWEET

The season for perennial irises starts in mid- to late spring, with the arrival of crested iris (*Iris cristata*). This winning little wildflower forms spreading clumps of pale purple-blue or white flowers atop 4- to 6-inch-tall stems. Enjoy crested iris as a groundcover in Zones 3 to 9, in a spot that gets partial to full shade. This little cutie likes

Mixers & Elixirs

IRIS GET-UP-AND-GROW MIX

4 parts bonemeal
6 parts hydrated lime

Mix the ingredients together and sprinkle around established plants in spring. Work it into the ground when the soil is dry enough, and your irises will be off to a flying start!

evenly moist, but well-drained soil with added humus, so toss an extra handful or two of compost into the hole at planting time.

❋ BEARDEDS BRING SUMMER BEAUTY

Late spring and early summer bring the divas of the perennial garden: the bearded irises. These handsome hybrids come in a true rainbow of colors, plus many other tints and shades—peach, bronze, brown, green, and even black. They range in height from 8 inches up to 3 feet or more, so you're sure to find one to fit any bed or border.

Once established, bearded irises spread to form broad clumps. Dividing these clumps every three years in mid- to late summer will keep them blooming freely and give you plenty to share, too. Carefully lift the clumps, then break apart the thick rhizomes. Discard any sections without leaves and those with visible holes, plump pinkish caterpillars (borers), or soft, rotted areas. Pull off any discolored foliage, then cut the remaining leaves back by half.

Replant within a few days after dividing, setting them so the tops of the rhizomes are just peeking through the soil. Firm the soil around them, then water well; they'll be all set to bloom again next year!

Try This!

Can't get enough of the bearded irises in early summer? Then it's worth searching for **reblooming** cultivars. Yep—there are actually beardeds that will bloom a second time in the summer or fall, if you treat them right! Two classic rebloomers are 'Baby Blessed' and 'Immortality'; but there are others, too. To encourage repeat flowering, give them an extra dose of fertilizer after their first flush of bloom, and keep them watered well during summer dry spells.

❋ TOUGH AND TROUBLE-FREE

Siberian irises (*I. sibirica*) are another great addition to sunny beds and borders for early-summer color. They produce good-looking clumps of flat, almost grasslike leaves, with slender, but sturdy 2- to 3-foot stems. Their delicate-looking blooms come in many shades of blue and purple, as well as white and yellow.

These trouble-free perennials can grow in Zones 2 to 9, in sun or light shade, with humus-rich, evenly moist soil. They can even tolerate soggy soil, so they're perfect for wet spots!

✿ RAISE THE FLAGS

Looking for some wet-soil standbys? Besides Siberians, there are several other irises that positively *thrive* in full sun and constantly moist soil, or even a few inches of standing water. Try either of these—they're sure to please!

Blue flag (*I. versicolor*): This native American wildflower has purplish blue flowers in early summer atop 2- to 3-foot-tall stems. Zones 2 to 8.

Yellow flag (*I. pseudacorus*): Growing 3 to 4 feet tall, yellow flag has—you guessed it!—yellow flowers in early summer. It can grow in as much as 10 inches of water. Zones 4 to 9.

✿ IRIS IQ

If you're an iris lover like I am, you already know how important it is to separate these showy beauties every three to five years so that they have plenty of room to bloom. What you may not realize is that because irises are such heavy feeders, they will soon deplete the soil of nutrients. So make sure you prepare their new beds well.

First, prepare a mixture of 1 part Epsom salts with 3 parts bonemeal. Then spread a layer of peat moss, dry shredded leaves, and the Epsom salt and bonemeal mixture at least 1 inch thick over the soil where

Quamash
Camassia esculenta

Spikes of starry late-spring blooms in all shades of blue to white

Mixers & Elixirs

IRIS ENERGIZER TONIC

½ cup of beer
Vitamin B₁ Plant Starter (mixed at 25 percent of the recommended rate)
2 tbsp. of dishwashing liquid
1 gal. of warm water

Mix the ingredients together in a bucket, and drench the soil around your newly planted irises to get them off on the right root!

you grow your irises, and work it into the top 6 inches of soil. After setting out your irises, give them a dose of my Iris Energizer Tonic (see page 239).

☀ SOME SHADY CHARACTERS

Here are two more out-of-the-ordinary irises to grace your shady garden:

✔ **Roof iris** (*I. tectorum*): Spreading clumps that are 12 to 18 inches tall when in bloom, with purple-blue or white flowers in late spring. Sun to partial shade; average, well-drained soil. Zones 5 to 9.

✔ **Stinking iris** (*I. foetidissima*): Grow this 1- to 3-foot-tall species not for its pale purple, early-summer flowers, but for its eye-catching scarlet seeds in fall. It only stinks (and not much) when you crush the leaves. Partial to full shade; evenly moist, well-drained soil. Zones 6 to 9.

Red baneberry
Actaea rubra

Fuzzy white flowers in spring followed by red berries; a wildflower for shady areas

Mum's the Word

Fall just wouldn't be the same without those end-of-summer standbys: chrysanthemums (*Chrysanthemum* x *morifolium*). Sure, it's easy to treat them like annuals and buy new plants each year. But with a little know-how, you can easily keep your favorites from year to year, and you can use the money you save to buy other perennials!

☀ PINCH 'EM AN INCH!

Ever notice that your mums seem to look a lot different the year after you plant them? When you buy them in late summer, they're dense and bushy, and they're covered with blooms in fall. The next year, they're tall and leggy, and they start flowering as early as midsummer. What's the deal?

The key to keeping your mums in top form is giving them a good pinch every now and then. When the plants are 6 to 8 inches tall, pinch or cut them back halfway, about $\frac{1}{4}$ inch above a set of leaves. Repeat four weeks later, and again in another four weeks if you have time. Don't pinch after August 1 in the North or August 15 in the South.

❀ THEY DON'T NEED A NIGHT LIGHT

If your mums aren't flowering when you expect them to, they may be staying up too late! Normally, mums produce leafy growth in spring and early summer. Once nights start getting longer again, the flower buds start to form—*unless* the plants are exposed to some light source at night, such as a street lamp. The plants get confused and may not form flower buds at all, or at least not until it's too late for them to flower before frost.

❀ DIVIDE AND CONQUER

Frequent division will help keep your garden mums healthy and free-flowering. Every two or three years, lift the clumps in spring, divide them, and replant the outer portions of the clump in a sunny spot with average, well-drained soil.

❀ LEAVE THEM BE

Don't be in a hurry to tidy up your mums after frost. Cut off the dead flowers if you want, but leave the stems standing;

MAKING ¢ents If you have to buy new mums each year because the last ones didn't survive, you might be planting the wrong mums. The big-bloomed **florist mums** you buy as potted gift plants are normally only suited for Zones 7 to 9. **Hardy** or **garden mums**, on the other hand—the ones you see for sale in late summer—are the ones you want; these should survive the winter just fine in Zones 5 to 9. Some mums are hardy even into Zones 3 or 4; one clue is a name that starts with the word "Minn" (like 'Minnpink').

they'll help insulate the crown from cold temperatures. For additional protection, cover the clumps with evergreen boughs or 6 inches of loose straw toward the end of November. In early spring, remove the mulch, then trim off the dead stems.

If Grandma got a flowering florist mum as a gift, she'd set it on a sunny windowsill with a southern, eastern, or northern exposure. (Keep the pot fairly close to the window, she'd always tell me, because mums prefer cooler temperatures.) When the threat of frost had passed, she cut the foliage all the way back, and planted the mum in a nice, sunny spot in her garden. If she was lucky, it would bloom again in the fall!

❋ RE-MUM-BER THIS TIP

If your mums die over the winter, the cold may not be to blame—the problem is likely too much moisture. So after the blooms fade, dig up the plants with as much soil as possible, and set them on top of the ground in a protected area. Then cover them lightly with mulch. Come spring, divide and replant them.

Perfect Peonies

These easy-care, long-lived perennials are a classic choice for cooler-climate perennial gardens. Peonies grow best in Zones 3 to 7, but even Zone 8 gardeners can enjoy them if they choose heat-tolerant (also called low-chill) cultivars, such as 'Festiva Maxima'. Read on for more tips on growing the prettiest peonies on your block.

❋ ON WITH THE SHOW

If you love peonies as much as I do, you want to make their flower display last as long as possible. By planting a selection of early-, midseason-, and late-flowering cultivars, you can extend their bloom time from just a week or two to well over a month!

❋ Making More Peonies

Plant peonies in a sunny, well-drained spot and give them proper care, and they'll continue to bloom for a good long time—20 years or more, if you're lucky! And to top that off, you can increase your peony plantings by dividing your plants from time to time. When a peony root is divided, each piece of root that has a bud attached to it will produce another plant just like its parent. What a deal! Just follow these three simple steps in late summer or early fall:

Step 1. Dig up the entire plant with a spading fork, shake the soil from the roots, or wash it off with a blast from the hose.

Step 2. Cut the clump into several divisions, each with at least three to five buds. Plant the divisions into compost-enriched soil, making sure that the buds are no more than 2 inches below the surface.

Step 3. Cover with soil, then press down firmly to eliminate any air pockets. Cut off any aboveground stems, then water and mulch well.

❋ Peony Problem Solver

Once established, peonies are pretty much trouble-free. But these tough plants do occasionally have some problems, so here's a few tips to help you out:

No flowers? One common cause is deep planting. (If the buds are more than 2 inches below the soil surface, dig up the clump, and set it slightly higher when you replant it.) Mulching too heavily can have the same effect. Other common causes include too much shade (they need at least 6

Reticulated iris
Iris reticulata

Dainty purple or blue blooms in earliest spring; thrives in sunny spots

Try This!

If you want the biggest possible peony blooms, pick off the side buds while they are still very small, leaving just the main end bud on each stalk. This will focus the plant's energy on producing one gigantic flower per stem. (Just make sure you stake each stem individually—these big blooms are really heavy!)

hours of sun a day); dry soil (water during dry spells); poor soil (add fertilizer); cold damage (protect with a light winter mulch); and overcrowding (divide the clump). Also, keep in mind that young plants may need a few years to reach flowering size.

Browned petals, or buds that don't open? Botrytis blight might be to blame. (To discourage this fungal disease, remove damaged buds and discolored leaves as they appear, and cut all remaining stems down to the ground after frost and destroy them.) Two other possibilities include thrips (spray with insecticidal soap) and temperatures above 85°F (pray for cooler weather).

> Don't worry about those ants crawling around on your peonies. They're busy gathering a sticky substance on the buds and won't do any harm to the plants or flowers.

🌼 PEONIES THAT GROW ON ... TREES?

It's true! There are actually plants called "tree peonies" (*Paeonia suffruticosa*). They grow so slowly that you'll seldom see one that's more than 5 feet tall. But even if the plants themselves aren't tree-sized, they produce gigantic blossoms—up to 8 inches across—with crinkled petals in white or shades of red, pink, peach, or yellow.

Unlike typical garden peonies, tree peonies have woody stems that don't die back to the ground each year. Once planted, they need no special care. Talk about trouble-free!

Roman hyacinth
*Hyacinthus
orientalis*
var. *albulus*

Each bulb sends
up multiple stalks
of fragrant white
flowers in spring

🌼 PROMOTE GOOD PEONY POSTURE

There's nothing sadder than a beautiful peony bloom that's flopped, facedown into the mud. And once your peony plants have fallen over, there's not much you can do except prepare to stake them *early* next year! Here are a few options to get you started:

☑ **Wire rings:** You can buy commercial wire peony hoops (basically, a three-legged wire ring surrounding a wire grid that the stems grow through). But you'll save a bundle if you make your own hoops out of 2-inch wire mesh, cut in a circle about 1 foot across. Simply toss the hoops over the just-emerging shoots; the stems will lift the hoops as they grow.

☑ **Plastic six-pack rings:** Turn trash into treasure by dropping these plastic rings over your peony shoots as they come up. They'll do a great job supporting the stems, and you won't even see them!

☑ **Old lamp shades:** Pick up old lamp shades at thrift shops and garage sales. Remove the covering, then set the wire skeletons over emerging peony plants to corral the stems.

 LIVING SINGLE

Hate staking with a passion? Then avoid it altogether by growing single-flowered peonies. These simple, but elegant blooms have fewer petals to catch and hold rain, so they're much less likely to fall over. Some of my favorites include snowy 'Krinkled White', coral pink 'Seashell', clear pink 'Bowl of Beauty', and red 'Scarlett O'Hara'.

Grandma loved to bring peony blooms indoors, so she made it a point to plant a few extra clumps in her yard. That way, she was never tempted to take too many blooms from just one plant. Her rule of thumb was to never take more than a third of the blooms from each clump, and she tried to leave as many of the leaves on the plant as possible. Once the flowering season was over, Grandma Putt also made sure she cut off the seedpods, so the plants wouldn't waste any energy producing seeds.

CHAPTER 13

THE BEST OF THE REST

Sure, you want to have a lot of the most popular perennials in your garden, but you also want some variety, too! In this chapter, I've gathered together a bounty of terrific tips on choosing and growing an *amazing* array of colorful, easy-care perennials that'll look great in your yard.

Flower Power!

Perennials are great, all-around garden plants. But if they have one flaw, it's that they tend to bloom for a fairly short time—just a few weeks each year. You can, however, have beautiful blooms over a much longer period of time by adding some of these long-flowering perennials to your yard.

✸ A BOUNTY OF BLOOMS

If you want color from early summer to frost in your perennial garden, be sure to tuck in some Jupiter's beard (*Centranthus ruber*). Also called red valerian, this prolific perennial is a snap to grow from seed. And if you start it indoors in late winter, your plants will start flowering their very first summer!

The 2-foot-tall plants form tidy clumps of blue-green leaves and branching stems topped with clusters of red, rose-pink, or white flowers. Pinching off the spent flower heads encourages bushier growth and more blooms. Give them full sun and average, well-drained soil; hold off on the fertilizer, or the stems may flop. Jupiter's beard grows best in Zones 4 to 8.

✸ COREOPSIS AMONG US

The bright blooms of sun-loving coreopsis (*Coreopsis*) are another must-have for extended perennial color. Here are some of your best bets for months of flowers:

❧ 'Early Sunrise' coreopsis (*C. grandiflora* 'Early Sunrise'): Eighteen-inch-tall plants with orange-yellow, double blooms from late spring to late summer or beyond. Start seeds

---

TOP 10 Perennials for Months of Flowers

Anise hyssop (*Agastache foeniculum*)

'Butterfly Blue' pincushion flower (*Scabiosa* 'Butterfly Blue')

Balloon flower (*Platycodon grandiflorus*)

Blanket flower (*Gaillardia* x *grandiflora*)

Catmints (*Nepeta*)

Coreopsis (*Coreopsis*)

Gaura (*Gaura lindheimeri*)

'Goldsturm' black-eyed Susan (*Rudbeckia fulgida* 'Goldsturm')

'Happy Returns' daylily (*Hemerocallis* 'Happy Returns')

Jupiter's beard (*Centranthus ruber*)

Rose campion
Lychnis coronaria

Glowing magenta blooms over rosettes of fuzzy, silvery foliage

TOOL TIME

The best trick for helping your perennials look their best and bloom the longest is also the easiest: Simply remove the spent flowers every few days, so they don't set seed. And the best tools for this task are a good pair of garden clippers and a basic, 5 gallon plastic bucket. You can often find these buckets for free, or for just a dollar or two, at fast-food restaurants, delis, and bakeries.

Keep your clippers and bucket in a handy spot, and carry them with you each time you go out in the garden. As you admire your beautiful flowers, snip off the dead ones and toss them into the bucket. Finish your tour with a trip to the compost pile to dump the clippings, and your bucket will be ready and waiting for your next stroll through the garden!

indoors in late winter, and you can get flowers the first year! Zones 4 to 9.

- Pink coreopsis (*C. rosea*): One- to 2-foot-tall, spreading mounds of needle-like leaves, covered with pink daisies from summer to early fall. It tolerates more moisture and more shade than most coreopsis. Zones 4 to 8.
- Threadleaf coreopsis (*C. verticillata*): Slow-spreading mounds of needle-like leaves with yellow, daisy-like blooms from early summer to fall. 'Moonbeam' has soft, yellow blooms on 15-inch-tall plants; 'Zagreb' is about the same size, with golden yellow flowers. Zones 3 to 9.

Gee Whiz—Geraniums!

Don't confuse these pretty perennials with the cold-tender geraniums (*Pelargonium*) that make such great windowbox and flowerbed annuals. Hardy geraniums (*Geranium*) look very different, forming mounds or clumps of lobed leaves and cupped or saucer-shaped blooms, usually in shades of purple, blue, pink, or white.

There are well over a dozen great species to choose from, and many more cultivars and hybrids. I've highlighted just two of the showiest below. Both of these thrive in full sun to light shade, in average soil that doesn't completely dry out.

- ☑ Bloody cranesbill (*G. sanguineum*): Low-growing (to 1 foot tall) mounds dotted with hot pink, bowl-shaped blooms through the summer. Zones 3 to 9.
- ☑ 'Johnson's Blue' geranium (*G.* 'Johnson's Blue'): An 18-inch-tall, clump-forming hybrid with clear blue, cupped blooms from late spring into early fall. Zones 4 to 8.

✺ BOLD AND BEAUTIFUL

If your definition of flower power is based on sheer size, you can't beat rose mallow (*Hibiscus moscheutos*). This brazen beauty grows anywhere from 2 to 8 feet tall, with saucer- or funnel-shaped flowers from early summer to fall. Each pink, red, or white flower extends 8 to 10 inches across. *WOW!* Give rose mallow sun or light shade and evenly moist soil. It grows in Zones 5 to 10.

Perennials for Posterity

One of the greatest things about perennials is that you don't have to plant them each year, like you do annuals. But most perennials do need to be dug up and divided every few years to stay vigorous and free-flowering. If you want to keep even this simple maintenance to a minimum, fill your garden with the longest-lived perennials—they'll thrive for five years or more without division.

✺ GONNA GET YOUR GOAT!

Goatsbeard (*Aruncus dioicus*) grows as big as a shrub, and it lives as long, too! Established clumps can grow up to 6 feet tall and wide. From early to midsummer, the bushy mounds of ferny green leaves are topped with huge plumes of creamy white blooms—a real showstopper.

In cooler areas, goatsbeard can take full sun; elsewhere, it appreciates a bit of shade. And while it can tolerate dry soil, it really loves moist soil with lots of added compost. Goatsbeard grows best in Zones 3 to 8.

Rose mallow
Hibiscus moscheutos

Show-stopping 6- to 8-inch-wide summer blooms on shrub-sized plants

✺ Indigo in Da Garden

Plant it and forget it—that's the rule for blue false indigo (*Baptisia australis*). This no-care perennial takes a few years to settle in, but once it's established, it returns year after year to grace your sunny garden with 4-foot spikes of blue blooms from late spring to early summer. As long as it has well-drained soil, this beauty is a winner anywhere from Zones 2 through 8.

✺ Carefree Hearts

Common bleeding heart (*Dicentra spectabilis*) has such delicate flowers, it's hard to believe how tough the plant itself really is! Left undisturbed, mature plants can grow 3 feet tall and spread to 4 feet across. From late spring to early summer, white-tipped, pink hearts dangle daintily from the graceful, arching stems.

In cool-summer areas (Zones 2 to 5), this durable perennial can grow in full sun; where summers get hot (Zones 6 to 9), give it partial shade. It likes humus-rich, evenly moist soil and may go dormant in summer if the soil dries out; if it does, simply cut the stems down and it will return the next year. Other than that, just leave it alone and enjoy!

✺ Not Yucky—Yucca!

If you like your perennials big and bold, yuccas (*Yucca*) definitely deserve a spot in your yard. One plucky yucca you're

---

Perfect Perennials

FOR POSTERITY

Plan your gardens around these long-lived beauties, and they'll still be alive and kickin' for the next generation to enjoy!

Balloon flower (*Platycodon grandiflorus*): Balloon-shaped buds open to blue, pink, or white flowers in summer. Zones 3 to 8.

Bugbanes (*Cimicifuga*): Fuzzy spikes of white flowers in summer and fall. Zones 3 to 8.

Daylilies (*Hemerocallis*): Trumpet-shaped blooms in a wide range of colors in midsummer. Zones 3 to 10.

Hostas (*Hosta*): Purple or white flowers in summer over clumps of heart-shaped leaves. Zones 3 to 8.

Peonies (*Paeonia*): Red, pink, white, or coral blooms in late spring to early summer. Zones 3 to 8.

likely to find for sale is Adam's needle (*Y. filamentosa*), with spiky, evergreen, blue-green leaves in eye-catching clumps that reach 30 inches tall and spread 4 feet or more across. 'Bright Edge' and 'Color Guard' have yellow-edged leaves; 'Golden Sword' leaves have a gold stripe down the center. But if great-looking leaves aren't enough, these long-lived plants also send up 5- to 6-foot-tall stems in summer, topped with clusters of cream-colored bells.

JERRY'S GEMS

For more ideas on long-lived perennials, visit old graveyards or abandoned homesteads in your area. **You'll see plants there that have been thriving for many, many years without any special care whatsoever!**

Give your yuccas full sun or very light shade, and any average soil that's not soggy. They grow in Zones 4 to 10. Individual clumps die after flowering, but new ones emerge soon after. There's no need to divide them, unless they get too big for the spot they're in!

Lovely Leaves

Think about gardens, and immediately, flowers come to mind. And why not? It's the bright blooms that catch our eye and entice us to start gardening in the first place. But gradually, most gardeners start to appreciate the beauty of leaves, too—the way their interesting color and striking textures provide dependable interest, even while flowers come and go.

❋ YOU WON'T BE-LEAF IT!

Once you actually start looking at leaves, you'll be amazed to find the many varied colors they come in. Besides every

Rough-leaved goldenrod
Solidago rugosa

Sprays of golden yellow blooms light up fall beds and borders

shade of green and silver, they can be practically any other color you can imagine. Here are just a few examples:

Black: Black mondo grass (*Ophiopogon japonicus* 'Nigrescens').

Blue: 'Halcyon' hosta (*Hosta* 'Halcyon').

Brown: New Zealand sedges (such as *Carex buchananii*).

Purple: 'Purple Ruffles' heuchera (*Heuchera* 'Purple Ruffles').

Red: Japanese blood grass (*Imperata cylindrica* 'Red Baron').

Yellow: Bowles golden sedge (*Carex elata* 'Aurea').

TOP 10

Perennials with Multicolored Leaves

'Alexander' whorled loosestrife (*Lysimachia punctata* 'Alexander')

'Brise de Anjou' Jacob's ladder (*Polemonium caeruleum* 'Brise de Anjou')

'Burgundy Glow' bugleweed (*Ajuga reptans* 'Burgundy Glow')

'Frosty Morn' sedum (*Sedum spectabile* 'Frosty Morn')

'Gold Band' sedge (*Carex morrowii* 'Gold Band')

Golden hakone grass (*Hakonechloa macra* 'Aureola')

Heucheras (*Heuchera*, many cultivars)

Hostas (*Hosta*, many cultivars)

'Tricolor' sage (*Salvia officinalis* 'Tricolor')

Zebra grass (*Miscanthus sinensis* 'Zebrinus'

❋ SPOTS AND SPLASHES

Multicolored—or variegated—leaves really liven up your flowerbeds and borders. Green with white edges, gold with green stripes, green and yellow with red splashes—the various combinations of colors and patterns are practically endless!

Planted among perennials with "ordinary" leaves, a clump of variegated foliage makes an eye-catching accent. For even more interest, plant it with a companion that picks up one of the leaf colors—for example, a white-flowered astilbe (such as *Astilbe* 'Bridal Veil') with the white-edged green leaves of 'Francee' hosta.

❋ SILVER IS GOLD

For sunny sites, silvery foliage simply can't be beat. Usually, the leaves themselves are green, but they look gray or silvery due to a covering of fine hairs that reflect the sunlight.

Silvery plants work great for setting off brightly colored blooms, but also look pretty with pastels. In fact, it's hard to think of a flower color that *wouldn't* look good against silver!

✻ NICE TO MEET YA, ARTEMISIA

One popular group of silvery perennials for full sun and well-drained, not-too-rich soil is the artemisias (*Artemisia*), also called wormwoods. Silvermound artemisia (*A. schmidtiana*) forms fluffy 12- to 18-inch-tall mounds of feathery foliage. It's best in cooler climates (Zones 3 to 7); hot, humid weather causes the clumps to flop open. (If they still flop, cut them back to 2 inches to get bushier regrowth.)

For a more upright plant, try 3-foot-tall 'Silver King' or 'Silver Queen' artemisia (*A. ludoviciana*). Both spread by creeping roots, so surround them with some kind of root barrier to keep them from taking over. They grow in Zones 3 to 8.

Royal fern
Osmunda regalis

Elegant clumps of lacy fronds pair perfectly with hostas in shady spots

✻ THE MANY HUES OF HEUCHERAS

It's tough to find perennials better than the heucheras for foliage interest! You may know them by their more familiar name "coral bells"—those are the species and hybrids grown for their showy red, pink, or white flowers. The ones with pretty leaves are simply called heucheras, or sometimes alumroots. Their usually evergreen, lobed leaves have scalloped or ruffled edges. They can be green with silver and/or maroon markings, deep purple with or without silvering, or even chocolate brown.

Heucheras can take full sun to full shade, but they prefer a spot with morning sun and afternoon shade. They grow best in Zones 4 to 8, in evenly moist, but not soggy, soil.

Try This!

The best fertilizer you can give leafy plants is ... *other leaves!* To make leaf mold, gather dry shredded leaves into plastic garbage bags and moisten them slightly. Close the bags and stack them in an out-of-the-way spot. By spring, you'll have a generous supply of humus-rich leaf mold to feed your perennials.

Rue
Ruta graveolens

Shrubby clumps of
silvery blue leaves
and yellow flowers
in early summer

Sizzling Summer Colors

As temperatures rise, so does the excitement in the
perennial garden! It's time to enjoy all those tropical
hues: sunny yellows, rousing reds, awesome oranges, and
regal purples. Read on to discover the many ways your
garden can reflect the glory of the summer season.

GO FOR THE GOLDS

To my mind, nothing says summer like bright yellow
blooms. Pastels are pretty in soft spring light, but the
strong sun of full summer calls for rich, golden yellow flowers. These bold beauties look equally good with ruby red,
tangerine orange, rich purple, and royal blue companions.
They also do a great job of pepping up plantings of pale-
flowered perennials.

There are many bright yellow summer perennials to
enjoy. Some of my favorites include black-eyed Susans
(*Rudbeckia*), coreopsis, 'Coronation
Gold' yarrow (*Achillea* 'Coronation
Gold'), daylilies (*Hemerocallis*, many
cultivars), oxeye (*Heliopsis
helianthoides*), perennial sunflowers
(*Helianthus*), sundrops (*Oenothera
fruticosa*), and whorled loosestrife
(*Lysimachia punctata*).

If you really want to heat
things up in your summer
garden, you can't do bet-
ter than red hot pokers
(*Kniphofia*)! Also called torch lilies, these
2- to 4-foot-tall perennials produce
dense bloom spikes tipped with reddish
buds that open into yellow flowers.
Give red hot pokers full sun and average
soil; they like a steady supply of moisture, but hate soggy soil, especially in
winter. Zones 5 to 9.

ORANGE YOU GLAD?

Few people are wishy-washy about
the color orange—they either love it
or hate it. But even if you don't like
orange in general, take a chance
and try it in your garden. There's nothing like orange flowers
to help blend bright yellow and red blooms. They're also
outstanding with bright blues and intense purples, and they
really pop against partners with deep red or purple leaves.

Ready to give orange a try? I suggest starting with

these: blackberry lily (*Belamcanda chinensis*), Boris avens (*Geum* x *borisii*), butterfly weed (*Asclepias tuberosa*), daylilies (*Hemerocallis*, many cultivars), 'Orange Perfection' phlox (*Phlox paniculata* 'Orange Perfection'), and Oriental poppy (*Papaver orientale*).

❋ RED-DY FOR FUN

Vibrant and exciting, red is a can't-miss addition to any bed or border. If your garden is small, a single clump of red flowers is probably enough; a larger garden can handle more, without the red becoming too overwhelming.

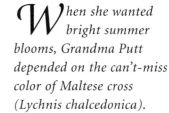

*W*hen she wanted bright summer blooms, Grandma Putt depended on the can't-miss color of Maltese cross (*Lychnis chalcedonica*). *This old-fashioned favorite is still a winner for today's gardens, with clusters of fire-engine-red flowers sitting atop sturdy 3-foot-tall stems in midsummer. Give it a spot with full sun and average, well-drained soil. Zones 3 to 8.*

Red partnered with golden yellow, orange, and violet creates a bright kaleidoscope of color. For a more elegant effect, combine red, pink, and white flowers, or try a striking contrast of red flowers against silvery foliage—*Wow!*

Here are some of the best reds for summer fun: bee balm (*Monarda didyma*), cardinal flower (*Lobelia cardinalis*), coral bells (*Heuchera sanguinea*), 'Fanal' astilbe (*Astilbe* 'Fanal'), 'Fire King' yarrow (*Achillea millefolium* 'Fire King'), 'Lord Baltimore' rose mallow (*Hibiscus moscheutos* 'Lord Baltimore'), Maltese cross (*Lychnis chalcedonica*), and 'Mrs. Bradshaw' avens (*Geum* 'Mrs. Bradshaw').

❋ VIBRANT VIOLETS

Blue flowers have an icy-cool appearance, but when you slide over into the violet and purple hues, the effect is totally different. These deep colors have an intensity that easily matches the rich reds and golds that grace summer gardens. They also make a lively contrast to bright white blooms and silvery foliage.

Purple- and violet-flowered perennials are hard to see

from a distance, so to get the best effect, plant them in a spot where you'll enjoy them close up. Use these to add a regal touch to your sunny summer garden: 'Black Knight' delphinium (*Delphinium* 'Black Knight'), clustered bellflower (*Campanula glomerata*), 'Dusky Challenger' bearded iris (*Iris* 'Dusky Challenger'), 'East Friesland' sage (*Salvia* x *superba* 'East Friesland'), 'Purple Profusion' spiderwort (*Tradescantia* 'Purple Profusion'), 'The King' phlox (*Phlox paniculata* 'The King'), and 'Velvet Star' daylily (*Hemerocallis* 'Velvet Star').

Get the Blues!

It's easy to fall in love with blue flowers. Sky blue, electric blue, royal blue, baby blue—all these and more have a magic all their own. But making the most of blue flowers takes a little bit of know-how, so I've put together some of my best secrets for giving your garden the blues.

❀ DELIGHTFUL DELPHINIUMS

Delphiniums are among the most beautiful of blue perennials—and they can also be the most tricky to grow. But not for those of you who live in areas with cold winters and cool summers (roughly Zones 3 to 5); these beauties will be the glory of your early summer garden! Give them full sun or light shade and evenly moist, but well-drained soil. Work plenty of compost into the planting area, and they'll be as happy as clams.

Where summers are hot, however, or where the soil tends to repeatedly freeze and thaw during the winter, most

Sea pink
Armeria maritima

Tidy tufts of grasslike evergreen leaves dotted with pink blooms in early summer

delphiniums can be a major hassle to keep healthy.
Fortunately, there are a few delphiniums that are a bit more
forgiving. In Zones 6 and 7, try cul-
tivars from the Belladonna Group
Hybrids (such as 'Bellamosum')
and the Connecticut Yankee Series
('Blue Fountains' is one).

☀ WAYS TO USE BLUES

When deciding where to plant blue-
flowered perennials, keep in mind
that their color tends to blend into
the background of green leaves.
Planting blue flowers in beds away
from your house will give the
impression that the beds are farther away, so your yard will look
bigger than it really is.

   On the other hand, if you have
a blue flower that you really like to
look at, plant it close by so it won't
get "lost" in the distance. Pairing
blue perennials with orange or yellow partners will also help them
show up better.

☀ BRIGHTEN YOUR BLUES

Once you've got the blues, it's
tempting to try planting an all-blue
garden. With so many blue-flowered perennials to choose from,
you'd think it would be easy. But in
reality, it's tough to come up with a
combination of all blue flowers that
doesn't look—well, dull.

   There's a simple solution—just toss another color into
the mix to liven things up a bit! A bed of blue and white

Perfect Perennials

FOR BLUE FLOWERS

Bring a bit of the sky to your backyard
with a planting of beautiful blue blooms
like these!

Bellflowers (*Campanula*): Full sun to partial
shade; average to rich, moist, but well-
drained soil. Zones 3 to 8.

Bluebeard (*Caryopteris* x *clandonensis*): Full
sun; average, well-drained soil. Zones 4 to 9.

Blue false indigo (*Baptisia australis*): Full
sun; humus-rich, evenly moist, but well-
drained soil. Zones 3 to 9.

'Butterfly Blue' pincushion flower (*Scabiosa*
'Butterfly Blue'): Full sun; average, well-
drained soil. Zones 3 to 8.

Catmints (*Nepeta*): Full sun to light shade;
average, well-drained soil. Zones 4 to 8.

'Johnson's Blue' geranium (*Geranium*
'Johnson's Blue'): Full sun to partial shade;
humus-rich, evenly moist, but well-drained
soil. Zones 5 to 9.

Siberian iris (*Iris sibirica*): Full sun to light
shade; evenly moist to wet soil. Zones 2 to 9.

Speedwells (*Veronica*): Full sun to partial
shade; average to humus-rich, well-drained
soil. Zones 3 to 8.

flowers and silvery foliage, for instance, is incredibly beautiful. Pale yellow perennials, such as yellow foxglove (*Digitalis lutea*), are also super for livening up blue borders.

✺ True-Blue Bloomers

For pure blue flowers, it's hard to beat leadwort (*Cerato-stigma plumbaginoides*). Despite its downright ugly name, this perennial is a real beauty, with clusters of small electric blue blooms in late summer and fall. In mid-fall, the green leaves turn orange and red, adding extra interest. The spreading 6- to 12-inch-tall plants make great groundcovers in Zones 5 to 9, in a site with full sun or light shade and evenly moist, but well-drained soil.

Mixers & Elixirs

NATURAL NUTRIENTS FOR NEGLECTED SOIL

6 parts greensand or wood ashes
3 parts cottonseed meal
3 parts bonemeal
Gypsum
Limestone

Mix the greensand or wood ashes, cottonseed meal, and bonemeal together. Add 2 cups of gypsum and 1 cup of limestone per gallon-size container of blend. Apply 5 pounds per 100 square feet of garden area a few weeks before planting perennials.

Pretty in Pastel

Bright colors not to your taste? Then pick from an abundance of pastel-flowered perennials to fill your gardens. Soft pink, butter yellow, baby blue, and lilac purple—all of these are lovely additions to beds and borders.

❀ Gardening with a Soft Touch

Take a tip from Mother Nature—spring is a super time for pastel colors in the perennial garden. The softer light of this season is kind to pale colors, so you can appreciate their delicate hues, even in sunny spots.

As the season swings toward summer, the sun gets more intense. In strong sunlight, pastels look washed out, and pale petals may even be scorched by the sun. So stick with brighter colors in your sunny areas, and plant summer-blooming pastels in some shade. The lighter colors will really brighten things up there!

❀ Hello Yellow

Soft yellows are particularly pretty for gardens close to the house—along a path, near a door, or around a deck, porch, or patio. At dusk, they show up almost as well as white flowers, and during the day, they blend beautifully with many other colors. Plus, pale yellow blooms often attract night-flying moths, so they'll add another dimension of interest to your garden in the evening.

❀ You Won't Rue the Day

If you want pastel flowers close to eye level, add meadow rues (*Thalictrum*) to your garden. These easy-to-grow perennials thrive in partial shade and evenly moist, but well-drained, compost-enriched soil. Here are three of my favorites:

✔ **Columbine meadow rue** (*T. aquilegifolium*): When you see the clumps of blue-green leaves, you'll think it's a gigantic columbine (*Aquilegia*)! But when it blooms, you'll see the difference; this perennial produces fluffy clusters of pink flowers atop 3-foot-tall stems in early summer. Zones 4 to 8.

Shooting star
Dodecatheon meadia

Pink or white spring blooms; dies back to the ground soon after flowering

Perennials with Pale Yellow Blooms

TOP 5

'Corbett' columbine (*Aquilegia canadensis* 'Corbett')

'Happy Returns' daylily (*Hemerocallis* 'Happy Returns')

'Moonbeam' coreopsis (*Coreopsis verticillata* 'Moonbeam')

'Moonshine' yarrow (*Achillea* 'Moonshine')

Yellow pincushion flower (*Scabiosa ochroleuca*)

✔ **Lavender mist** (*T. rochebrunianum* 'Lavender Mist'): Looks much like the former, but taller—to 5 feet. Zones 4 to 7.

✔ **Yellow meadow rue** (*T. flavum* ssp. *glaucum*): Also looks like columbine meadow rue, but with light yellow blooms on 4-foot-tall stems. Zones 5 to 9.

TOOL TIME

If you're like me, you tend to misplace trowels, clippers, and other small tools as you're working in your garden. Well, here's a great tip: Mount an old mailbox on a post in one of your flowerbeds, and use it to store small tools, string, seed packets, and all those other little items that are so easy to lose track of. Besides providing convenient tool storage, the mailbox makes a nice decorative accent!

✹ Think Pink

With so many pretty pink flowers to choose from, it's tempting to fill your whole yard with them. And why not? Pink flowers hold up well in the sun, and they bring welcome color to shadier spots, too.

If you have nothing but pink, though, your gardens can look too cotton-candy sweet. But it's easy to get around that—just pep things up with some purple- or yellow-flowered partners.

✹ Crazy for Foxgloves

Foxgloves (*Digitalis*) are a classic choice for soft-colored flowers from early to midsummer. Give them full sun to light shade (partial shade south of Zone 6) and well-drained, compost-enriched soil that doesn't dry out totally. Here are two worth trying:

• Common foxglove (*D. purpurea*): A classic sight in cottage gardens, this 3- to 6-foot-tall plant with spotted pink or white flowers is commonly either biennial or a short-lived perennial. Strawberry foxglove (*D.* x *mertonensis*) is more dependably perennial, with plump, rose-pink blooms on 3-foot-tall stems. Zones 3 to 8.

• Yellow foxglove (*D. lutea*): Spikes of small, pale yellow flowers on 3-foot-tall stems with smooth green leaves. *D. grandiflora* also has soft yellow flowers, but the individual blooms are much bigger, and the plants have hairy leaves. Zones 3 to 9.

The Whitest Whites

What could be more elegant than a garden of all-white flowers? It's an experiment that many gardeners are tempted to try at least once. Read on for tips to help you make the most of these pristine perennials in your yard.

Showy
stonecrop
Sedum spectabile

Broad clusters
of pink
late-summer and
fall flowers;
beloved by
butterflies

☀ VARIATIONS ON A THEME

White's white, right? Not always! When you start combining white-flowered perennials, you'll notice there are many different kinds of white: creamy white, pinkish white, bluish white, greenish white, and bright white. Next to flowers that are pure white, flowers with a touch of color can look drab.

You can get around these differences, though—simply separate white flowers with lots of green or silvery foliage, so the blooms aren't right next to each other. From a distance, they'll all look like the same white, and close up, you can enjoy the differences without unpleasant clashes.

☀ START SMALL

Before you decide to plant your whole yard in white flowers, try a small bed or border first. White's nice in small quantities, but too much of any good thing gets boring after a while. For extra interest, add companions with blue or silvery foliage; white-variegated plants look super with white flowers, too.

The same quality that makes white flowers show up at night makes them a super choice for shade gardens. There are lots to choose from, but here are a few of my favorites: anemones, 'Bruce's White' phlox (*Phlox stolonifera* 'Bruce's White'), foamflowers (*Tiarella*), goatsbeards (*Aruncus*), snakeroots (*Cimicifuga*), and white baneberry (*Actaea alba*).

☀ KEEP 'EM CLEAN

Keep in mind that white flowers tend to look yucky as they die—brown flowers among the whites really stand out. So, you'll need to pinch off the spent blooms more often than you would for other colored blooms in order to keep your garden looking good.

Perfect Perennials

FOR WHITE FLOWERS

Crisp, white flowers make you feel cool, even on the hottest summer day. Here are just a few of the prettiest white flowers you can grow:

Boltonia (*Boltonia asteroides*): Full sun; average, well-drained soil. Zones 3 to 9.

'Bridal Veil' astilbe (*Astilbe* 'Bridal Veil'): Partial shade; humus-rich, evenly moist, but well-drained soil. Zones 4 to 8.

'David' phlox (*Phlox* 'David'): Full sun to partial shade; evenly moist, but well-drained soil. Zones 3 to 8.

Foamflowers (*Tiarella*): Partial to full shade; humus-rich, evenly moist, but well-drained soil. Zones 3 to 8.

Gaura (*Gaura lindheimeri*): Full sun; average, well-drained soil. Zones 5 to 9.

'Honorine Jobert' anemone (*Anemone* x *hybrida* 'Honorine Jobert'): Full sun to partial shade; humus-rich, evenly moist, but well-drained soil. Zones 4 to 8.

Perennial candytuft (*Iberis sempervirens*): Full sun; average, well-drained soil. Zones 3 to 9.

WAYS WITH WHITE

White flowers are so bright, they're the first to catch your eye when you look at a bed or border. Dotting white flowers throughout your yard can provide a pleasing sense of repetition, visually tying all of your plantings together. But if your yard is on the small side, consider keeping the whites closer to the house, and saving softer blues and purples for outlying borders. Otherwise, the whites will draw your eye right out to the end of your property, and your yard will look smaller than it really is!

LIGHT UP THE NIGHT

If you're like many gardeners, you may find that you only have time to enjoy your garden for a few minutes each evening. But as the light fades, so do most colors. To create a garden you can enjoy on *your* schedule, plan a planting of white flowers and silvery foliage. These beauties will catch any light that's available— they look especially great in moonlight! An evening garden is really nice next to a deck, porch, or patio, where you can relax and enjoy your flowers before bedtime.

Glorious Grasses

Grasses aren't just for lawns anymore! Ornamental grasses come in all shapes, sizes, and colors, for sun or shade, wet soil or dry, so there's sure to be at least one that's perfect for your perennial garden.

 GRASSES FOR EVERY GARDEN

What can grasses do for you? Anything any other garden plant can do! Here are some great ways to work grasses into your yard:

Add them for seasonal interest. Some grasses look best in spring, others show off in summer, and still others put on a great show in fall. There are even grasses with evergreen foliage or long-lasting seedheads for winter!

Enjoy them as screens. Tall-growing grasses are super as temporary hedges. They also work well for providing warm-weather privacy around swimming pools, decks, and patios.

Grow them for wildlife shelter and food. If you enjoy having birds visit your yard, grasses are a must-have! Besides providing excellent shelter, some grasses produce seeds that wild birds will enjoy feeding on all winter long.

Include them in beds and borders. The narrow leaves of grasses make a great textural contrast to broad-leaved perennials, such as hostas. Variegated grasses add color, and tall-growing grasses provide height.

Plant them along paths. Low-growing grasses are excellent

Siberian iris
Iris sibirica

A border favorite for early summer, with graceful blue, purple, or white flowers

TOP 10 **Grasses for Fall and Winter Interest**

Blue oat grass (*Helictotrichon sempervirens*)

Feather reed grass (*Calamagrostis* x *acutiflora*)

Flame grass (*Miscanthus* 'Purpurascens')

Fountain grass (*Pennisetum alopecuroides*)

Japanese blood grass (*Imperata cylindrica* 'Red Baron')

Japanese silver grass (*Miscanthus sinensis*)

Pampas grass (*Cortaderia selloana*)

Ravenna grass (*Erianthus ravennae*)

Switch grass (*Panicum virgatum*)

Wild oats (*Chasmanthium latifolium*)

choices for edging paths and walkways. They add lots of interest, without attracting bees to bother passersby!

Use them as problem solvers. If you have a tough spot, there's a grass to fill it. Slopes, wet spots, hot areas, dry sites—grasses can handle them all. Plus, grasses need minimal care to look their best!

TOOL TIME

Handheld pruning or grass shears will work just fine for cutting back smaller grasses in late winter. Larger grasses call for more powerful tools, like electric hedge shears, or even a power trimmer with a blade attachment. Before cutting, wrap a piece of twine around the clump, about a foot or two above the ground, to gather the leaves and stems together. That way, you'll have just one neatly tied bundle of grass to pick up when you're done, rather than a mess of scattered stems.

🌼 Easy and Pleasin'

Grasses that flower in spring or early summer (called cool-season grasses) seldom need any maintenance—just groom out any dead-looking leaves with a rake or your fingers. Later-flowering kinds (called warm-season grasses) look best if you cut their top growth down to about 4 inches in late winter.

🌼 Divide and Multiply

If your ornamental grass clumps die out in the center, dig them up and divide them. (Divide cool-season grasses in fall and warm-season grasses in spring.) Replant only the vigorous outer portions of each clump.

What if your grass is too big to dig up? Then use a spade to cut out pie-shaped wedges, and lift out only the wedges. (Fill the holes that are left with soil.) Or, use a post-hole digger to clean out the center of the clump, fill it with fresh soil, and set a small plant of the same type of grass in the middle to fill it in.

Siberian squill
Scilla siberica

Clumps of
starry, bright blue
blooms in early
to midspring

🌼 Made for the Shade

Everybody thinks of grasses for sun, but there are gorgeous grasses for shade, too. One group that's positively made for the shade is the sedges (*Carex*). These close relatives of true grasses come in a range of heights and leaf colors. The most popular choice for partial to deep shade and moist soil is Japanese sedge (*C. morrowii*). It forms dense mounds of slender, semi-evergreen leaves. Its cultivar, 'Variegata', has white-striped leaves; 'Gold Band' has yellow stripes. Japanese sedge is hardy in Zones 5 to 9. Two other great grasses for shade are golden hakone grass (*Hakonechloa macra* 'Aureola') and wild oats (*Chasmanthium latifolium*).

Wonderful Wildflowers

Bring the beauty of nature closer to home by adding some wildflowers to your yard. If you have lots of space, you might try a meadow planting to fill a sunny spot, or a woodland garden under a group of trees. Small gardens can have wildflowers, too—just tuck them into your existing gardens, and enjoy their beauty alongside their more cultivated cousins.

❋ EARLY RISERS

One special group of wildflowers is the early bloomers known as spring ephemerals. These delicate beauties emerge in early spring, do their thing, and then retreat back into the ground by midsummer. This makes them a perfect choice for planting under decidu-

JERRY'S GEMS

If you decide to purchase wildflower plants, make sure that they are "nursery propagated," meaning that someone has grown them in cultivation. Plants labeled merely as "nursery grown" or with no notes about their origin may have been wild-collected, stuck in a pot for a few weeks, and then set out for sale. Sure, they may be a little cheaper, but it's worth paying more for plants that were produced responsibly, without harming natural populations.

ous trees—you have a bounty of color in spring, and the plants will store up all the energy they need before the trees fully leaf out. Some of the most beautiful and easiest to grow spring ephemerals include bloodroot (*Sanguinaria canadensis*), May apple (*Podophyllum peltatum*), and Virginia bluebells (*Mertensia virginica*).

A tip: Because spring ephemerals die totally to the ground—leaves and all—make sure you intersperse them with ferns, hostas, and other perennials that will stay around to fill the empty spaces from midsummer on.

SHADY CHARACTERS

Want to add some wildflowers to your shady garden? Then consider these key points:

๛ Most woodland wildflowers grow best in light shade—with a few hours of morning sun or with dappled shade all day.

๛ Adequate moisture is a must for most, so be prepared to water them well during extended dry spells.

๛ Good drainage is critical, too. Soggy soil will cause delicate wildflowers to rot.

๛ Shade-loving wildflowers thrive in humus-rich soil, so work plenty of compost into the soil before planting, and mulch with chopped leaves through the year.

FIVE STEPS TO A MAGNIFICENT MEADOW

Want to try your hand at a meadow garden? It's easier than you think! With a little work up front and some patience afterward, you'll enjoy a great-looking addition to your yard,

Silvermound
artemisia
*Artemisia
schmidtiana*

Dense, rounded mounds of lacy silver leaves

that'll attract wildlife, as well. Follow these simple steps:

Step 1. Choose the right site. Perennial meadow wildflowers do best with lots of sun (at least six hours of full sun a day) and relatively infertile soil. Most prefer well-drained conditions and can even take some drought, although there are fine choices for wetter sites, too.

Step 2. Prepare the site. First, remove the existing weeds and grass by spraying with an herbicide or by smothering them with sheets of clear plastic for a few weeks during the summer.

Step 3. In fall or early spring, rake the area lightly to scratch up the surface. Scatter the seeds over the area, then rake again, and water to mix them with the soil.

Step 4. Water lightly, but often during the first three to four weeks, to encourage good germination. Pull any weeds that appear.

Step 5. Each year, mow your meadow in the fall or early spring. During the growing season, keep after the weeds. By the third year, your perennial wildflowers should be coming into their flowering glory, and they'll just keep getting better each year after that!

Perfect Perennials

FOR SUNNY MEADOWS

Bring the beauty of nature to your backyard with a meadow planting of these pretty, sun-loving perennials.

Bergamot (*Monarda fistulosa*): Shaggy heads of lavender-pink flowers in mid- to late summer. Zones 3 to 9.

Black-eyed Susan (*Rudbeckia hirta*): Dark-centered, golden daisies from summer into early fall. Zones 3 to 9.

Butterfly weed (*Asclepias tuberosa*): Clusters of orange or yellow flowers in midsummer. Zones 3 to 9.

Gayfeathers (*Liatris*): Fuzzy spikes of purplish pink flowers from mid- to late summer. Zones 3 to 9.

Goldenrods (*Solidago*): Clusters of golden yellow flowers in late summer and fall. Zones 4 to 9.

New England aster (*Aster novae-angliae*): Showy blooms in shades of purple, pink, or white in fall. Zones 3 to 8.

Purple coneflower (*Echinacea purpurea*): Rosy pink daisies from midsummer to fall. Zones 3 to 9.

PART 4

LIGHT UP YOUR LIFE

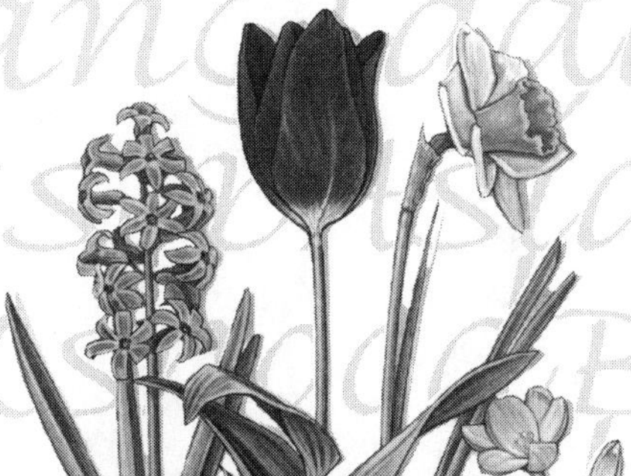

WITH BULBS!

CHAPTER 14

BULB BASICS

Bulbs are flowers-in-waiting—prewrapped packages
of leaves and flowers ready to burst into bloom.
The good news is that bulbs are practically
foolproof. However, even the most experienced green
thumbers can use a little refresher course on how to
get the best from these beautiful bloomers.

Tuber U

"Bulb" is a general term that describes a large group of very different plants, including true bulbs, corms, tubers, tuberous roots, and rhizomes. What do all of these plants share? They all have the ability to store food in specialized, underground parts. This stored energy lets them grow fast when conditions are right, and it helps them breeze right through the tough times (such as dry spells), when they are dormant.

'Single Early' tulip

Tulipa 'Single Early'

Classic midspring tulip with goblet-shaped blooms in a wide color range

 WHAT'S IN A BULB?

According to the experts, a **true bulb** is actually a stem that's been flattened into a platelike structure. Roots emerge from the bottom of the plate. On top of the plate are fleshy, scalelike leaves surrounding an embryonic flower bud. There are two types of true bulbs:

Tunicate bulbs have leaf scales that are closely wrapped around the flower bud. If you cut a true bulb (like an onion) in half, you'll see distinct rings formed by the tightly packed leaves. Tunicate bulbs are generally covered by a dry, papery shield called a tunic. Examples include daffodils, tulips, and hyacinths.

Imbricate bulbs have thicker leaf scales that are much more loosely arranged, and they normally don't have any sort of covering. Lilies are imbricate bulbs.

Two bulb-related terms you're likely to see are **bulblets** and **bulbils**. Bulblets are small new bulbs that form underground around a bulb. Bulbils are small new bulbs that appear aboveground, where the leaves join the stem.

CORM FORMS

A **corm** is a swollen, underground stem base that's a solid mass of storage tissue. (If you were to slice through it, you wouldn't see any rings.) Roots grow from the base, and

Try This!

Tulips, daffodils, and other bulb flowers are the stars of the spring garden. But even "yardless" gardeners can enjoy colorful spring flowers in containers suited for entryways, decks, patios, and balconies. Other great early bloomers for pots include crocuses, hyacinths, and grape hyacinths (*Muscari*).

Once the weather heats up, keep the show going by filling containers with summer-blooming bulbs. Tuberous begonias (*Begonia* Tuberhybrida Hybrids) and caladiums (*Caladium bicolor*) are perfect for pots in shady spots, while cannas, dahlias, and lilies really light up sunny spots in summer.

growth points (or eyes) on the upper side produce top growth. Corms are usually covered by dried leaf bases from the previous season's growth.

As a corm sends up leafy growth and flower stems, its stored food is used up, and the corm shrinks. A new corm then forms on top of the old one. Additional small corms—called cormels or cormlets—form around the base of the corm. Examples of corms include crocuses, gladiolus, and freesias.

TUBER, OR NOT TUBER?

Tubers are kind of like corms, but they don't have any sort of covering. Their growth points are scattered over their surface (not just on the top), and both their roots and their shoots come from these "eyes."

Some tubers, such as those of caladiums (*Caladium bicolor*), shrink as the season goes on, then produce new tubers. Hardy cyclamen (*Cyclamen*), tuberous begonias (*Begonia* Tuberhybrida Hybrids), and other tuberous plants have tubers that keep expanding in size from year to year.

THE ISSUE OF THE ROOT

One more specialized structure is the **tuberous root**. Unlike a tuber, which is stem tissue, tuberous roots are swollen roots that are modified to store food. (They also produce fibrous roots that do normal root things, like absorbing water and nutrients.) Growth points can be scattered all over the surface, but they're usually gathered where the previous year's stem joined the roots. Dahlias have tuberous roots; so do daylilies (*Hemerocallis*).

▭ RHIZOME WISDOM

Another type of modified stem is called a **rhizome**. It is a thickened stem that grows horizontally. Roots grow from the bottom half of the rhizome, and shoots develop from growth points on the upper side. Calla lilies (*Zantedeschia*), cannas, and bearded irises are all examples of rhizomes.

Sneezeweed
Helenium autumnale

An abundance of yellow, orange, or red daisylike flowers for the fall garden

Delightful Dutch Dandies

A flower garden just isn't complete without a few bulbs. It's super-easy to plant a few tulips or daffodils in fall, and you'll be rewarded with an abundance of blooms to celebrate the return of spring. But that's just the beginning—there are dozens of other great bulbs that bloom all through the growing season, so you can have fabulous flowers and foliage nearly all year long!

▭ GO WILD WITH BULBS

Blooming bulbs offer a wide variety of colors, heights, and flowering periods. Since bulbs are easy to grow, let your imagination run wild as you plan your garden. Here are some tips for success with bulbs:

❧ Note the blooming period for each bulb you want to grow. Plant

MAKING ¢ents If you're lucky enough to get some potted bulbs as a gift, don't toss them out when they're finished flowering! Treat them like any other houseplant (lots of light, regular feeding, and occasional fertilizing) until after the last frost date, then plant them in your garden. It may take a year or two for them to flower again, but then they'll return, year after year, to grace your garden with their beauty.

shorter, early-blooming bulbs among tall, late-season flowers. The late bloomers will camouflage the withered foliage after the shorter flowers have faded.

❧ If your garden or planters are visible from indoors, try using bulbs that bloom in colors that complement your curtains or porch decor.

❧ Plant scattered clusters of early-flowering bulbs, such as crocuses, throughout your lawn to get that "natural" look.

Hardy bulbs need low temperatures to develop good roots and buds. So don't mulch them too early, or you'll cause premature leaf growth, which will weaken them. New plantings of tulips and daffodils benefit the most from mulching once the ground is frozen; older beds, in milder climates, really don't need it.

HIDDEN TALENTS

The only downside to bulbs is that some go dormant soon after they bloom. Fortunately, there's a simple solution to the problem of ugly, dying foliage—camouflage it. Plant your bulbs among some bushy perennials, or fill in around them with annuals. The foliage of the annuals or perennials will hide the yellowing bulb leaves, and no one will be the wiser!

Snowdrop
Galanthus nivalis

Welcome spring with these nodding white blooms; dependable and trouble-free

KEEP 'EM HIGH AND DRY

For a glorious spring display, plant spring-flowering bulbs in the fall. They thrive in full sun, but will actually do just fine in almost any location, as long as the soil is well-drained. Bulbs will rot in standing water, so avoid planting them in areas of your yard that are prone to flooding, like at the bottom of a hill.

LAYER BULBS FOR LONGER BLOOM

Got a small garden? Increase your flower power by layering your bulbs to get two, three, or even four times the flowers from the same amount of space!

Simply dig a hole about 10 inches deep, then plant

large bulbs, like lilies or giant onions (*Allium giganteum*). Replace enough soil to barely cover those bulbs, then set in slightly smaller bulbs, such as tulips. Add more soil, then maybe some grape hyacinths (*Muscari*) or dwarf daffodils; cover them, too. If you have room, finish up with a layer of small bulbs, such as crocuses. In spring, scatter seeds of sweet alyssum (*Lobularia maritima*) or some other annual over the area, and you'll have a bounty of beauty to enjoy for months on end!

▸ ANTI-SQUIRREL STRATEGY

You carefully planted a bunch of bulbs yesterday, and today, they're scattered all over the garden. What's the story? Probably squirrels! It's not so much the bulbs that they're after; it's the loosened soil that seems to attract them like a magnet.

To deter these pesky critters from digging up your new bulbs, lay some chicken wire over the area immediately after planting, and cover it with mulch. You can remove the wire any time the following year; squirrels don't seem to dig established bulbs.

▸ WHICH END UP?

Have you ever held a bulb in your hand, turning it this way and that, trying to figure out which is the top and which is the bottom? Just about every one of us at one time or another will plant a bulb the wrong way around. While setting a bulb upside down won't kill it, it does put the new shoot at a disadvantage, because it has to reverse course to grow up and out.

With some bulbs and tubers, it's anyone's guess as to which is the top and which is the bottom, but for most,

Mixers & Elixirs

BEST BULB DEFENSE

To defend your bulb beds from slithering snakes, mix up a batch of this sandy send-off:

1 part builder's sand
1 part diatomaceous earth

Mix the ingredients together and sprinkle a 3-inch-wide band around the area to be protected. Snakes won't dare cross this rough stuff. Now that's what I call drawing a line in the sand!

there's an obvious difference. The top of a bulb comes to a point (either blunt or sharp), while at the base, there is usually some sign of roots or a basal plate from which the roots originate. Remember—look for the nose, not the toes, and plant your bulbs "heads up"!

Bulbs Look Best in Bunches

The biggest mistake people make when planting bulbs in fall is to plant one bulb here and one bulb there, not realizing how sparse they're going to look come spring. Whether you're planting 20 bulbs or 200, you'll get the biggest bang for your gardening buck by planting them close together in groups!

WELCOME, FRIENDS!

When you're looking for more places to tuck in some bulbs, don't forget your foundation plantings! The traditional evergreen shrubs around the base of a house provide year-round form and height, although not much in the way of visual interest. But when you add bulbs, these boring beds will come to life with color, creating a much more welcoming face for your home.

If your home has a formal front, choose formal-looking bulbs, like hybrid tulips (*Tulipa*) and Dutch hyacinths (*Hyacinthus orientalis*). Or complement a more cottagey-type home with drifts of daffodils (*Narcissus*), clumps of crocus, or an abundance of ornamental onions (*Allium*).

Snowdrop anemone
Anemone sylvestris

Snow-white flowers and deeply cut green leaves in spring; spreads by creeping roots

CHAPTER 15

YEAR-ROUND BULBS

Sure, everyone thinks about bulbs for spring, and
why not? These beauties are among the earliest
risers after winter loosens its grip, and they keep
the show going all through the spring. But don't
let the fun stop there—keep the color coming
with summer- and fall-flowering types, too!

Small Bulbs to Welcome Spring

Great things come in small packages! These diminutive darlings have dainty, but durable blooms that laugh at chilly temperatures, and even laugh in the face of snow!

▸ TIMING COUNTS

Getting a great display of bulbs in spring takes a little advance work—namely, you've got to plant in the fall. In the North, early to midfall is the best time to get spring-flowering bulbs in the ground; in the South, midfall to early winter is the ideal season.

TOP 10 Bulbs for Early to Midspring

Dutch crocus (*Crocus vernus*)

Glory-of-the-snow (*Chionodoxa luciliae*)

Grecian windflower (*Anemone blanda*)

Reticulated iris (*Iris reticulata*)

Siberian squill (*Scilla siberica*)

Snow crocus (*Crocus chrysanthus*)

Snowdrops (*Galanthus nivalis*)

Spring snowflake (*Leucojum vernum*)

Striped squill (*Puschkinia scilloides*)

Winter aconite (*Eranthis hyemalis*)

▸ 'SNO JOKE

Some of the earliest bulbs to make their appearance can bloom even through the snow. Get the spring season off to a fast start with either or both of these beauties:

❧ **Snowdrops** (*Galanthus*): Nodding white blooms marked with green appear among grasslike leaves. Giant snowdrops (*G. elwesii*) grow 5 to 8 inches tall; common snowdrops (*G. nivalis*) are only about 4 inches tall. Partial shade; moist, but well-drained soil, enriched with compost. Zones 3 to 9.

❧ **Winter aconite** (*Eranthis hyemalis*): These compact buttercup relatives produce cupped yellow blooms and green rufflike leaves on 2- to 3-inch-tall stems. Full sun to partial shade; moist, but well-drained soil, with added compost. Zones 4 to 9.

PLANT 'EM PROMPTLY

It's best to plant bulbs as soon as possible after you bring them home. If you find yourself with unplanted bulbs after cold weather has arrived, plant them anyway, because they won't keep indoors until next year. I've often found that if you put them into the ground, they're likely to surprise you by flowering in the spring.

ANEMONES, ANYONE?

Say hello to spring with the delightful daisylike blooms of Grecian windflowers (*Anemone blanda*). The white, pink, or blue flowers appear atop 6-inch-tall stems, clad in ferny green leaves in early to midspring. Soak the rhizomes in warm water overnight, then plant them about 3 inches deep in fall. Give them a site with partial shade and moist, but well-drained soil, enriched with compost. Zones 4 to 8.

BREAK THE RULES WITH BULBS

Usually, you want to put short plants near the front of your flowerbeds and tall plants near the back. But I suggest you break that rule when it comes to siting small bulbs in your garden. Go ahead and plant them near the back of beds and borders. By the time the perennials come up, the bulbs will be finished flowering, and the perennial foliage will cover up the yellowing bulb leaves.

EASY EARLY IRISES

Iris lovers rejoice—you don't have to wait for summer to enjoy your favorite flowers. The group of tiny treasures known collectively as reticulated irises (because of the net-

Try This!

Here's a super-smart tip to try: Plant small bulbs—such as crocus and 'Tête-à-Tête' daffodil—so they'll come up through the foliage of low-growing perennials, like bugle-weed (*Ajuga reptans*). The leaves of the perennial will help hold up the bulbs when spring winds blow. Plus, they'll keep soil from splashing up on the flowers when April showers fall!

Snow-in-summer
Cerastium tomentosum

Carpets of woolly-white leaves sprinkled with white blooms in early summer

tinglike covering on their bulbs) produce their fragrant blooms in late winter and early spring. Plant them 3 to 4 inches deep in fall, in a sunny spot with humus-rich, well-drained soil. Here are two to try:

✔ Danford iris (*Iris danfordiae*): Yellow flowers on 3- to 5-inch-tall stems. Zones 5 to 8.

✔ Reticulated iris (*I. reticulata*): Blooms in shades of purple and blue on 6-inch stems. Zones 3 to 8.

When spring bulbs start peeking above the surface, scatter some all-purpose fertilizer around them. And if spring showers are lacking, make sure you water to keep the soil from drying out—at least until the bulb leaves wither away.

▸ THREE'S A CHARM

Spring is a super season for blue blooms, thanks to several early bulbs that are small in size, but big on charm. All three of these appreciate a site with full sun to partial shade and average, well-drained soil:

• Glory-of-the-snow (*Chionodoxa luciliae*): Starry, light purplish blue flowers with lighter centers atop 4- to 6-inch-tall stems. Zones 3 to 9.

• Siberian squill (*Scilla siberica*): Deep blue, nodding blooms on 6- to 8-inch-tall stems. Zones 4 to 8.

• Striped squill (*Puschkinia scilloides*): Looks much like Siberian squill, but the blooms are very pale blue with darker blue stripes. Zones 3 to 9.

▸ YOU CAN FOOL MOTHER NATURE

If you want to see your bulbs bloom a bit earlier than nature intended, plant your spring-flowering bulbs in a warm, sunny spot, such as against a wall. The result? Beautiful blooms a week or two earlier than usual.

If, on the other hand, you want to *delay* the bloom time, plant your bulbs in a cooler spot, such as on a northern hillside.

SAY CHEESE!

I love spring bulbs, but once they die back to the ground, I have a devil of a time remembering where I've planted them! If you have the same problem, here's a tip: Take lots of pictures of your garden in spring. That will give you a permanent record of where the bulbs are, so when it comes time to plant more in the fall, you can dig without worrying about disturbing your established bulbs.

Bigger Bulbs for Mid- to Late Spring

Of course, spring wouldn't be the same without daffodils, tulips, and other larger, colorful spring bulbs. These Dutch dandies are the perfect partners for early-flowering perennials!

GRAPE IDEAS

You want dependable? You want colorful? Then you want grape hyacinths (*Muscari*)! These vigorous bulbs often start sending up leaves in late fall, but that's nothing to worry about; even if the leaf tips get a bit nipped by the cold, the flowers will still appear in abundance in midspring. They look spectacular planted in masses, especially in curving drifts to create a streamlike effect. Or pair them with multicolored Double Early tulips for a knock-your-socks-off burst of bright color.

   Grape hyacinths thrive in full sun or partial shade and compost-enriched, well-drained soil. Plant them in fall,

Solomon's plume
Smilacina racemosa

Shade-loving, with arching stems tipped in fuzzy white plumes in late spring

Solomon's seal
*Polygonatum
biflorum*

White bells dangle
below gracefully
arching stems in
spring; superb for
shady areas

3 to 4 inches deep. Several species are available, but they
are all pretty similar, with clusters of grape-shaped, purple-
blue blooms atop 6-inch-tall stems. Grape hyacinths are
hardy in Zones 4 to 9.

SOME BULBS WON'T WAIT

Don't keep tulips, daffodils, or hyacinths past the fall season to plant in spring. They need a long period of cool temperatures to put down their roots before they will bloom, so
they *must* be planted in the fall to bloom properly the following spring.

CHOOSE THESE BLUES

Ring in spring with a bounty of bluebells! These trouble-
free bulbs form generous clumps of clustered, bell-shaped
blooms in shades of blue, pink, or white. Plant the bulbs 3
inches deep, in a spot with full sun or partial shade and
moist, but well-drained soil, enriched with compost.

☑ **English bluebells** (*Hyacinthoides
non-scripta*): Lavender-blue
bells dangle from gracefully
arching 8- to 12-inch-tall
stems. Zones 4 to 9.

☑ **Spanish bluebells** (*H. hispanica*): Purple-blue flowers
atop upright, 10- to 12-inch-
tall stems. In bulb catalogs,
you may see this beauty listed
under a number of botanical
names, including *Endymion
hispanicus, H. campanulata,
Scilla campanulata,* and *S. hispanica.* Pink- and white-flowered cultivars are also available. Zones 4 to 9.

Mixers & Elixirs

TEA TIME FOR APHIDS

Aphids start showing up near the end of spring,
and they love lush bulb shoots. If these pests are
bugging your bulbs, give them a sip of this tantalizing "tea":

½ cup of parsley flakes
2 tbsp. of minced garlic
3 cups of water

Mix all of the ingredients together, and boil down
to 2 cups. Strain and cool. Put two cups of the tea
in your 20 gallon hose-end sprayer, and apply to
your beds and borders.

CROWNING GLORY

If you like your bulbs big and bold, you'll *love* crown imperials (*Fritillaria imperialis*)! They're kind of pricey, but they're not the sort of bulbs you plant by the dozens—just three crown imperial bulbs create a can't-miss garden accent. The bottom half of each 3- to 4-foot-tall stem bears whorls of slender, bright green leaves; the upper half is crowned with orange, yellow, or red bells topped with a tuft of more leaves.

You can remove the faded flowers from bulbs, but don't you dare touch the foliage! It needs to stay in place until it withers to provide the bulbs with food for next year's flowers.

Crown imperials thrive in full sun or partial shade and moist, but well-drained soil in Zones 5 to 8. Set them about 8 inches deep, and plant them on their sides so water doesn't collect on and rot the bulbs. I do have to tell you one more thing—crown imperials have a strong scent that some describe as pleasantly musky and others call *eau de skunk*. Either way, it's probably best to plant them away from your house, so you can see them, but not smell them!

Super Summer Blooms

Most people think about bulbs for spring, but summer's also a super time to enjoy bulbs in your beds and borders. This is the season for some of the biggest and brightest blooming bulbs, including lilies (*Lilium*) and gladiolus, to name just two!

TOUGH OR TENDER?

Summer-blooming bulbs are kind of a mixed bag. Some of them, like lilies, are hardy in most climates (meaning you

**Spanish
bluebells**
*Hyacinthoides
hispanica*

Easy and
dependable, with
nodding blue,
pink, or white
bells in spring

plant them in fall or spring, and leave them in the ground year-round). Others are cold-tender, so if you live north of Zone 8, you'll plant them in spring and dig them up in fall, for winter storage indoors. Examples of tender bulbs include cannas and dahlias.

PERFECT PERUVIAN LILIES

If you enjoy indulging in florist flowers, you may already be familiar with Peruvian lilies (*Alstroemeria*). The multi-petaled, funnel-shaped blooms come in a wide range of colors, including shades of orange, pink, salmon, red, and white, usually with deep red striping on the upper petals. They obviously make great cut flowers, but they're also great in the garden, usually growing 3 to 4 feet tall.

Plant the bulbs about 8 inches deep, in full sun or light shade and humus-rich, moist, but well-drained soil. They appreciate a summer mulch and regular watering. They'll overwinter in the ground in Zone 7 and south, and they may even live over in Zone 6 with a generous winter mulch. Elsewhere, dig them up in fall and store the bulbs indoors for the winter.

Mixers & Elixirs

BULB SOAK

Prepare bulbs, tubers, and corms for planting by soaking them in this solution:

1 can of beer
2 tbsp. of dishwashing liquid
¼ tsp. of instant tea granules
2 gal. of water

Mix all of the ingredients together in a large bucket, and carefully soak the bulbs into the mix before planting.

BE A CANNA FAN

If you can't get to the tropics for your summer vacation, bring the tropics to your garden—with cannas! These brassy beauties bear broad, 1- to 2-foot-long leaves that may be plain green, bluish green, deep purple, or striped with yellow or white. As they bloom through the summer, they send up strong stems that can be anywhere from 2 to 6 feet tall, with huge, showy blooms in shades of red, yellow, orange, pink, or coral. These heat-lovers thrive in full sun and moist, but well-drained soil. Rich soil and ample moisture will encourage the lushest growth.

▷ PUT CANNAS IN THE CELLAR

In Zone 7 and south, cannas usually overwinter outdoors just fine. Elsewhere, cut the plants down to within 6 inches of the ground when the foliage has been nipped by frost. Then dig them up without making any special effort to shake the soil loose from the roots. Pack the plants close together with sand around them in shallow boxes; place them in a cellar or room where the temperature stays between 40° and 50°F. Take a look at your cannas occasionally during the winter, and if they look a bit shriveled, moisten the sand just slightly.

▷ SUMMER BELLS

Summer hyacinths (*Galtonia candicans*) may not look much like their spring-flowering cousins, but their late-summer flowers are equally welcome in the garden. Summer hyacinths grow 3 to 4 feet tall, with spikes of scented, pure-white bells, at a time when many other flowers have given up for the season. Their fragrance and light color make them ideal for planting around decks or patios, where you relax on late summer evenings. They look great in containers, too!

Give summer hyacinths full sun and evenly moist, but well-drained soil. Plant them in spring, about 8 inches deep. In Zone 6 and south, the bulbs will overwinter fine with some winter mulch. In colder areas, dig up the bulbs in fall, and store them indoors for the winter.

BEST BULBS FOR SUMMER BLOOM

Tuck some of these bulbs into your beds and borders, then expect a spectacular summer show of color!

Crocosmia (*Crocosmia*): Sprays of bright orange or red flowers. Zones 6 to 9.

Foxtail lily (*Eremurus*): Brushy spikes of yellow, pink, or white blooms. Zones 6 to 9.

Honey garlic (*Nectaroscordum siculum*): Clusters of nodding pink and white bells. Zones 4 to 9.

Lilies (*Lilium*): Trumpet-shaped blooms in a wide range of colors. Zones 4 to 8.

Ornamental onions (*Allium*): Tiny purplish, pinkish, or white flowers in rounded clusters. Zones 4 to 9.

Pineapple lilies (*Eucomis*): Spikes of cream-colored to pinkish flowers topped with a tuft of leaves. Zones 6 to 9.

Spike gayfeather
Liatris spicata

Fuzzy spikes
of pinkish purple
flowers in summer;
great for cutting
or border accent

▭ SPRING INTO SUMMER

Give summer bulbs a jump on the growing season by starting them indoors in early to midspring. Fill 6- to 8-inch-
wide pots halfway with potting soil. For dahlias, put one
clump of tuberous roots in each pot. With tuberous begonias (*Begonia* Tuberhybrida Hybrids) and smaller lilies, you
can fit three or five bulbs per pot; larger lily bulbs and caladiums (*Caladium bicolor*) may fit only three or even just one
bulb per pot. Add more potting soil so the bulb tips are just
covered, and moisten with water.

Set the planted pots under plant lights, on a warm and
bright windowsill or on a sunny and warm enclosed porch.
Water as needed to keep the soil from drying out. Once outdoor temperatures are dependably above 50°F, even at
night, the bulbs can go outside. Carefully remove them from
their pots and plant them in the garden, or leave them in
their pots and slip them into a showier display pot to enjoy
them as container plants.

Flowers for Fall

**The cooler days of fall tell us that the growing season is
coming to a close, but they also bring on a final bounty
of bulb blooms for gardeners to enjoy.**

▭ FALL FUN WITH ONIONS

Most ornamental onions are outstanding for early summer
gardens, but a few species put off their display until later in
the year. Like their earlier-flowering relatives, these onions

love full sun and do fine in average, well-drained soil. Here are two to try:

🌿 **Curly chives** (*Allium senescens* var. *glaucum*): This cutie produces clusters of pink flowers atop 6- to 8-inch-tall stems from late summer into early fall. My favorite part, though, is the nearly evergreen, blue-gray leaves that are twisted, creating swirling clumps. Zones 5 to 9.

🌿 **Garlic chives** (*A. tuberosum*): This one's a beauty—and mighty tasty, too! It produces dense clumps of edible green leaves accented with rounded clusters of starry white, fragrant flowers from late summer to midfall. It's a snap to grow from seed—in fact, I suggest you pinch off the spent flowers, or you'll have lots of garlic chives popping up in your garden! Zones 4 to 8.

📣 THESE GLOVES FIT, SO WEAR THEM!

Even if you're one of those folks who don't normally wear gloves while gardening, bulb-planting time is a good time to change your habits. Your hands can get pretty grubby planting bulbs, and in some cases, the bulbs themselves can irritate your hands. I find disposable gloves are a good solution: They're inexpensive, they're good at keeping your hands clean, and they're form-fitting enough that you can easily pick up even small bulbs without fumbling. Buy a small box of these gloves in the painting-supplies section of your local hardware store, and you'll have plenty for years to come!

📣 DON'T CROAK—PLANT CROCUSES!

Put your fall garden in the pink by planting autumn crocuses (*Colchicum autumnale*) as summer comes to a close. These late bloomers aren't related to spring-flowering crocuses, but they do share similar-looking flowers. Autumn crocuses send up their 1-foot-long, green straplike leaves in spring; the foliage yellows and dies back in early summer. It isn't until early fall that the 6-inch-tall, pink flowers appear.

Look for these bulbs for sale in late summer, and plant them immediately. (If you delay, the bulbs may actually flower in your house, and this can weaken them.) Set them about 3 inches deep in a site with full sun or light shade and average, well-drained soil. Keep in mind that the big spring leaves can smother daintier companions, and then leave a gap in the garden when they die back. So it's smart to plant them around the base of shrubs, or where they can come up through a low-growing groundcover. They do best in Zones 4 to 8.

TOP 5 — Bulbs for Fall Flowers

Autumn daffodil
  (*Sternbergia lutea*)

Crinums (*Crinum*)

Hardy cyclamen
  (*Cyclamen hederifolium*)

Showy crocus
  (*Crocus speciosus*)

Spider lily
  (*Lycoris radiata*)

Spotted
bellflower
*Campanula
punctata*

White to pink
nodding summer
bells, spotted
inside with
purple or red

🔊 GREAT LATE BLOOMERS

Besides autumn crocuses, a fair number of other fall-flowering bulbs send up their foliage in winter or spring, and their flowers in fall. All of them adapt to full sun or light shade and average, well-drained soil. Scatter these seasonal surprises among your shrubs, or naturalize them in grassy areas—just remember that you can't mow until midsummer, when the leaves die back, and you have to stop mowing again when the flower buds appear.

✔ Magic lily (*Lycoris squamigera*): Also called surprise lilies, these bear rose-pink trumpets in clusters atop 2-foot-tall stems in late summer to early fall. Zones 5 to 8.

✔ Naked ladies (*Amaryllis belladonna*): Clusters of fragrant pink trumpets appear atop 2- to 3-foot-tall stems in late summer and early fall. Zones 7 (with winter mulch) to 10.

✔ Nerine (*Nerine bowdenii*): Eighteen-inch-tall stems topped with funnel-shaped pink flowers in fall. Zones 8 to 10.

CHAPTER 16

A Bulb for Every Bed and Border

Bulbs are a snap to grow, so they're super
for beginners, and they're versatile enough to
excite even the most experienced gardener.
What more could you ask for?

A Rainbow of Colors

If bright blooms are your bag, then bulbs belong in your garden! They come in every color you can imagine, so you're sure to find at least one that's perfect for every spot.

Bulbs for Knock-Your-Socks-Off Color

Asiatic lilies (*Lilium* Asiatic Hybrids)

Cannas (*Canna*)

Crimson flag (*Schizostylis coccinea*)

Crocuses (*Crocus*)

Crown imperial (*Fritillaria imperialis*)

Daffodils (*Narcissus*)

Gladiolus (*Gladiolus*)

Ornamental onions (*Allium*)

Persian buttercup (*Ranunculus asiaticus*)

Tulips (*Tulipa*)

DUTCH DARLINGS

Dutch irises (*Iris* Dutch Hybrids) are my favorite spring bulbs for bringing indoors as cut flowers. Their beautiful white, yellow, purple, blue, or bicolor blooms open atop sturdy 1- to 2-foot-tall stems—which make them perfect for formal arrangements or casual bouquets.

    Don't depend on last year's Dutch irises for a good show in the garden, though. Chances are, they won't bloom well—or maybe not at all—their second year. But, if you plant new bulbs each year in early spring, you'll be sure to have top-notch blooms in just a few weeks!

A HONEY OF A BULB

Spotted calla lily
Zantedeschia albomaculata

Cupped blooms in white, cream, or yellow with a dark throat; silvery spotted leaves

Here's a bulb with a difference! Known as honey garlic (*Nectaroscordum siculum*, also called *Allium siculum*), it's a true beauty, with nodding, bell-shaped flowers that bloom in early to midsummer. Each bloom is delicately shaded with cream, pink, and green, creating an elegant mother-of-pearl color that you just can't get from any other plant. Plant this bulb where it will come up through bushier companions, because its leaves die back about the time the flowers open. Give it full sun to light shade and average, well-drained soil in Zones 6 to 9.

BUTTER UP YOUR GARDEN

Can't-miss color and big, bold blooms make Persian butter-cups (*Ranunculus asiaticus*) the stars of the spring or summer garden. The ruffled, petal-packed flowers come in a range of rich colors, including rousing red, glowing gold, bright pink, clear orange, and pure white. Warm-climate gardeners can plant these tubers in fall for early color; in cooler climates (Zone 6 and north), plant them in spring for summer excitement. They make super container plants, too!

Persian buttercups die back quickly after they flower, so be sure to plant them with annual or perennial companions that will fill in by midsummer. In Zones 7 through 10, they may come back a second year, but for the biggest blooms, plant new tubers each year.

ALL THAT JAZZ

Colorful bulbs are super for livening up boring sites, such as expanses of paving—like along a driveway. They also sparkle against bland-colored walls, such as stucco and neutral-colored siding. You'll be amazed at how a handful of bulbs can really jazz things up!

JERRY'S GEMS

Bulbs don't need a lot of fancy food, and they don't demand—or even particularly like—hard-to-get gourmet items. When I plant my bulbs, I work a handful of my Bulb Breakfast (see page 60) into the soil in each hole before setting in the bulb. Or, you can use a handful of compost and a teaspoonful of bonemeal instead. The only other feeding I give my bulbs is in early spring. When I notice they've begun to stick their noses out of the ground, I spread a handful of all-purpose garden food (4-12-4 or 5-10-5) over the soil. That's all there is to it!

BASIC BLACK

If you're looking for a real conversation piece in your garden, look no further than Persian fritillary (*Fritillaria persica*). This odd duck sends up 1- to 3-foot-tall stalks topped with spring spikes of nodding, dusky purple flowers that are just about as close as you can get to black in bulbs. It prefers full sun and average, well-drained soil in Zones 5 to 8. Set a clump of these bulbs against a light background; otherwise, the dark blooms will blend in and be nearly impossible to see!

Fabulous Bulbs for Fragrance

Sweet or spicy, fruity or flowery—bulbs offer all these scents and more! Adding fragrant bulbs to your beds and borders is a great way to enjoy their aromas in and around your home.

GLADS TO MAKE YOU HAPPY

Like the look of gladiolus flowers, but wish they packed a bit more perfume? Try Abyssinian gladiolus (*Acidanthera bicolor* var. *murielae*, also sold as *Gladiolus callianthus*). In late summer to early fall, they produce spikes of pure white, funnel-shaped blooms with chocolate-colored center markings. Their blossoms are beautiful, but that's not all—just a few flowers can perfume your whole garden as well. Abyssinian gladiolus also grow well in pots, and they make great cut flowers, too.

Plant these tender bulbs about 6 inches deep in spring, a few weeks before the last frost date for your area. Give them a spot in full sun with average, well-drained soil. When the leaves start to die back, dig up the bulbs, and store them indoors, as you would for regular gladiolus.

DELIGHTFUL DAFFODILS

If you're like me, you love the cheerful spring blooms of daffodils—both in the garden and in indoor bouquets. If there's

Spotted geranium
Geranium maculatum

Pretty woodland wildflower with loose clusters of pink or white flowers in spring

one downside to daffodils, though, it's that most of them have little or no fragrance. When you want bright color *and* fragrance, turn to the group called jonquils (*Narcissus jonquilla* and its cultivars). These gorgeous, golden-bloomed bulbs have a rich perfume that carries far and wide. 'Sundial' is a real cutie, with nearly flattened cups. For a softer color, try pink and white 'Bell Song' or ivory-colored 'Curlew'.

FREESIAS FOR FREE

Fabulous freesias are a common sight in flower shops, but you can also grow these colorful, sweetly scented blooms in your own garden. Plant the corms about 2 inches deep after all danger of frost has passed. (Make another planting three to four weeks later for blooms through the summer.) Unless you live in a frost-free area, dig up the corms in fall, and store them indoors for the winter.

LILIES MAKE SCENTS

Lilies are a must-have for anyone who loves fragrant flowers. Watch out, though—not all lilies are created equal! The widely grown Asiatic Hybrids come in a wide range of bright colors, but they're duds when it comes to perfuming the air. For good fragrance, check out some of the lesser-known lilies, like the summer-blooming Trumpet or Aurelian Hybrids. These beauties usually have clustered, outward-facing or nodding, trumpet-shaped flowers in shades of red, pink, orange, yellow, and white. Oriental Hybrids bloom slightly later—toward the end of summer—and typically have flat-faced, star-shaped flowers in shades of red, pink, and white (often with darker spots).

One word of warning, though: If you're sniffing lilies

MAKING ¢ents Fragrant bulbs produce some of the best loved—and most expensive!—florist flowers. You can save a bundle by growing these beautiful bulbs right in your own backyard. Tuck a few into a corner of your vegetable garden for cutting; add them to flowerbeds to enjoy in your yard; or plant them in pots to perfume a deck, porch, or patio. For just pennies a bulb, you can have all the fragrant flowers you'll ever need!

My Grandma Putt just adored fragrant flowers, so tuberoses were tops on her list. This old-fashioned favorite is still hard to beat for perfumed blooms, so if you like fragrance, too, you need to give tuberoses a try.

These Mexican natives hate cold soil, so in all but the warmest climates, you'll need to do what Grandma did: Plant them 3 inches deep and 8 inches apart in mid- to late spring, and dig them up again in fall for indoor storage. An even easier option is to plant them in pots, then just bring the containers into a frost-free spot for the winter.

in the garden, watch that you don't stick your nose too close to the pollen-covered anthers. (The anthers are those powdery-looking bits that dangle from the end of short stalks in the middle of the blooms). Otherwise, you're likely to have a nice coating of bright red or orange pollen on your snout! And, if you bring the blooms indoors, cut off the anthers, so they don't drop pollen and stain your furniture.

Spring starflower
Ipheion uniflorum

Late-spring blooms in many shades of blue; trouble-free

Perfect Bulbs for Pots

Here's a novel idea—instead of planting all your bulbs in the ground, try putting some in pots! You'll have no more hassles digging planting holes or worrying about critters chewing up your buried bulbs. When the bulbs are in bloom, move them to an area where you'll see and enjoy them; when they're finished, simply set them out of sight, and replace them with newer bloomers!

BUILD UP YOUR BULBS

To get even more bang from your container bulbs, plant them on top of each other! Even a relatively shallow pot (about 6 inches deep) can hold two layers of bulbs; deeper planters (at least 10 inches deep) can support four layers, or even more!

Layering bulbs is super-simple: Just spread at least 3 inches of potting soil over the bottom of the pot, then set in the largest bulbs. Add more potting soil to barely cover them, then add a layer of the next smallest bulbs. (You can set the bulbs much closer in pots than out in the garden; an inch or so of space in between is fine.) Keep going until the tips of the smallest bulbs are within an inch of the pot's rim. Top with more potting soil to cover the tips, water well, and set the pot in a sheltered place outdoors for the winter. Come spring, you'll have months of flowers to look forward to!

OUT OF AFRICA

Give your pots and planters the blues with a heaping helping of African lilies (*Agapanthus*). These tropical-looking beauties produce clumps of rich green, straplike leaves and leafless stalks topped with clusters of trumpet-shaped blue (or sometimes white) flowers through the summer season. Most African lilies are hardy only south of Zone 7, so if you live in a colder climate, growing them in pots makes bringing them indoors a snap!

CALLING ALL CALLAS!

Calla lilies (*Zantedeschia*) make spectac-ular container plants, even when they aren't in flower. Their arrowhead-shaped leaves are typically deep green and glossy, and they often have showy white speckling. Their fas-cinating summer flowers almost look fake, due to their odd

Try This!

Want to spruce up a plain clay pot to suit some special bulbs? Here are a few fun ideas:

• To give a bright new terra cotta pot an aged look, spray it with sour milk and set it in a shady, out-of-the-way spot for a few weeks. Pretty soon, you'll see moss starting to grow on it!

• Cover the outside of a clay pot with acrylic primer, then paint it the color of your choice. Experiment with fun effects, like painting contrasting stripes, or dabbing on different colors with pieces of sponge or old wadded-up socks.

• Gather pebbles (or buy a bag of aquarium gravel) and attach them to the outside of a clay pot with clear silicone adhesive. Cover the whole pot in random patterns, or create a design of your choice.

shape—essentially a deep cup (called a spathe) with one side pulled out into a flattened "lip" and a yellowish upright spike (called a spadix) in the center. The spathe is usually white or bright yellow, but can also be pink or reddish orange.

Give calla lilies full sun, and water them regularly to keep the potting soil evenly moist. Fertilize every two to three weeks to encourage best growth and flowering. North of Zone 9, bring potted calla lilies indoors before frost, and store them in a cool, dry spot for the winter.

TOP 10 Bulbs for Pots and Planters

Caladiums (*Caladium bicolor*)

Cannas (*Canna*)

Crocuses (*Crocus*)

Daffodils (*Narcissus*)

Dahlias (*Dahlia*)

Grape hyacinths (*Muscari*)

Hyacinths (*Hyacinthus orientalis*)

Lilies (*Lilium*)

Tuberous begonias (*Begonia* Tuberhybrida Hybrids)

Tulips (*Tulipa*)

RUN WITH THE BIG BULBS

You might not think of tall-growing bulbs like lilies and cannas for containers—but why not? If you have a large planter, like a wooden half-barrel, a few large bulbs shooting up from the middle can make a great centerpiece. The trick is to tuck some bushy and trailing plants (like verbenas) into the same pot, so they'll cover up the often-boring bulb stems, and provide color when the bulbs aren't in bloom.

Shady Solutions

It's true—most bulbs simply love the sun. But don't despair if your yard's mostly on the shady side; there are beautiful bulbs for you, too! Some are designed to make good use of whatever sun they can get, while others actually prefer some shade.

⌦ EARLY BULBS CATCH THE SUN

Spring-blooming bulbs are a perfect choice for gardens that are heavily shaded by trees in summer. These early risers send up their flowers and leaves while sun is plentiful, storing all the energy they need for next spring's show. By the time the tree leaves start blocking out the sun, the bulbs are finished for the year, and their leaves die back. The site could be totally dark until the following spring, and the bulbs wouldn't care, because they are snug as a bug in a rug, underground!

Squirrel corn
*Dicentra
canadensis*

Wildflower with
white spring
hearts, ferny
foliage; dies back
after flowering

BEST BULBS FOR SHADY SPOTS

If your garden runs on the shady side, give these beautiful bulbs a try!

Caladiums (*Caladium bicolor*): Large, heart-shaped green leaves heavily marked with red, pink, or white. Zone 10 (grow as an annual elsewhere).

Checkered lily (*Fritillaria meleagris*): Nodding, creamy white or deep purple blooms with darker markings. Zones 4 to 8.

Daffodils (*Narcissus*): Showy yellow or white spring blooms with yellow, white, pink, or orange center trumpets. Zones 4 to 9.

English bluebell (*Hyacinthoides non-scripta*): One-sided spikes of nodding, bell-shaped blue flowers in spring. Zones 4 to 9.

Hardy cyclamen (*Cyclamen*): Heart-shaped, deep green leaves heavily mottled with silver, and pink or white flowers in either fall or early winter. Zones 6 to 9.

Italian arum (*Arum italicum*): Arrowhead-shaped green leaves that are heavily mottled with creamy white appear in fall and die back by midsummer. Zones 5 to 9.

LET THERE BE LIGHT (BULBS)

In shady spots, light-colored bulb blooms show up much better than rich, deep hues. White, pale yellow, and pink flowers really leap out of the gloom; so do bulbs with white-marked leaves, such as caladiums (*Caladium bicolor*). Blue-flowered bulbs can look great in shade, too, but you really need to plant them in masses (in clumps of at least a dozen) in order for them to stand out—otherwise, they'll just blend into the background.

DON'T KEEP 'EM IN LINE

Straight lines are fine for a formal effect, but for a shady woodland garden, a more natural approach is the way to go. So, instead of planting your shade-loving bulbs in rows or blocks, scatter 'em around in random-looking drifts or irregularly shaped groupings. That will make it look like the bulbs just popped up on their own!

Orchids outdoors? You bet! Unlike the fussy indoor orchids that need lots of pampering, Chinese ground orchid (*Bletilla striata*) is tough enough to grow right in your garden. In spring and early summer, this shade-loving beauty sends up 1- to 2-foot-tall stems topped with clusters of bright pink or white flowers. Best of all, it can overwinter outdoors with no extra fuss in Zones 7 to 9. If you're willing to give it some winter mulch, Chinese ground orchid can survive outdoors, year-round, as far north as Zone 5! And it makes a super container bulb as well. What more could you ask for?

WINNING WILDFLOWERS

Here's a group of bulbs that are absolutely made for the shade! As a kid, I knew these woodland wildflowers under a bunch of different names: dogtooth violets, adder's tongues, fawn lilies, and trout lilies. Whatever you call them, they're real beauties. Unlike many bulbs, dogtooth violets (*Erythronium*) produce foliage that's as pretty as their flowers: broad green leaves that are dotted with brown or cream spots.

Plant the oddly shaped roots as soon as you get them. They like to

be set deep, so dig a generous hole about 8 inches deep.
Work several handfuls of compost into the planting hole,
then plant the roots upright (not on their sides). Hardy in
Zones 3 to 9, dogtooth violets don't need any special care to
thrive, and they'll come back better and better every spring!

Fantastic Foliage

**Terrific tulips, dazzling daffodils, cheerful crocuses—when
you mention the word "bulbs," it's their bright blooms
that come to mind. But believe you me—some bulbs produce leaves that are every bit as pretty as their flowers!**

SHADY CALADIUMS

You can't talk about bulbs with fabulous foliage without
mentioning caladiums (*Caladium bicolor*). These tropical
beauties produce showy clumps of huge, heart-shaped
green leaves that are heavily spotted, netted, or veined
with varying amounts of white, pink, red, and maroon.
They need warmth to thrive, so start the tubers indoors in
pots two to three months before your last frost date. Wait
until all danger of frost is past before you plant them in
partial shade with evenly moist, well-drained soil. Dig the
tubers up in fall, and store them indoors in a warm, dry
place until starting again in spring.

SPOTS AND SPECKLES

Sure, you grow tulips for their beautiful flowers. But since
the foliage is around for several weeks longer than the flow-

Star-of-
Bethlehem
*Ornithogalum
umbellatum*

Green-striped,
white spring
flowers open in
the afternoon,
close at night

ers, choosing tulips with good-looking leaves gives you much more excitement for no extra effort.

My favorite foliage-interest tulips are the Greigii Hybrids, which have maroon striping and/or speckling on their leaves. 'Red Riding Hood', with rich, red blooms on 6-inch-tall stems, is an easy one to find. Other hybrids occasionally have white striping on their foliage. The Triumph tulip 'New Design', for example, offers yellow-flushed salmon-pink flowers on 20-inch-tall stems with white-edged leaves.

I'm sure you've heard the saying, "The bigger the bulb, the bigger the flower." Well, let me share a little secret with you—sometimes bigger isn't necessarily better! It all depends on how you plan to use the bulbs in your landscape. Bigger bulbs work best to accent walkways or to plant around lamp posts, and in any other areas that will be seen up close. Put smaller bulbs to better use in mass plantings, especially those that will be seen from a distance.

A WINNER FOR WINTER

Here's a plant that sure has things backwards! Italian arum (*Arum italicum* 'Pictum') emerges from below-ground tubers in fall, forming a 1- to 2-foot-tall clump of amazing, arrowhead-shaped, deep green leaves heavily marbled with creamy white. It looks, for all the world, like you left one of your tropical houseplants outside for the winter!

In spring, Italian arum sends up interesting hooded flowers to bloom among the leaves. As summer approaches, the leaves die back to the ground, until the only parts left standing are the stalks of bright Christmas-red berries in July—neat!

Italian arum grows best in Zones 5 to 9, in a spot with spring sun and summer shade. It likes humus-rich soil and lots of moisture, so keep it well mulched with compost, and water it during dry spells.

CRAZY FOR CYCLAMEN

Don't confuse handsome, hardy cyclamen (*Cyclamen*) with the cold-tender kind sold as a potted gift plant; the tougher species can survive outdoors as far north as Zone 5 with some winter mulch. *C. hederifolium* sends up its heart-shaped, deep green, silver-mottled leaves in mid- to late fall, and the foliage looks great all through the winter. The leaves finally die back by early summer, so the pink, early-fall flowers appear without any leaves in sight. *C. coum* is similar, but it blooms in late winter or early spring, above the leaves. Both species thrive in partial shade and humus-rich, well-drained soil.

MAKING ¢ents

Tropical-looking cannas (*Canna* x *generalis*) are some of the best bulbs for super summer foliage (and flowers too, of course). But buying new plants of the best colored-leaved cannas every year can really break the bank—costing $10, $15, or even more for a single rhizome! Fortunately, there's no reason to buy your favorite cannas more than once; these cooperative plants multiply readily, and are easy to overwinter indoors where they aren't hardy (Zone 7 and north). You need only a small piece to get started, so you may even be able to beg or trade with a gardening friend, and get started for free!

Go Wild!

Planting bulbs in random, irregularly spaced drifts in grassy areas or under trees is certainly not a new idea— Mother Nature has been doing it for thousands of years! But it's worth rediscovering this age-old technique— which we now call naturalizing—to bring a touch of natural beauty right to your backyard.

CREATIVE CROCUSES—AND MORE

If you want to get creative with your landscape and not have everything all tidily arranged in beds and gardens, try planting crocuses, Siberian squill (*Scilla siberica*), and other small

Summer hyacinth
Galtonia candicans

Tall, summer-blooming spikes of white flowers; nice in beds, borders, and large pots

Sundrops
Oenothera fruticosa

Glowing yellow
cups open from
red-tinged buds in
summer; great for
hot, dry sites

bulbs right in your lawn. That's right, *in* your lawn! They
provide lots of early spring color, and when they're done
blooming, you simply mow the tops off. They'll return the
following year almost without fail. Now that's what I call
low-maintenance landscaping!

GIVE 'EM A FIGHTING CHANCE

You'll have the best luck with naturalized bulbs if you plant
them where the lawn is fairly sparse, such as under trees.
Thick turf can be tough for bulbs to push up through!

MOWING MATTERS

Keep in mind that you'll need to wait until the bulb leaves
start turning yellow before you mow, and that may not be
until early summer. By then, the grass can get pretty tall.
You're best off keeping naturalized bulbs in less visible
areas, such as a side yard or a wooded
area, so you're not tempted to trim
off their leaves before they have
stored all the energy they need for
next spring's show.

TINY TURF TREASURES

Some lawn grasses, like buffalo grass,
look great in warm weather, but turn
brown soon after the first frost. To
spruce up the boring, off-season turf,
tuck in a bunch of small, spring-blooming bulbs, such as reticulated iris (*Iris
reticulata*) and lady tulips (*Tulipa clu-
siana*). The bulb leaves will make the
lawn look green earlier, and the slower-
growing turf will be ready for its first
mowing right about the time the bulb
leaves die back.

TOP 10

Bulbs for Planting in Grass

Daffodils (*Narcissus*)

Grape hyacinths (*Muscari*)

Grecian windflower (*Anemone blanda*)

Lily leek (*Allium moly*)

Showy autumn crocus (*Colchicum speciosum*)

Showy crocus (*Crocus speciosus*)

Siberian squill (*Scilla siberica*)

Snowdrops (*Galanthus*)

Spanish bluebells (*Hyacinthoides hispanica*)

Summer snowflake (*Leucojum aestivum*)

DON'T DROP 'EM!

You'll often hear the advice to toss your naturalized bulbs onto the ground, then plant them where they fall. The theory is fine—this way, the bulbs will fall at natural-looking random spacings. But in practice, dropping bulbs on the hard ground can bruise them, leading to rot later on—definitely a bad return for your efforts! You'll get much better results if you hand-place your bulbs where you want them to grow.

GIVE ME AN H!

With tiny bulbs, like crocuses, you'll save lots of time by planting them in small groups, rather than individually. Use a spade or edging tool to cut a 6- to 8-inch-long slit in the turf, then cut two more equal slits at each end of the first to make an "H." Peel back the two flaps of turf (the top and bottom of the "H"), plant a handful or two of bulbs in the exposed soil, then replace the flaps of turf and step on them to settle them back in place.

> **TOOL TIME**
>
> Need to make lots of little bulb-planting holes in a hurry? A big, old screwdriver, or a similar-looking weeding tool, called an asparagus fork, is the perfect tool. Just jam it in the ground, swirl it around a few times, and *voilà*—instant hole!
>
> For setting out a few daffodils, tulips, and other large bulbs, a trowel makes a handy tool for scooping out individual planting holes. But if you have a whole bunch of bulbs to plant, speed up the process by using a bulb auger—a corkscrew-like bit that attaches to a handheld power drill. You'll be glad you did!

CHAPTER 17

CLASSIC BULB
FAVORITES

Even if you don't grow any other bulbs, you
need to give these old standbys a try. There are
all kinds of reasons why they're so popular:
They're easy to find, they're easy to grow,
they're reasonably priced, and best of all, their
flowers are *absolutely fantastic!*

Crocus Hocus-Pocus

The perky blooms of petite crocuses are a surefire sign of spring. Even if more snow falls, these sturdy little bulbs don't miss a beat—they'll keep on flowering anyway! Crocuses like a site with full sun and do fine in average, well-drained soil.

Switch grass
Panicum virgatum

Tall ornamental grass with gray- or blue-green foliage that turns yellow in fall

BLOOM AND GROW THROUGH THE SNOW

As a group, crocuses are among the first bulbs to flower in spring, and the species called snow crocus (*Crocus chrysanthus*) is the very earliest of the early bloomers. These little gems often make their appearance in late winter, poking their 2-inch-tall blooms through the last of the snow and ice. You'll usually see the corms sold as a cheerful combination of mixed colors, but you can often find single colors if you buy bulbs by mail order. 'Blue Bird', for example, is cream-colored inside the bloom and purplish blue on the outside; 'Goldilocks' is bright yellow with deep purple markings.

LET 'EM LOOSE IN YOUR LAWN

Looking for a different way to enjoy crocuses in your garden? Try planting them in your lawn! They'll spruce up the turf in late winter and spring, then their grasslike leaves will blend right into the real grass. Many crocuses are great for this technique—called naturalizing—but one of the best is *C. tommasinianus*. Its 3- to 4-inch-tall pale to reddish purple blooms show up well against the grass, and its corms multiply readily, so you'll have more and more flowers as the years go by. Just make sure you wait until the crocus leaves turn yellow before you mow, so they have a chance to store plenty of food for the following year. For more tips on naturalizing bulbs, see "Go Wild!" on page 301.

> **Try This!**
>
> Tired of squirrels digging up your newly planted crocus corms? Baby those bulbs by dusting the area with baby powder, after planting, to keep the pesky critters at bay.

DUTCH DANDIES

Crocuses are all pretty compact, but the biggest of the bunch are the Dutch crocuses (*Crocus vernus*). They bloom in early to midspring, with 4- to 5-inch tall flowers in white, yellow, or shades of purple. Like snow crocuses, Dutch crocuses are most often sold as mixed colors, and they look great all together in bloom. But, if you prefer single colors, you can get those, too. 'Yellow Mammoth' (also sold as 'Dutch Yellow') has good-sized bright yellow flowers. 'Joan of Arc' ('Jeanne d'Arc') is pure white, while 'Pickwick' has white blooms striped with purple.

SPRING FLOWERS IN FALL

We normally think of crocuses for spring color, but did you know that there are fall-flowering crocuses, too?

That's right! There are several late-blooming species, but some have a reputation for being a little fussy. *C. speciosus* is a good one to start with, because it's fairly adaptable to different growing conditions and climates. It looks very much like the typical spring species—large, purple-blue or white, yellow-throated blooms up to 6 inches tall—but it sends up its flowers in September and October.

Look for fall crocus corms for sale in late summer, and plant them as soon as you get them; they'll flower in just a few weeks! They're hardy in Zones 3 to 8, so just leave them in the ground, and they'll come back better every fall!

MAKING ¢ents

Guess what—you can grow the world's most expensive spice right in your yard! I'm talking about saffron crocus (*C. sativus*). The small red parts (called stigmata) in the center of each rich purple, 2-inch-tall bloom are the source of saffron—a spice used to add yellow coloring and delicate flavoring to foods, including rice and noodle dishes.

Plant saffron crocus corms as soon as you get them in late summer for bloom the same year. They like lots of sun, and well-drained soil is a must. They are hardy in Zones 5 to 8. When they flower, pick the red stigmata, dry them, and store in an airtight glass container for later use.

Darling Daffodils

Delightful and dependable—that's what daffodils (*Narcissus*) are! These trouble-free bulbs are hardy just about everywhere, tolerate just about any growing conditions, and don't have any pests or diseases to speak of—plus, they make great cut flowers. Plant them once, and daffodils are sure to brighten your spring for many years to come.

Tall bellflower
Campanula americana

Blue flowers atop
3- to 6-foot-tall
stems in
late summer

TIPS FOR TOP-NOTCH DAFFODILS

I consider daffodils to be no-fail bulbs, because it's nearly impossible to have bad luck with them. In fact, you'll often see clumps of daffodils coming up where the home they originally surrounded has long since disappeared—the bulbs have outlasted the people who planted them! Here are some tips to help you make the most of these easy bulbs:

🌱 Daffodils like full sun, but can take partial shade; in fact, sites under deciduous trees are ideal!

🌱 A spot with moist soil in spring is fine, but avoid sites where water sits in winter; daffodils absolutely hate cold and soggy soil.

🌱 Avoid planting daffodils as individuals—they look best when they're planted with their buddies in groups of a half-dozen bulbs or more.

Grandma Putt's WISDOM

*D*affodils look super in spring, but then you have the ugly yellowing foliage hanging around to look at for several weeks. Well, my Grandma Putt had a simple solution for that—she'd plant her daffodils with later-rising perennials, like daylilies (Hemerocallis), hostas, and ferns. The new perennial shoots did a great job covering up the dying daffodil leaves, and Grandma got twice the flowers from the same amount of garden space!

HERE COMES THE SUN

A daffodil-lined path or patio is truly a beautiful sight—*if* it gets sun from all sides. But here's something you might not know: Daffodil flowers like to face the sun, so if they're shaded on one side, they'll turn toward the light. That could mean that most or all of the flowers are facing directly away from you. So, if possible, plant daffodils where the shade is behind them, so they'll face you instead!

> **Try This!**
>
> Wire clothes hangers make perfect stakes for propping up floppy daffodils (and other bulbs, too). Fold the triangular base in half (so the two corners are together), then squeeze tightly to form a post with a hook sticking out of one side. If needed, tie the post with string or wire to keep it together. Now, bend the hook to one side so that it can curve around the stem of a bulb flower that needs some support. Shove the post into the ground next to the plant, and you're all set.

DIG DEEP

For the biggest blooms, don't skimp on daffodil planting holes. Set the bulbs about three times as deep as the bulbs themselves are tall. For example, if a bulb is 2 inches tall, set it 6 inches deep.

DAFFODIL DYNAMOS

Daffodils come in an amazing array of flower forms: with long center trumpets, short cups, or practically no cup at all. There are even double-flowered daffodils, with petal-packed centers, instead of cups or trumpets. I love them all, but my favorites are the ones that produce multiple flowers on each stem. Most daffodils come one flower per stem, but with multiflowered (or cluster-flowered) daffodils, you get anywhere from 2 to 20 flowers from a single bulb! Multiflowered types include the Triandrus cultivars (such as pale yellow 'Hawera' and pure white, fragrant 'Thalia'); the Tazetta cultivars (such as orange and white, fragrant 'Geranium'); and the super-scented Jonquilla cultivars (like white 'Curlew' and rich yellow 'Quail').

GIMME A D!

Searching for something different for your spring garden? Look no further than hoop petticoat daffodil (*Narcissus bul-*

bocodium). This little cutie may be small in size—it grows only 6 inches tall—but it's certainly big on charm! Its name comes from the curious large-cupped flowers, which some people apparently think look like an old-fashioned hoop skirt. To me, the flowers look more like mini-megaphones, shouting out cheers for spring. Hoop petticoat daffodils are hardy in Zones 4 to 8.

Glorious Glads

The beautiful bulbs known as gladiolus (*Gladiolus*)—or glads—certainly give you lots to be happy about! Each easy-to-plant corm sends up a sturdy stalk, topped with funnel-shaped blooms with satiny petals in nearly every color imaginable. They're gorgeous in the garden, and even better as cut flowers.

WINTER CARE FOR GORGEOUS GLADS

The common, large-flowered glads (*G.* x *hortulanus*) are actually capable of surviving winter temperatures as low as 0°F, as long as they're protected with a 3- to 6-inch layer of mulch, like partially rotted leaves. But most folks dig up their glads whenever the foliage begins to turn color, or when it has been killed by frost. Leave the tops attached until they become brittle; then you can easily remove them, along with the loose scales and withered corms of the preceding year. Spread the plants out in shallow boxes or paper grocery bags, and keep them in a dry place between 40° and 50°F until spring.

Tall gayfeather
Liatris scariosa

Dense spikes of pale purple blooms in mid- to late summer; a butterfly magnet

THEY'LL THANK YOU FOR YOUR SUPPORT

When your glads start poking up through the soil, give them a dose of 5-10-5 fertilizer (at a rate of 1 cup per 25 feet of row), then water to wash the fertilizer into the soil. When the spikes are about a foot tall, they'll need some kind of support. Either stake them, or mound up 4 to 6 inches of soil around the base of the stems.

THWART THRIPS

The main pest of glads are tiny insects called thrips, which cause off-color streaking on petals and silvery markings on the leaves. If your gladiolus have been attacked by thrips, dig up the corms, brush off any loose soil, then place them in paper bags along with 2 tablespoons of mothball crystals for every 100 corms. Twist the mouth of the bag closed, and keep them at about 70°F for three or four weeks. Then remove the corms and store them as described in "Winter Care for Gorgeous Glads" on page 309.

You'll usually find the corms of common glads for sale in spring. Set the smallest corms (those less than ½ inch in diameter) about 3 inches deep; the largest corms (over 1 inch across) about 6 inches deep; and the medium-sized corms 4 to 5 inches deep. And here's a bonus tip: To have flowers over a longer period, don't plant all the corms at one time. Plant a handful to start, then another batch two weeks later. Keep going at two-week intervals from midspring through midsummer, and you'll have waves of blooms to enjoy all summer long!

GLAD TO BE BACK

For glads that come back dependably, year after year, without any extra fuss, try hardy gladiolus (*G. byzantinus*). They grow only 2 to 3 feet tall (shorter than the usual 4-foot-tall common glads), so they never need staking, and they're dependably hardy in Zones 5 to 10. These easy-care cuties bloom in late spring to early summer, with deep green leaves and eye-catching magenta flowers that are sometimes striped with pink or white.

GLADS FOR FREE!

Want to grow more of your favorite glads? It's easy to do! When you dig up the corms in fall for winter storage, break off the withered, old corms and discard them; then pick off the small cormels that have formed around the new corms. When you replant the following spring, put the fattest corms back in the spotlight, and plant the small cormels about an inch deep in a nursery bed or a corner of your vegetable garden. Dig them up in fall, then replant the now-larger cormels 2 inches deep the next spring. By their third year, they'll be big enough to take center stage!

Mixers & Elixirs

KNOCK 'EM DEAD TONIC

Get rid of whatever's bugging your bulbs with this surefire insect killer:

6 cloves of garlic, chopped finely
1 small onion, chopped finely
1 tbsp. of dishwashing liquid
1 qt. of warm water

Mix all of the ingredients together, and let the mix sit overnight. Strain out the solids, pour the liquid into a handheld sprayer, and blast the bugs dead!

Three-lobed coneflower
Rudbeckia triloba

Dark-centered yellow daisies bloom for 2 months or more atop 2- to 5-foot-tall stems

Lovely Lilies

To get the most from your lilies, you need to treat them well, right from the start. Give them a little tender loving care, and you'll be rewarded with lovely lily blooms year after year.

LOCATION, LOCATION, LOCATION

I just love lilies; they're the darlings of my flower garden. If you've never had the pleasure of tending to these beauties, you may not realize that you need to choose their location very carefully to ensure good growth. Here's what they need to get off to a good start:

Perfect drainage: A gentle slope will do. If your site is level and your soil is heavy, you need to build raised beds for the bulbs.

Every time Grandma Putt sent me out to plant lily bulbs, she'd come with me to make sure I picked a good planting spot. She had two special rules: Never plant new lily bulbs where other lilies failed to grow, and never plant them in soggy soil. Where the soil was a little on the heavy (clay) side, she'd have me tilt the bulb a bit in the planting hole, so water didn't collect between the scales of the bulb and cause them to rot.

Air circulation: A good breeze can keep many garden pests and diseases away from your lilies.

Sunlight: At least 6 hours a day of sunshine. Filtered sunlight or semi-shade brings out the more delicate colors, but makes for weak stems and soft flowers. Don't plant lilies near walls, walks, or driveways that reflect sun or heat.

Torch lily
Kniphofia uvaria

Late-summer show-offs with orange and yellow flower spikes

DON'T DELAY

Lily bulbs are never completely dormant, so it's critical to get them back into the ground as soon as possible after you buy them or dig them up. If the bulbs you buy are slightly limp, place them in moist peat moss for a few days. They'll soon freshen up, and you should then plant them immediately.

MORE MULCH, PLEASE!

Lilies love a good mulch of well-rotted cow manure, rich compost, or decaying leaf mold. Keep it nice and thick by applying it several times during the growing season. The mulch keeps the soil cool, discourages weeds, and eliminates the need for surface cultivation, which might hurt the stems of your growing lilies.

CONSIDER THE LILIES

Lots of people mistakenly refer to the common orange roadside daylily (*Hemerocallis fulva*) as tiger lily. The roadside daylily first sends up a clump of straplike leaves, then, in early July, nonleafy flower stems topped with orange, trumpet-shaped blooms that each stays open only one day. Commonly known as tawny daylily, ditch lily, and many other names, this plant is a very vigorous spreader.

The real tiger lily (*Lilium lancifolium*, also known as *L. tigrinum*) is a bulb that blooms around the same time. It sends up a single 4- to 5-foot stalk topped with several flowers. The petals are bright orange with dark speckles, and the petals curve backwards. Look for black mini-bulbs that form where each leaf joins the stem—they're another clue that you've found a true tiger lily.

The secret to keeping your lilies strong and healthy is to feed them two or three times during the growing season. Scatter a handful of balanced fertilizer every few feet, along with a pound of wood ashes every 20 square feet.

If your soil and water are alkaline, then scatter a pinch or two of agricultural sulfur over the soil, and water it in two or three times during the growing season. Also, work a handful of peat moss into each planting hole. It is slightly acidic, which is ideal for lilies.

PERFECT PARTNERS

Lilies tend to bloom atop tall stems, so plant them where they can rise up through bushy companions to hide their "bare ankles." Their bright blooms look especially good against a darker background, such as a hedge, fence, or wall.

Terrific Tulips

These big-bloomed beauties are perfect for bridging the gap between the small spring bulbs and the sun-loving, big bulbs of summer. Here are some of my best tips for top tulips!

🚩 GET 'EM IN THE GROUND

Get your tulip bulbs in the ground as soon as you can after the first hard frost. For best blooms, year after year, from the large-flowered types, dig deep—work the soil to a depth of 18 inches—then set the bulbs 10 inches deep and 6 inches apart. Shorter, smaller-flowered "species" tulips don't need such deep planting; 3 to 6 inches is fine.

🚩 MOISTURE MATTERS

Don't let the soil around your tulips dry out while they are growing. Generally, they need about an inch of water a week. A soaker hose works best, so you don't get water on the leaves or flowers (which can lead to discolored petals or disease problems).

🚩 CHANGE THEIR BEDS

Take a tip from the pros: Don't plant tulips in the same bed for more than three years in a row. Repeated plantings in the same soil, year after year, are an open invitation to diseases, such as fire blight. After three years, either change the location of your tulip bed for two or more years, or replace all of the soil in the current bed.

MAKING ¢ents

Where winters are on the warm side (Zones 8 to 10), you'll need to put a bit more thought into buying your bulbs. You see, most spring-flowering bulbs need some kind of winter chilling to grow and bloom properly, and they won't get that where the soil stays warm year-round. But instead of spending extra money on "prechilled" or "precooled" bulbs, save some dough and give them the cold shoulder yourself! Buy regular (non-cooled) bulbs, then stick them in your refrigerator for eight weeks before planting in late fall or early winter.

KEEP THE COLOR COMING

Love tulips, but hate having to replant them every year or two to get good blooms? Give species tulips a try! These cuties come in a wide range of heights, colors, and flower forms. Their smaller blooms aren't as dramatic as the large-flowered hybrids, but they are much more reliable for color year after year. Some of the best bets for surefire species tulips include *Tulipa batalinii*, *T. humilis*, *T. saxatilis*, and *T. tarda*.

HANDS OFF!

It's tempting to trim away tulip tops as they turn yellow—but don't do it! If you want top-notch blooms next spring, your bulbs need all the time they can get to store food for those flowers. Snap off the seedpods as you see them, but wait until at least half of the leaf surface has turned brown before cutting it off.

MORE FLOWERS, LESS LABOR

The classic, large-flowered tulips are true beauties, and spring just wouldn't be the same without them! But did you know that you can get two or three times the flowers from the same space if you try cluster-flowered tulips? Unlike large-flowered types, which produce one flower atop each stem, cluster-flowered types (often called bouquet tulips) can have anywhere from two to five blooms on each stem. Hybrids with multiple flowers per stem include 'Antoinette', which starts out yellow and ages to salmon, coral-colored 'Toronto', and rich red *Tulipa praestans* 'Fusilier'.

If you're tired of rodents treating your tulip bulbs like their own private snack bar, try this trick. When you plant, surround the tulip bulbs with a ring of daffodil bulbs! Besides providing extra color, the bad-tasting daffodil bulbs will keep critters at bay.

Tuberous begonia
Begonia Tuberhybrida Hybrid

Big-bloomed beauties flower for months; good for pots in shady spots

CHAPTER 18

A BOUNTY OF BULBS

With so many great bulbs to choose from, it's
tough to figure out just where to start. Sure, crocuses,
daffodils, glads, lilies, and tulips are the most popular,
and with good reason—they're downright beautiful when
they bloom! But don't stop with them—there are lots
more bulbs to brighten up your yard and gardens.

Amaryllis among Us

If you're easily addicted to things, you'd better *not* start growing amaryllises (*Hippeastrum*)! You'll get hooked, dollars to doughnuts, and before you know it, you'll have them blooming all over your house. But come to think of it, that's not such a bad thing after all!

Turk's-cap lily
Lilium superbum

Bright orange, purple-spotted flowers atop 4- to 6-foot-tall stems in summer

⬛ GET POTTED

When planting amaryllises in pots, make sure you start with a good-quality, rich potting soil. That way, you can expect to have a healthy plant for many years to come. Buy packaged potting soil, or mix equal parts of good garden loam, peat moss, and perlite or vermiculite to make your own. If you have any fertilizer (preferably 5-10-5) left over from your garden, stir a little into the potting soil before planting, but don't go overboard—a teaspoon per 6-inch pot is plenty! After planting, feed potted bulbs monthly with a liquid fertilizer at 10 percent of the recommended rate.

⬛ CONTAIN YOURSELF

When it comes to planting your amaryllis, you can use plastic, ceramic, or clay pots—your choice. I like brightly colored plastic ones myself, but you can still buy beautiful ceramic pots and jardinieres, as well as the old standbys—unglazed terra cotta pots. If you choose to use an unglazed pot, soak it in water overnight before planting, or it'll suck the water out of the potting soil and away from the bulb's roots. And, if you use hand-me-down pots, be sure to scrub them thoroughly with soap, hot water, and a touch of bleach, so your amaryllis bulbs won't catch any lingering germs.

JERRY'S GEMS

So, what do you do with your potted amaryllis bulbs once they're done blooming? I keep mine in their pots, and then sink them in the ground for the summer. Come fall, I cut the foliage back to 3 inches, lift the pots out of the soil, set them in a cool, dry area, and keep them damp (not wet). Pretty soon, the bulbs produce new growth, and they're back in bloom before I know what hit me!

 PUT THEM IN THEIR PLACE

I like to pot my amaryllis bulbs around September or October, but I've known folks who have successfully potted them right on up to spring. Amaryllises bloom best when they can crowd a pot with their large bulbs and roots, so don't give them too much elbow room. Set the bulb in place, spreading the roots carefully. Then add a little potting mix, and gently pack it around the bulb, making sure the bulb is centered in the pot. Keep filling and firming until the bottom two-thirds of the bulb are covered with soil. (Amaryllis likes to keep its nose clean, well above soil level.) Pat the soil down around the bulb, and water generously; then don't water again until new growth appears.

> **Grandma Putt's WISDOM**
>
> *To keep pests away from her houseplants, my Grandma Putt would sprinkle a few mothball crystals directly onto the soil surface in all of her pots. Why, in no time at all, the plants were bug-free! If you try this trick, make sure you keep the treated plants out of reach of children and pets.*

 THE TRUTH ABOUT AMARYLLIS

Twin-leaf squill
Scilla bifolia

Short spikes of delicate blue blooms for spring color in shady spots, under shrubs

If your amaryllis isn't producing blooms, it could be that you're giving it too much to drink—or giving it the cold shoulder. Overwatering is one of the fatal mistakes amaryllis growers make, and the result is a plant that fails to bloom. The other big mistake is not keeping your amaryllis in a warm place. Whatever you do, don't expose the bulb to below-freezing temperatures, or I can guarantee you that it will refuse to bloom.

Now, you may be discouraged by this picky plant, but once you get the hang of it, and give your amaryllis just the right water and temperature conditions, it will reward you with a bonus—baby bulbs! Since the amaryllis is a true bulb, you can collect the bulblets that develop beside the main bulbs, and grow lots of new plants from them. Now that's what I call a great return on your investment!

Awesome Onions

Want to spice up your flower garden? Then add some of the ornamental onions (*Allium*) to it! These fun and easy bulbs don't need a lot of fuss and muss—just give them full sun and average, well-drained soil. In return, their bright and colorful flowers will come back to delight you year after year.

⬤ GO FOR THE GLOBES

My favorites in this big group of bulbs are the giant onions (*A. giganteum*). They bloom in early summer, with grapefruit-sized globes of rosy purple flowers sitting atop sturdy flower stems that grow up to 4 feet tall. For a similar effect on a slightly smaller scale, check out Persian onion (*A. aflatunense*), with apple-sized globes of lavender-purple flowers on 3-foot-tall stems. Or, go to the other extreme with the hybrid 'Globemaster'—its rich, reddish violet spheres can be as big as a soccer ball! Best of all, these three look great for months after their flowers fade, thanks to their fascinating, long-lasting seedheads.

⬤ HOLY MOLY

If you want to enjoy ornamental onions as early as possible, try some of the spring-blooming species. Lily leek or golden garlic (*A. moly*) struts its stuff in late spring, with starry yellow blooms on 6- to 12-inch-tall stalks. If rosy pink flowers are

Try This!

Tired of losing track of your bulbs' names? Try any or all of these quick-and-easy label ideas!

🧅 Cut vinyl miniblind strips into 4- to 6-inch-long pieces with scissors, then write the names on one end of each with a pencil (not pen). Set them into the soil so that just a half-inch sticks out above the ground. They'll last for years!

🧅 Buy a box of tongue depressors at a craft shop. These wooden sticks will last a few years, and just one box will give you hundreds of labels for pennies apiece.

🧅 Save pieces of broken clay pots, and use permanent marking pens to jot the names on them. They're an interesting addition to the garden—and definitely different!

Mixers & Elixirs

HOT BUG BREW

Even ordinary garlic can make a great-looking addition to your flower garden. And after you've enjoyed the curiously curled flower stalks, you can dig up the cloves and concoct this super-duper pest spray!

3 hot green peppers (canned or fresh)
3 medium cloves of garlic
1 small onion
1 tbsp. of dishwashing liquid
3 cups of water

Purée the peppers, garlic, and onion in a blender. Pour the purée into a jar, and add the dishwashing liquid and water. Let stand for 24 hours, then strain out the pulp with cheesecloth or panty hose. Use a handheld sprayer to apply the remaining liquid to bug-infested bulbs and perennials, making sure to thoroughly coat the tops and undersides of all the leaves.

your preference, then you need 6-inch-tall *A. oreophilum* (also sold as *A. ostrowskianum*). Both are hardy in Zones 4 to 9.

GET A WHIFF OF THIS!

When you first cut the stem of an ornamental onion, make sure you hold your nose! It'll smell just like its humble relatives (onion and garlic). Fortunately, the odor disappears once the stem is in water. In spite of the scent, ornamental onions make excellent cut flowers—they come in a rainbow of colors, and they last a surprisingly long time in arrangements.

A GARDEN RAINBOW

Most of the best-known ornamental onions produce rosy purple blooms, but that's just the beginning—these beautiful bulbs come in many other colors, too! Here's a rundown of just a few:

Black onion (*A. nigrum*, also known as *A. multibulbosum*): Early-summer clusters of white blooms, each with a black center; grows 2 to 3 feet tall. Zones 6 to 10.

Blue globe onion (*A. caeruleum*): Dense globes of true-blue blooms on 1- to 2-foot-tall stems in June. Zones 3 to 8.

Drumstick allium (*A. sphaerocephalon*): Oval, golf-ball-size, red-violet flowers on 3-foot stems from late May through June. Zones 4 to 8.

Small yellow onion (*A. flavum*): Clusters of yellow flowers in July; grows 8 to 12 inches tall. Zones 4 to 9.

Beautiful Begonias

Looking for a colorful, graceful bulb with loads of flowers to light up a shady spot? If so, then tuberous begonias (*Begonia* Tuberhybrida Hybrids) are just the plants for you! They don't mind some sun in early morning or late afternoon, but at other times, indirect or dappled light is the order of the day.

RISE 'N' SHINE!

For the earliest possible begonia blooms, start the tubers indoors in late winter. Set them in flats or boxes of damp peat moss, and press them down (but don't cover them up). Keep them in a warm spot, such as on top of your refrigerator. Once the tubers sprout, transplant them to 6-inch pots. Wait until all danger of frost has passed before you move them outside.

If you don't mind waiting a few weeks for the flowers, you can start the tubers outdoors instead. Wait until the nighttime temperatures stay above 50°F, then set the tubers 1 to 1½ inches deep in soil that you've enriched with rotted manure or compost.

MAKING ¢ents If you want lots of tuberous begonias, you can save yourself a bundle of dough by growing them yourself from seed. These seed-grown hybrids (called 'Non-Stop' begonias) are vigorous and uniform, with an abundance of 3-inch semidouble flowers in a range of bright colors. Plus, they stay small and mounded—perfect for hanging baskets!

GIVE 'EM A GOOD SUPPORT SYSTEM

Tuberous begonia stems are pretty brittle, and they can snap under the weight of their huge blooms. To keep your plants from breaking, stake them right at planting time. That way, you won't accidentally spear the tuber with the stake if you try to insert it later. As the stem grows, tie it to the stake, every few inches, with strips cut from old panty hose. For extra protection, keep your begonias in a spot that's sheltered from strong winds.

Virginia bluebells
Mertensia virginica

Wildflower with pink buds opening to sky-blue bells; dies back after flowering

WATER WISELY

To keep those beautiful begonia blooms coming, keep the soil evenly moist; begonias absolutely hate to dry out. Also, apply a mild fertilizer, such as my Flower Feeder Tonic (see page 85), every two to three weeks during the growing season.

Most tuberous begonias have both male and female flowers. How can you tell the boys from the girls? Well, there's no need to turn them over—just look at them! The boys have the big, ruffly double blooms, and they're usually flanked by a smaller, single girl bloom on each side. To help the showy boy flowers last longer, pinch off the girls; that'll keep your begonia from wasting energy on seeds.

ROOM TO GROW

Besides rot (usually due to soggy soil), mildew is the main problem that can bother tuberous begonias. To prevent problems, avoid crowding the plants together; they need good air circulation around the leaves and stems. Lightly misting the leaves with water each morning can also help keep your plants healthy and happy.

BABY THOSE BEGONIAS

When frost threatens, it's time to bring your tuberous begonias indoors. If you're growing them in pots, you can store them in the same pots; just let the soil dry out, and keep them in an area that stays around 50°F through the winter.

If your begonias are growing in the ground, dig them up before the first frost, and pack them close together in a shallow box with soil around their roots. When the tops have withered, remove the tubers, and dust them with sulfur. Pack them in a shallow, topless box with leaf mold or peat moss around them, and keep them in a dry 50°F location for the winter.

GET AN EARLY START

Tuberous begonias grow best when the days are warm and the nights are fairly cool. If you live in an area where the

summers are stifling hot, but the winters are mild, try starting your tuberous begonias in the fall. They'll be in bloom
by February or March, and they'll look spectacular well into
May or June!

Dashing Dahlias

**Delightful dahlias can fill your garden with flowers in
practically every color of the rainbow from midsummer
until frost. The blooms range from 1 inch to 1 foot
across, and the plants themselves can be anywhere from
1 to 7 feet tall. And, if you enjoy lots of different flower
forms—daisies, pompoms, powderpuffs, and more—
dahlias definitely deserve a place in your garden!**

LET THE SUN SHINE

For top-notch results, plant dahlias in full
sun (except in the warmest areas of the
country, where afternoon shade is desir-
able). And don't let the soil dry out after
planting, because dahlias require lots of
moisture, from the time growth begins until
they're done blooming.

JERRY'S GEMS

To get the most
out of your
dahlias, here's
a little secret I
use—pinch the tips off the
plants when they are about
1 foot tall, to make them
stronger and bushier.

OFF TO A GOOD START

After the last threat of frost has passed, plant your dahlia
tubers in any good garden soil, 4 to 5 inches deep, with an
eye (or sprout) upright. Before planting, work compost, peat
moss, and 5 pounds of 0-20-20 fertilizer per 100 square feet

into the soil. Once the plants are up and growing, give them a light application of fertilizer, such as my Perennial Planting Potion on page 65.

My Grandma Putt always encouraged her dahlias to do double duty by cutting the shoots when they were 6 inches tall. She cut them off 1 inch above the soil line, then stuck them in a pot in a mixture of half light sand and half compost. After watering lightly, she'd cover the pot with a clear glass jar (I use a plastic bag), and set them in a spot with bright, but indirect, light. In four to six weeks, they were rooted and ready to transplant in the garden. The original plants? They were better off, too—much bushier and sturdier than their untrimmed relatives!

FALL INTO WINTER

When frost has blackened dahlia foliage, cut the tops down to within a few inches of the ground. Then dig up the roots carefully (early in the morning), turn them upside down to drain any moisture from the hollow stems, and leave them exposed to sunshine until that afternoon.

One storage method is to wrap each clump of roots in newspaper, and pack them in a ventilated barrel or crate. Another method is to put the roots in a box that is 6 to 8 inches deep, and fill in and around them with peat moss or sand. Store them in the coolest place available, provided that the temperature doesn't ever fall below freezing. (In Zone 8 and south, you can leave your dahlias in the ground all winter long; there's no need to dig!)

LABEL, LABEL—WHO'S GOT THE LABEL?

The trickiest part of carrying over dahlias from one year to the next can be keeping their names straight. Of course, if you're growing mixed colors, that's not a problem. But if you want to keep your deep red 'Arabian Night' separate from your light pink 'Park Princess', you'll need some way to identify them during storage, because their roots all look alike! I've experimented with a lot of different labeling methods, and the winner, hands down, is a simple marking pen. After drying the roots, but before packing them for storage, use a medium-tipped, permanent marking pen to write the name right on the roots. Come spring, you'll know exactly who is who—and have no more worries about mixed-up labels!

🚩 EARLY RISERS FOR FASTER FLOWERS

Want to enjoy dahlia flowers weeks before anyone else in your neighborhood? Give your tubers a jump on the growing season by starting them indoors! Pot them up in early to midspring, and keep them in a warm room. When sprouts appear, make sure they get plenty of light. Plant them out in the garden after all danger of frost has passed, and you'll have beautiful blooms to enjoy a month earlier than your neighbors will!

Wand flower
Sparaxis tricolor

Summer flowers
in a rainbow
of colors;
store indoors
in cold winter
climates

Elephant's Ears Made Easy

If you have young ones in your family, then you definitely need to plant an elephant's ear for them. No, it won't grow an elephant! The name comes from the leaves, which can reach gigantic proportions. But they sure will add a touch of the tropics to any yard!

🚩 HERE'S AN EARFUL!

"Elephant's ear" is the name you'll hear most often applied to the species *Colocasia esculenta* (also called *C. antiquorum*), although it's also known as taro. Its large bulbs send up huge heart- or arrowhead-shaped leaves—each 2 to 3 feet long—atop stems that can be anywhere from 3 to 8 feet tall. These plants are definitely a can't-miss addition to any garden, but for even more excitement, look for the cultivars 'Black Magic' (with purple-black leaves) and 'Illustris' (with purplish stems and green leaves that have purple-black patches between the leaf veins). Elephant's ear can be hardy into Zone 8, but the showy cultivars tend to be less hardy (Zones 9 and 10).

Another plant with a similar name is upright elephant's ears (*Alocasia macrorrhiza*). The tips of its leaves point upward, rather than hang down like regular elephant's ears. It's equally handsome and enjoys the same growing conditions. Why not give both a try?

☞ THE INSIDE SCOOP

Give your elephant's ears a head start by planting them indoors 8 to 10 weeks before the last frost date in your area. Set them about 2 inches deep in good potting soil, and keep them warm— about 75°F. Wait until all danger of frost has passed before moving them outdoors for the summer.

☞ MOISTURE'S A MUST

Elephant's ears thrive in a sunny or shaded spot in soil that's been loosened up with peat moss, sand, and compost or rotted manure. Lots of moisture is a must if you want the really big leaves.

In fact, elephant's ears grow beautifully along the edge of water gardens, with a few inches of water over the tops of their tubers.

☞ EAR'S LOOKING AT YOU, KID!

If you live in the Deep South, your elephant's ears can stay outside for the winter; elsewhere, you'll have to dig them up

---

TOOL TIME

Need an extra watering can? Don't go out and buy a new one—recycle your old laundry detergent bottles instead. Start with a large liquid laundry detergent bottle that has a handle. Wash it out thoroughly. Then drill a couple of holes in the cap, fill up the bottle with water, replace the cap, and *voilà*—instant watering can! Use the handle to carry it out to the garden, then simply turn the bottle upside down to water your plants. An added bonus is that these plastic bottles tend to be brightly colored, so you're not going to lose track of them in the garden.

after the first fall frost. Or, you can make your life easier, and grow them in pots in a mixture of 2 parts potting soil, 2 parts peat moss, 1 part sifted compost, and 1 part sand. They won't get as big, and they'll need watering more often, but they'll be a whole lot easier to bring inside for the winter. Move the pots indoors before frost, and grow the plants in bright, but indirect, sunlight.

COLD STORAGE

Don't have room to grow your elephant's ears as houseplants over the winter? Then dig them up before the first frost, cut off the top growth, and set the tubers in a shady spot to dry for a few hours. Pack them in barely moist peat moss or sand, and keep them at about 50°F until it's time to pot them up in late winter.

Mixers & Elixirs

ELEPHANT'S EAR ELIXIR

Give your elephant's ears an earful of this tonic, and watch 'em grow!

1 can of beer
1 cup of all-purpose plant food
¼ cup of ammonia

Mix the ingredients together, and pour them into a 20 gallon hose-end sprayer. Fill the balance of the sprayer with water. Every three weeks, spray the plants until the liquid runs off the leaves.

White turtlehead
Chelone glabra

Tall stems with lilac-blushed white blooms in late summer and fall

Hiya, Cynth!

Grown in the garden or planted in pots, hyacinths have a charm all their own. Besides their many colors, they offer incredible fragrance—just a few clumps can perfume your whole yard!

DUTCH DANDIES

Dutch hyacinths (*Hyacinthus orientalis*) don't demand much in return for their fabulous flowers: Just give them full sun and average, well-drained soil. Set the bulbs about 6 inches deep. Space them about 10 inches apart if you plan to plant pansies or other flowers around them; 6 inches apart is fine if you're growing hyacinths by themselves. Dutch hyacinths can be grown in Zones 4 to 8, but they perform best in Zones 5 to 7.

 SHOW YOUR TRUE COLORS

Looking for a patriotic way to welcome spring? Why not try a planting of red, white, and blue hyacinths? If you have the room, you could even re-create a whole American flag with these colorful flowers!

HANDLE WITH CARE!

It's a good idea to wear gloves when handling hyacinth bulbs. Here's why: Their jackets contain a substance that can cause itching or skin irritation.

COLOR CLUES

Most times, when you buy mixed bulbs, there's no way to tell what colors you have until they bloom. But guess what—with hyacinths, the answer is skin deep! The bulbs with tan skins produce white or yellow flowers, the reddish ones will have red or pink flowers, and the purplish ones will produce purple or blue blooms.

THANKS FOR YOUR SUPPORT

Are your hyacinths too heavy to hold their heads up high? Give them a little support, and they'll stand up tall! It's easy

---

MAKING ¢ents

Here's a great way to fill up your garden without breaking the bank: Grow more hyacinths from the bulbs you already have! Dig up bulbs in the fall, and pick off the small bulbs that have divided off the original ones. Set the big bulbs back in the garden, and plant the small bulbs in a corner of your vegetable garden, or another out-of-the-way spot. Leave them there until they bloom once, then move them back into the flower garden the following fall.

to do—just use a piece of heavy wire about 10 inches long (the straight part from the base of a wire coat hanger is perfect). Right before the flowers open, slip the wire into the top of the spike, down through the stem, and into the bulb. Just be sure not to forget that the wires are there, when you go to snip off the spent flower stems.

THE NAME GAME

Hyacinths are so popular, it's no wonder that many bulbs share the name. It can get pretty confusing for us gardeners, though! Here's a quick rundown of the various kinds of hyacinths and their proper botanical names, so you can be sure you're getting the ones you want:

Dutch hyacinth (*Hyacinthus orientalis*)

Grape hyacinth (*Muscari*)

Roman hyacinth (*Hyacinthus orientalis* var. *albulus*)

Summer hyacinth (*Galtonia candicans*)

Wild hyacinth (*Camassia*)

Wood hyacinth (*Hyacinthoides hispanica*)

EASY AND ELEGANT

The dense flower spikes of Dutch hyacinths are certainly showy, but if you like your flowers a little more delicate-looking, there are hyacinths for you, too! Roman hyacinths (*H. orientalis* var. *albulus*) are an old-fashioned favorite, with multiple spikes of pink, blue, or white flowers, that are much less formal-looking than their heavily hybridized cousins. They are wonderful for forcing, and they perform

Try This!

Here's a neat trick to keep squirrels away from your bulbs—after planting new areas, lay old window screens (still in their frames) on the ground, and cover them up with a thin layer of soil or mulch. The screens weigh just enough to foil the squirrels, and the mesh allows for air circulation and lets rain soak through. After a few weeks, the soil will have settled and the squirrels will dig elsewhere. Remove the screens, and store them for use the next time you plant new bulbs.

Wild columbine

Aquilegia canadensis

Dainty red and yellow blooms dance at the tips of slender stems in spring

much better outdoors in warm climates (Zones 6 to 8) than Dutch hyacinths. True Roman hyacinths can be hard to find, but fortunately, breeders have come up with a replacement, called multiflowering or 'Festival' hyacinths. Give them a try—you'll love 'em!

For Something Completely Different

Are you ready to step outside the everyday realm of daffodils, crocuses, and tulips? Then check out some of these fun and quirky bulbs. They're guaranteed to attract plenty of attention!

Wild oats
Chasmanthium latifolium

Shade-tolerant ornamental grass with good-looking seedheads; lasts well into winter

▭ PINING FOR PINEAPPLE LILIES

Hang on, Carmen Miranda fans—here's a bulb that looks good enough to grace a fruit-filled hat any day! Pineapple lily (*Eucomis*) looks remarkably like its namesake, with star-shaped flowers packed into dense, cylindrical clusters topped with a tuft of leaves. *E. bicolor* (usually hardy in Zones 8 to 10) has green leaves and white flowers, while *E. punctata* (Zones 6 to 10) has either green or purplish leaves and white or pink-tinged blooms. Both grow fine in full sun or partial shade and average, well-drained soil.

▭ GLORY, GLORY—HALLELUJAH!

This bulb's breathtakingly beautiful blooms will definitely brighten up any porch or patio. Glory lily (*Gloriosa superba*) is one-of-a-kind among bulbs, thanks to its climbing habit.

In the North, its yellow and scarlet or orange and red blooms brighten the summer garden; in the Deep South, it'll grow and bloom all year round! It makes a handsome houseplant, too.

Outdoors, plant the tuberous roots with their tips 4 inches deep in compost-enriched soil, preferably in full sun. Apply a 5-10-5 fertilizer once a month during the growing season. In Zone 7 and north, dig up the roots in the fall, and store them as you would dahlias (see "Fall into Winter" on page 324). Or, enjoy glory lily as a houseplant, by potting up the roots in a mixture of equal parts potting soil, peat moss, and clean sand. Keep the soil moist, and fertilize every 12 weeks during the growing season. The dormant period usually lasts from October through January; during this time, withhold both water and fertilizer.

ACHIMENES: FIT FOR A KING

It's tough to beat achimenes—pronounced uh-KIM-in-eez— for pots, planters, and hanging baskets. Also known as monkey-face pansy or orchid pansy, this amazing little bulb blooms its heart out from spring through fall, with loads of small, but colorful, trumpet-shaped blossoms on graceful, trailing stems. The flowers come in many colors, including purple, pink, yellow, blue, and red.

These African violet relatives absolutely hate the cold, so growing them in pots makes it easy to bring them indoors when frost threatens. Their rhizomes look like tiny pinecones, and they're very fragile, so handle them with care. In late winter or early spring, pot them up about 1 inch deep and 3 inches apart in a mixture of 2 parts peat moss, 1 part potting soil, and 1 part clean sand. Water

Grandma Putt's WISDOM

After a day spent grubbing around in the garden, your fingernails can get grimy. When I was a youngster, my Grandma Putt used to get pretty tired of nagging me to scrub my nails, so she had me try this trick: Before heading out to the garden, I lightly scratched my fingernails over a bar of soap. Come cleanup time, the dirt and soap would wash right out!

Mixers & Elixirs

FABULOUS FOLIAR FORMULA

For the biggest, brightest, shiniest leaves in town, feed your leafy bulbs and perennials this fantastic formula every three weeks:

1 can of beer
½ cup of fish emulsion
½ cup of ammonia
¼ cup of blackstrap molasses
4 tbsp. of instant tea granules

Mix all of the ingredients together in a 20 gallon hose-end sprayer and apply thoroughly, until it starts running off the leaves.

carefully, then set them in bright, indirect sunlight. After all chance of frost has passed, move them outdoors to a spot in light shade. When they stop flowering, let them die back, and stop watering. Store them at around 60°F until February, then start watering again.

RAISE THE FLAGS

If you're looking for something bold and red for your perennial garden, take a look at *Schizostylis*, otherwise known as crimson flag. Their spikes of rousing red blooms appear in late summer and into fall. They need full sun or partial shade, and are dependably hardy in Zones 7 to 9. Crimson flag can make it through the winters as far north as Zone 5 with a generous winter mulch.

Now here's a story I just have to share: I once told a cousin of mine that *Schizostylis* grew well in damp soil, and suggested that she plant some down by the stream in back of her house. She later informed me that *Schizostylis* couldn't be found anywhere in her little town, but that she did set out some crimson flags, and they were flourishing. Someday, I just may get up the nerve to tell her that they're one and the same!

Winecups
*Callirhoe
involucrata*

Cupped magenta
blooms in summer
on low-growing
stems that
weave among
other plants

CHAPTER 19

PERFECT PAIRINGS

Sure, bulbs are beautiful—but you can't have a great
garden with just bulbs alone! You'll get the very best from
your bulbs if you pair them up with a bunch of carefully
chosen companions. Besides physically helping to hold
up the bulb blooms, annuals, perennials, and shrubs add
extra color, height, texture, and seasonal interest to
complement your bulbs all year round.

Annuals for Afterward

Annuals and bulbs—now that's what I call a match made in heaven! Whether you're looking to beef up your bulb display or fill in after bulb flowers are gone, annuals are a simple, but stunning, solution.

COMPATIBLE COMPANIONS

It can take a lot of bulbs to make a really good show, but what if you can't afford as many bulbs as you need to fill a big space? Try planting the bulbs a little farther apart than recommended (add 3 to 4 inches to the suggested spacing), then fill in with early-flowering annuals, once the bulbs poke their noses above the soil.

PERFECT PARTNERS

Besides cutting down on the bulbs you'll need to buy, combining bulbs and annuals is a wonderful way to create fabulous color combinations. Here are a few ideas to get you started:

❧ Deep blue 'Blue Jacket' Dutch hyacinths with yellow pansies (*Viola* x *wittrockiana*).

❧ 'White Triumphator' tulips underplanted with sky-blue forget-me-nots (*Myosotis*).

❧ Yellow 'Tête-à-Tête' daffodils rising out of violet and yellow Johnny-jump-ups (*Viola tricolor*).

DIG IN

If you're planting bulbs in a bed where you grow only annuals in the summer, plan on lifting your bulbs out of the soil right after they bloom. That way, you can dig up the bed and prepare it for planting without having to worry about skewering the bulbs. To my mind, it's easiest to just toss the used bulbs onto my compost pile; then I buy cheap, new bulbs in the fall for that spot. But if you want to save the bulbs from year to year, dig them up carefully, when the flowers fade, and transplant them to a corner of your vegetable garden, or some other out-of-the-way spot. Then, in the fall, dig them up and move them back to the display bed.

◀ SELF-SOWN LATE SHOW

To get even more mileage from annuals, use them to fill the spaces left *after* the bulbs themselves are gone. Self-sowing annuals are particularly good for this, because once you plant them the first year, they'll come back on their own each year after that!

Start the process by scattering the seeds around emerging bulb shoots and carefully scratching or pressing them into the soil. By the time the bulbs start turning yellow, the annuals will be up and raring to grow! Some of my favorite self-sowing annuals include California poppy (*Eschscholzia californica*), corn poppy (*Papaver rhoeas*), bachelor's button (*Centaurea cyanus*), and love-in-a-mist (*Nigella damascena*).

◀ SPECIAL SPACE FILLERS

Fall-flowering bulbs offer a special challenge—and annuals are up to the job! Autumn crocus (*Colchicum*), magic lilies (*Lycoris squamigera*), naked ladies (*Amaryllis belladonna*), and other late bloomers send up their leaves in fall, then the foliage dies back by midsummer. But you don't want to plant a tall annual to fill the spot, because the bulbs will make a return appearance, to flower in late summer or fall. Two of my favorite low-growing annuals, for following the foliage of fall-blooming bulbs, are dusty millers (*Senecio cineraria*) and moss rose (*Portulaca grandiflora*)—there are many others, too!

Winter aconite
Eranthis hyemalis

Cheerful yellow flowers over a ruff of green leaves; super for late-winter and early-spring color

Annual transplants are another good way to go for filling spaces left by dormant bulbs. I recommend that you buy small transplants in cell packs (usually six per pack). Besides being cheaper, these smaller plants are easy to tuck in without disturbing the bulbs.

Perennials: Partners for Life

Don't want to bother with setting out annuals with your bulbs each year? Then the answer's simple—just plant perennials! These dependable bulb buddies can add extra color in time for the spring show, and perennials can also fill the space left when spring bulbs retreat back underground for the season.

▭ PERFECT PERENNIALS FOR SPRING BULBS

The possibilities for perfect perennial-and-bulb pairings in spring are practically endless! In areas that will stay sunny all summer long, interplant bulbs with low-growers like wall rock cress (*Arabis caucasica*), cushion spurge (*Euphorbia polychroma*), and moss phlox (*Phlox subulata*). In areas where trees will provide some summer shade, great bulb companions include primroses (*Primula*), lamium (*Lamium maculatum*), and barrenworts (*Epimedium*). All of these perennials will produce beautiful blooms in spring, then stick around to provide good-looking leaves for the rest of the year.

▭ DAFFY DELIGHTS

I love all bulbs, but daffodils are definitely my all-time favorites. They're easy to plant, they come back dependably year after year,

---

Perfect Perennials

FOR PLANTING WITH SPRING BULBS

Cushion spurge (*Euphorbia polychroma*): Neatly mounded, 1-foot-tall clumps covered with bright yellow blooms from midspring to midsummer. Zones 5 to 9.

Lamb's ears (*Stachys byzantina*): Spreading, 6- to 8-inch-tall carpets of soft, furry-feeling silvery gray leaves from early spring through fall. Zones 4 to 9.

Lungworts (*Pulmonaria*): Pink-turning-blue blooms atop 1-foot-tall stems with showy, silver-spotted leaves. Zones 5 to 8.

Pasqueflower (*Pulsatilla vulgaris*): Nodding pink, purple-blue, or white cupped blooms atop fuzzy 8-inch stems from early to late spring. Zones 5 to 7.

Wild bleeding heart (*Dicentra eximia*): Twelve- to 18-inch-tall clumps of lacy leaves accented with reddish, pink, or white flowers from mid- to late spring. Zones 4 to 8.

and they have big, colorful flowers. And, if that's not enough, they're practically pest and disease-free—even critters won't bother them! The only downside is that the foliage can look absolutely awful as it ripens.

Instead of cutting off the leaves, which will weaken the bulbs, I have a better solution: Plant these bulbs among later-rising perennials! In spots that are sunny all season long, daylilies (*Hemerocallis*) are ideal for following daffodils; where spring sun gives way to summer shade, hostas make perfect partners.

SUMMER BULB BUDDIES

Tall summer bulbs, like lilies (*Lilium*) and glads, often bloom atop long, lanky stems. Since these stems aren't much to look at, it makes perfect sense to cover them up with other plants. Besides hiding the bulbs' "bare ankles," bushy perennials help support the often top-heavy bulbs stems—and that means no more staking! Some of my favorite perennials for pairing with tall bulbs include Shasta daisies (*Chrysanthemum* x *superbum*), 'Powis Castle' artemisia (*Artemisia* 'Powis Castle'), and 'Six Hills Giant' catmint (*Nepeta* 'Six Hills Giant').

Wreath goldenrod
Solidago caesia

Arching sprays of bright yellow flowers in fall; adds welcome color to shady spots

Superb Shrubs

You may not think of pairing bulbs with shrubs, but hey—why not? Besides looking great with the showy blooms, shrubs stick around all year, so you can enjoy their leaves, flowers, and form long after the bulbs have come and gone.

Zebra grass
Miscanthus sinensis
'Zebrinus'

Tall clumps of
arching green
leaves banded
with yellow; great
in borders, and
with shrubs

GET DOWN WITH BULBS

Bulbs are perfect for sprucing up the space around the base of big mature shrubs, where the grass is often sparse and scrawny. They'll get sun in the spring, then go dormant by the time the shrubs leaf out again for summer.

SHRUBS AND BULBS FOR EVERY SEASON

Pairing flowering shrubs and bulbs is a fabulous way to turn an ordinary yard into a real showplace. Best of all, these eye-catching combinations are easy to plan and even easier to plant! Just be aware of when your shrub blooms, then select bulbs that flower at the same time. Choose bulbs in a similar color to create an elegant echo for the shrub, or pick a contrasting color to create a dramatic contrast. Here are a few ideas to get you started:

Spring: Silvery gray pussy willow (*Salix discolor*) with white Dutch crocus (*Crocus vernus*); bright yellow forsythia underplanted with bright blue Siberian squill (*Scilla siberica*) or yellow 'Tête-à-Tête' daffodils (*Narcissus* 'Tête-à-Tête').

Early summer: Purple lilac (*Syringa*) with rosy purple giant onions (*Allium giganteum*).

Midsummer: Electric reddish pink 'Knockout' rose with white 'Casa Blanca' Oriental Hybrid lily (*Lilium* 'Casa Blanca').

Fall: Glossy abelia (*Abelia* x *grandiflora*)—with pink flowers and reddish pink fall color—underplanted with pink 'Waterlily' autumn crocus (*Colchicum* 'Waterlily').

Here's a way to get even more mileage out of your bulb-and-shrub combinations: Toss in a few groundcovers, too. Besides adding ground-level flowers and foliage, the bulbs and groundcovers make a great low-maintenance alternative to maintaining a yucky-looking lawn in these tough spots.

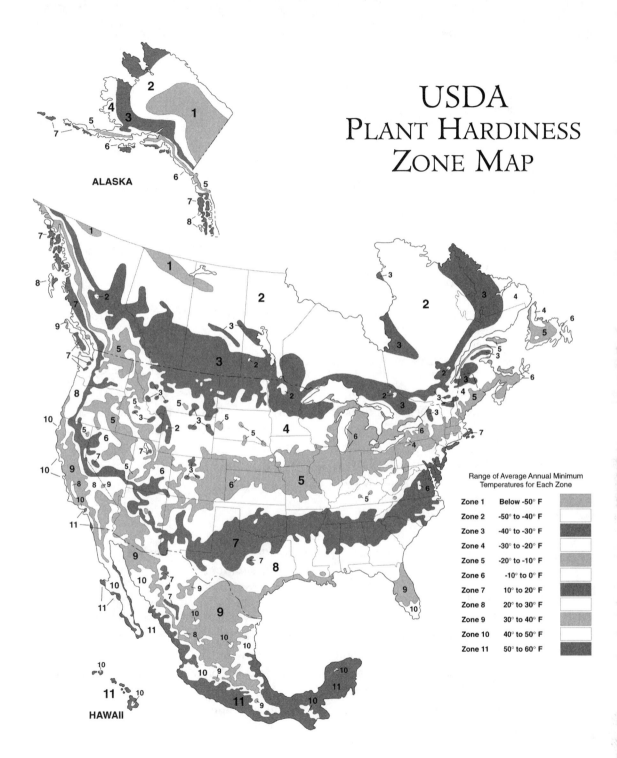

USDA
PLANT HARDINESS
ZONE MAP

ALASKA

HAWAII

Range of Average Annual Minimum
Temperatures for Each Zone

Zone 1	Below -50° F
Zone 2	-50° to -40° F
Zone 3	-40° to -30° F
Zone 4	-30° to -20° F
Zone 5	-20° to -10° F
Zone 6	-10° to 0° F
Zone 7	10° to 20° F
Zone 8	20° to 30° F
Zone 9	30° to 40° F
Zone 10	40° to 50° F
Zone 11	50° to 60° F

BONUS PERENNIAL POTIONS

If you're as crazy about growing perennials as I am, I know you'll enjoy learning a few more ways you can put these dependable and versatile plants to work. So, here's a dandy dozen of my new, favorite perennial potions—things you can eat, soak your tired tootsies in, use to control pests in and around your house and garden, and more— and best of all, each and every one is made from perennials!

HORSETAIL ANTI-FUNGUS SPRAY

Horsetail (*Equisetum*) loves wet soil in the garden, so it's great for soggy spots where nothing else will grow. This vigorous perennial spreads quickly, though, so keep it under control by picking lots of the stems to make this great fungus-fighting tonic:

⅛ cup of dried horsetail stems
1 gal. of water

Put the stems and water in a large pot. Bring to a boil, then let simmer for at least 30 minutes. Let cool, then strain out the stems. Store the leftover liquid concentrate in a glass jar. To use, mix 1 part concentrate with 10 parts water. Spray disease-prone plants, such as bee balm (*Monarda didyma*) and garden phlox (*Phlox paniculata*), every four to seven days to prevent powdery mildew and other fungal problems.

RUE INSECT SPRAY

You'll most often see rue (*Ruta graveolens*) in herb gardens, but this good-looking perennial has what it takes to shine in flower gardens, too—showy yellow blooms, plus beautiful blue-gray leaves. And, if that's not enough reason to grow it, it's also useful as an insect control spray!

4 cups of water
1 cup of rue leaves, mashed
Baby shampoo

Add 2 cups of water to the rue leaves, then let sit overnight. Strain out the leaves, then dilute the remaining liquid with 2 more cups of water and pour into a handheld sprayer. Add a few drops of baby shampoo to help the spray stick, then apply to pest-plagued plants.

ANISE HYSSOP WINDOW WASH

Bees and butterflies love the long-lasting, spiky purple flowers of anise hyssop (*Agastache foeniculum*)—and so do I! But this perennial is more than just a pretty face; its fragrant leaves make a great-smelling addition to this homemade window cleaner:

3 cups of fresh anise hyssop leaves and/or
*   flowers*
3 cups of white or apple cider vinegar
3 cups of water

Place the anise hyssop in a quart-size glass jar, then pour in the vinegar. Put the lid on the jar, shake, and let it sit for a week. (During that time, shake the jar daily, and add more vinegar, if needed, to keep the leaves and/or flowers covered.) Strain, then add $1/3$ cup of the remaining liquid to 3 cups of water, and pour into a handheld sprayer. Spray on windows, and wipe clean with a soft, dry cloth.

TANSY PEST REPELLENT

Send leaf-eating pests packing with a simple spray made from this pretty, yellow-flow-ered perennial. Tansy (*Tanacetum vulgare*) grows quickly, so feel free to harvest as much as you need; you won't hurt the plant!

3 cups of fresh tansy leaves
2 cups of boiling water
2 cups of room-temperature water

Pour the boiling water over the leaves, cover, and let stand until cool. Strain out the leaves, then dilute the remaining liquid with the room-temperature water. Pour into a handheld sprayer, and spray plants thoroughly.

DANDY HOREHOUND CANDY

The fuzzy, silvery leaves of horehound (*Marrubium vulgare*) are a beauty in beds and borders, and they make a mighty tasty treat, too! Here's an old recipe my Grandma Putt liked to use for horehound drops:

1 cup of fresh horehound leaves
1 cup of water
2 cups of granulated sugar
2 tbsp. of corn syrup
Powdered sugar

Combine the leaves and water in a non-aluminum saucepan. Bring to a boil and simmer, covered, for 20 minutes. Let cool, then strain out the leaves. Add sugar and corn syrup to the liquid in the pan. Stir, while bringing to a boil, then simmer until the liquid reaches the hard-crack stage (330°F). Remove from the heat, and pour the hot mixture into a lightly buttered baking pan. Score the surface after it's cool enough to be firm, and break the pieces apart as soon as the candy is cool enough to handle. Dust a bit of powdered sugar over the pieces to keep them from sticking together; store in a closed container in a cool place.

Fragrant Pest Fighter

People love perfumed perennials, but pests sure don't! Next time you're out in the garden, gather the ingredients for this aromatic pest-control spray:

½ cup of fresh tansy (Tanacetum vulgare) or mugwort (Artemisia vulgaris) leaves
½ cup of fresh lavender (Lavandula) flowers and/or leaves
½ cup of fresh sage (Salvia officinalis) leaves
Boiling water
2 cups of room-temperature water
1 teaspoon of Murphy® Oil Soap

Place the herbs in a 1-quart glass jar; fill with boiling water, cover, and let it sit until cool. Add ⅛ cup of the liquid to the 2 cups of room-temperature water and the Murphy's. Pour into a handheld sprayer, and apply it to your plants to keep pesky pests at bay.

Super-Simple Lavender Soap

Get your hands squeaky clean after a day of gardening with this sweet-smelling—and easy-to-make—lavender soap.

10 tbsp. of Castile soap, finely grated
8 tbsp. of boiling water
2 tbsp. of dried lavender flowers, crushed into a powder
4 drops of lavender oil (available at craft stores)

Put the soap and boiling water in a bowl, then set the bowl over a pot of hot water. Stir until the soap and water mixture is smooth, then remove the bowl from the hot water, and stir in the powdered lavender flowers and lavender oil. Store the scented soap in a glass or plastic container, and use as needed to clean grimy hands.

Fragrant Closet Fresheners

Chase moths away and keep your clothes smelling sweet with sachets (small muslin bags) filled with these fragrant and pest-repelling perennial flowers and foliage.

2 cups of dried mugwort (Artemisia vulgaris) leaves
1½ cups of dried lavender (Lavandula) flowers
1½ cups of dried tansy (Tanacetum vulgare) leaves and/or flowers
½ cup of dried southernwood (Artemisia abrotanum) leaves
¼ cup of dried sweet woodruff (Galium odoratum) leaves
5 to 6 small muslin sachet bags (available at craft stores)

Crush all of the ingredients with your fingers, and put them in a large glass jar. Close the lid tightly, shake the jar, and let it sit for two or three weeks (shake again every day or two). Place ½ to 1 cup of the finished blend into each muslin bag, tie closed with string or ribbon, and hang in your closets or place in drawers.

WINDOW SCREEN SPRAY

Put a stop to those annoying gnats that sneak through your window screens with this easy-to-make elixir. You can use any of the following perennials: bee balms (*Monarda*), common yarrow (*Achillea millefolium*), southernwood (*Artemisia abrotanum*), tansy (*Tanacetum vulgare*), or mugwort (*Artemisia vulgaris*).

3 cups of fresh flowers and/or leaves
3 cups of boiling water

Put the leaves and/or flowers in a large bowl or pot, and pour the water over them. Cover and let sit for 30 minutes. Strain, then spray the remaining liquid on your window screens (from the inside).

SOOTHING SWEET FLAG BATH

Soak away your cares with this super-soothing bath made from sweet flag (*Acorus calamus*). This good-looking, moisture-loving perennial produces handsome clumps of iris-like leaves, but it's not the leaves in this relaxing elixir—it's the roots.

½ pound of sweet flag roots, chopped
8 pints of water

Put the roots and water in a pot, and bring to a boil. Simmer for 30 minutes, then strain out the root pieces. Add the remaining liquid to your bath water, and you'll feel the day's tensions fade away.

FABULOUS FOOT SOAK

Relief for those swollen, aching feet is as close as your perennial garden!

1 qt. of boiling water
*¼ cup of dried mugwort (**Artemisia vulgaris**) leaves*

Pour the water over the leaves, and let it sit for 20 minutes. Strain out the leaves, and add the remaining liquid to your foot bath to make those old dogs feel young again.

HOMEMADE DRY CLEANER

If you have yucca or soapwort (*Saponaria officinalis*) growing in your garden, you've got the fixings for a super-gentle, "dry cleaning" solution for delicate fabrics, baskets, and other nonwashable items.

¼ cup of powdered dry yucca root or soapwort root
3 cups of boiling water

Put the powdered yucca or soapwort roots in a blender and add the boiling water. Cover, and blend on high for two to three minutes. Allow the mixture to settle for a few seconds before removing the lid. Scoop out the suds with your hand, a cloth, or a soft brush, and rub them into the item you want to clean. Let the foam dry, then simply brush it off.

Flower Fixers, Magical Mixers & Excellent Elixirs

All-Purpose Bug/Thug Spray

To kill flower garden insects and diseases in one fell swoop, whip up a batch of this all-purpose spray:

3 tbsp. of baking soda
2 tbsp. of Murphy® Oil Soap
2 tbsp. of canola oil
2 tbsp. of vinegar
2 gal. of warm water

Mix all of the ingredients together, and mist-spray your perennials to the point of run-off. Apply in early spring, just as the bugs and thugs are waking up. (For related text, see page 137.)

All-Purpose Perennial Fertilizer

This power-packed mix will keep perennials "in the pink."

1 part bloodmeal
3 parts bonemeal
3 parts greensand or wood ashes

Mix the ingredients in a bucket or in a wheelbarrow. Apply 3 to 5 pounds per 100 square feet before planting and work it into the soil, or scatter 2 tablespoons around each clump of established perennials in the spring and scratch it lightly into the soil with a hand fork. (For related text, see page 186.)

ALL-SEASON CLEAN-UP TONIC

Apply this tonic in early evening every two weeks during the growing season to keep pests and diseases at bay:

1 cup of baby shampoo
1 cup of tobacco tea*
1 cup of antiseptic mouthwash
Warm water

Mix all of the ingredients in a 20 gallon hose-end sprayer, filling the balance of the jar with warm water. Liberally apply this mixture to your beds and borders. (For related text, see page 134.)

*Place three fingers of chewing tobacco in an old nylon stocking and soak in a gallon of hot water until the mixture is dark brown.

APHID ANTIDOTE

To keep aphids and other pests off your prized perennials, mix up a batch of this amazingly potent antidote:

1 medium onion, chopped finely
1 tbsp. of dishwashing liquid
Water

In a blender, thoroughly blend the onion in a quart of water. Strain off the clear juice, and mix 2 tablespoons of it per gallon of water with the dishwashing liquid. Pour it into a handheld sprayer, and apply liberally to your flowers at the first sign of aphid trouble. (For related text, see page 139.)

BEETLE JUICE

This recipe isn't for the squeamish, but nothing beats it for fighting beetles!

¹/₂ cup of beetles (dead or alive)
1 tsp. of dishwashing liquid
Water
Cheesecloth

Mix the beetles and 2 cups of water together in an *old* blender. Strain the mix through cheesecloth and stir in the dishwashing liquid. Pour ¹/₄ cup into a 1 gallon handheld sprayer and fill the rest of the jar with water.

Drench the soil around new plants with this beetle juice to keep beetles from getting started. If they're already on the scene, spray plants from top to bottom, making sure to coat both sides of the leaves. Freeze any extra juice—and be sure to label it clearly! (For related text, see page 140.)

BEST BULB DEFENSE

To defend your bulb beds from slithering snakes, mix up a batch of this sandy send-off:

1 part builder's sand
1 part diatomaceous earth

Mix the ingredients together and sprinkle a 3-inch-wide band around the area to be protected. Snakes won't dare cross this rough stuff. Now that's what I call drawing a line in the sand! (For related text, see page 275.)

BULB BATH

To keep your bulbs bug-free, treat them to a nice warm bath before putting them into their planting bed. Here's what you'll need:

2 tsp. of baby shampoo
1 tsp. of antiseptic mouthwash
¼ tsp. of instant tea granules
2 gal. of warm water

Mix all of the ingredients in a bucket, then carefully place your bulbs into the mixture. Stir gently, then remove the bulbs one at a time and plant them. When you're done, don't throw the bath water out with the babies. Your trees, shrubs, and evergreens would love a little taste, so don't let it go to waste. (For related text, see page 57.)

BULB BREAKFAST

10 lbs. of compost
5 lbs. of bonemeal
2 lbs. of bloodmeal
1 lb. of Epsom salts

Mix all of the ingredients together in a wheelbarrow. Before setting out your bulbs, work this hearty breakfast into every 100 square feet of soil in your bulb-planting areas.

Don't neglect individually planted bulbs, either. Work a handful of compost and a teaspoon of bonemeal into the soil in each hole before setting in the bulb. (For related text, see page 60.)

BULB SOAK

Prepare bulbs, tubers, and corms for planting by soaking them in this solution:

1 can of beer
2 tbsp. of dishwashing liquid
¼ tsp. of instant tea granules
2 gal. of water

Mix all of the ingredients together in a large bucket, and carefully soak the bulbs in the mix before planting. (For related text, see page 284.)

CATERPILLAR KILLER TONIC

To keep caterpillars in check and away from your flowers, mix up a batch of this tonic:

½ lb. of wormwood (**Artemisia**) *leaves*
2 tbsp. of Murphy® Oil Soap
Warm water

Simmer the wormwood leaves in 2 cups of water for 30 minutes or so. Strain out the leaves, then add the remaining liquid and the Murphy's to 2 more cups of warm water. Apply with a 6 gallon hose-end sprayer to the point of run-off. Repeat as necessary until the caterpillars are history! (For related text, see page 142.)

CHAMOMILE MILDEW CHASER

Chamomile is an excellent control for powdery mildew, so put it to good use with this elixir. Apply at the first sign of trouble (or as a preventive measure in damp weather), and every week throughout the growing season to perennials that are particularly prone to this fungal disease:

4 chamomile tea bags
1 qt. of boiling water
2 tbsp. of Murphy® Oil Soap

Make a good strong batch of tea using the tea bags and boiling water, letting it steep for an hour or so. Let the tea cool, then mix with the Murphy's. Apply with a 6 gallon hose-end sprayer. (For related text, see page 158.)

COMPOST BOOSTER

1 can of beer
1 can of regular cola (not diet)
1 cup of ammonia
½ cup of weak tea water*
2 tbsp. of baby shampoo

Pour this mixture into your 20 gallon hose-end sprayer, and saturate your compost pile every time you add a new foot of ingredients to it. This'll really get things cookin'! (For related text, see page 76.)

*Soak a used tea bag in a mix of 1 gallon of warm water and 1 teaspoon of dishwashing liquid until the mix is light brown.

COMPOST TEA

This solution is great as an all-around perennial pick-me-up. Simply put several shovelsful of compost or manure into a large trash can, and fill the can to the top with water. Allow the mixture to sit for seven days, stirring it several times each day. To use, dilute with water until it is light brown. Give each plant about a cup of this tea every two weeks, and your feeding worries will be over! (For related text, see page 78.)

CONTAINER PLANT TONIC

2 tbsp. of whiskey
1 tbsp. of all-purpose 15-30-15 fertilizer
½ tsp. of unflavored gelatin
½ tsp. of dishwashing liquid
¼ tsp. of instant tea granules
Water

Put the whiskey, fertilizer, gelatin, dishwashing liquid, and tea in a clean 1 gallon milk jug, and fill it up with water. Mix, then mark the jug "Container Plant Tonic." Add ½ cup of this fortified mix to every gallon of water you use to water your potted perennials. (For related text, see page 205.)

DEER BUSTER EGG TONIC

2 eggs
2 cloves of garlic
2 tbsp. of hot sauce
2 tbsp. of cayenne pepper
2 cups of water

Put all of the ingredients in a blender and purée. Allow the mixture to sit for two days, then pour or spray it all over and around the plants you need to protect. (For related text, see page 166.)

DISEASE DEFENSE

Wet, rainy weather can mean an outbreak of fungus in your flower garden, especially in late winter and early spring. Keep your perennials and bulbs happy and healthy with this elixir:

1 cup of chamomile tea
1 tsp. of dishwashing liquid
¹/₂ tsp. of vegetable oil
¹/₂ tsp. of peppermint oil
1 gal. of warm water

Mix all of the ingredients together in a bucket. Mist-spray your plants every week or so before the hot weather (75°F or higher) sets in. This elixir is strong stuff, so test it on a few leaves before completely spraying any plant. (For related text, see page 154.)

DOG-GONE-IT!

Man's best friend can be your flower garden's worst enemy. To keep dogs away from their favorite digging areas, liberally apply this mix to the soil:

2 cloves of garlic
2 small onions
1 jalapeño pepper
1 tbsp. of cayenne pepper
1 tbsp. of hot sauce
1 tbsp. of chili powder
1 qt. of warm water

Chop the garlic, onions, and pepper finely, then combine with the remaining ingredients. Let the mix sit for 24 hours, then sprinkle it on any areas where digging dogs are a problem. (For related text, see page 165.)

EASY WEED KILLER

Weeds trying to take over your wonderful wildflower meadow? Give those pesky plants a shot of this spray to send them packing:

1 gal. of white vinegar
1 cup of table salt
1 tbsp. of dishwashing liquid

Mix these ingredients in a handheld sprayer, and apply liberally to weeds. Just make sure you don't get it on plants you want to keep! (For related text, see page 266.)

ELEPHANT'S EAR ELIXIR

Give your elephant's ears an earful of this tonic and watch 'em grow!

1 can of beer
1 cup of all-purpose plant food
¼ cup of ammonia

Mix the ingredients together, and pour them into a 20 gallon hose-end sprayer. Fill the balance of the sprayer with water. Every three weeks, spray the plants until the liquid runs off the leaves. (For related text, see page 327.)

FABULOUS FOLIAR FORMULA

For the biggest, brightest, shiniest leaves in town, feed your leafy bulbs and perennials this fantastic formula every three weeks:

1 can of beer
½ cup of fish emulsion
½ cup of ammonia
¼ cup of blackstrap molasses
4 tbsp. of instant tea granules

Mix all of the ingredients together in a 20 gallon hose-end sprayer and apply thoroughly, until it starts running off the leaves. (For related text, see page 332.)

FERN FOOD

To keep your outdoor ferns looking lush, give them a dose of this milky brew!

2 cups of milk
2 tbsp. of Epsom salts

Combine the milk and Epsom salts in your 20 gallon hose-end sprayer, and give your ferns a generous drink until they are saturated. (For related text, see page 87.)

FLOWER BED BONANZA

After fall cleanup, spray all of your perennial beds with this mixture:

1 can of beer
1 can of regular cola (not diet)
½ cup of dishwashing liquid
½ cup of tobacco tea*

Mix all of the ingredients together in a bucket, then apply liberally with your 20 gallon hose-end sprayer. (For related text, see page 102.)

*Place three fingers of chewing tobacco in an old nylon stocking and soak in a gallon of hot water until the mixture is dark brown.

FLOWER FEEDER TONIC

1 can of beer
2 tbsp. of fish emulsion
2 tbsp. of dishwashing liquid
2 tbsp. of ammonia
2 tbsp. of hydrogen peroxide
2 tbsp. of whiskey
1 tbsp. of clear corn syrup
1 tbsp. of unflavored gelatin
4 tsp. of instant tea granules
2 gal. of warm water

Mix all of the ingredients together. Feed all of your perennials and bulbs with this mix every two weeks in the morning for glorious blooms all season long. (For related text, see page 85.)

FLOWER POWER TONIC

Whenever Grandma Putt brought a new perennial to her garden, she gave it a little extra-special TLC. First, she'd fill the hole with plenty of organic matter, and then follow that up with a dose of her Flower Power Tonic. That got them up and growing on the right root!

2 lbs. of dry oatmeal
2 lbs. of crushed dry dog food
1 handful of human hair
½ cup of sugar

Mix all of these ingredients in a 5 gallon bucket. Work a handful of this mix into the base of each hole before planting your prized perennials. (For related text, see page 52.)

FUNGUS FIGHTER TONIC

Molasses is great for fighting diseases in your flower garden. So at the first sign of trouble, try this tonic:

½ cup of molasses
½ cup of powdered milk
1 tsp. of baking soda
1 gal. of warm water

Mix the molasses, powdered milk, and baking soda into a paste. Place the mixture into the toe of an old nylon stocking, and let it steep in the warm water for several hours. Then strain, and use the remaining liquid as a fungus-fighting spray for your flower garden every two weeks throughout the growing season. I guarantee you'll have no more fungus troubles! (For related text, see page 156.)

GARDEN CURE-ALL TONIC

At the first sign of insects or disease, mix up a batch of this tonic to set things right:

4 cloves of garlic
1 small onion
1 small jalapeño pepper
Warm water
1 tsp. of Murphy® Oil Soap
1 tsp. of vegetable oil
Warm water

Pulverize the garlic, onion, and pepper in a blender, and let them steep in a quart of warm water for 2 hours. Strain the mixture through cheesecloth or panty hose, dilute the liquid with three parts of warm water. Add the Murphy's and vegetable oil. Pour into a handheld sprayer and apply to your perennials and bulbs several times a week. (For related text, see page 130.)

HOMEGROWN DAISY SPRAY

If you grow painted daisy (*Tanacetum coccineum*)—also called pyrethrum daisy—you have the makings for this great homemade pest spray.

⅛ cup of 70% isopropyl alcohol
1 cup of packed, fresh painted daisy
    flower heads

Pour the alcohol over the flower heads and let sit overnight. Strain out the flowers, then store the extract in a labeled and sealed container. When you need it, mix the extract with three quarts of water to make a spray that controls a wide range of garden pests. (For related text, see page 232.)

HOT BUG BREW

Even ordinary garlic can make a great-looking addition to your flower garden. And after you've enjoyed the curiously curled flower stalks, you can dig up the cloves and concoct this super-duper pest spray!

3 hot green peppers (canned or fresh)
3 medium cloves of garlic
1 small onion
1 tbsp. of dishwashing liquid
3 cups of water

Purée the peppers, garlic, and onion in a blender. Pour the purée into a jar, and add the dishwashing liquid and water. Let stand for 24 hours, then strain out the pulp with cheesecloth or panty hose. Use a handheld sprayer to apply the remaining liquid to bug-infested bulbs and perennials, making sure to thoroughly coat the tops and undersides of all the leaves. (For related text, see page 320.)

HUMMINGBIRD TONIC

If you know there are hummers in your area, try this mixture to lure them into your yard:

1 part granulated sugar
4 parts water

Heat the mixture to a boil, and stir until all the sugar has dissolved. Let the mixture cool and put it in your feeders.

Once hummers start coming, decrease the solution to about 1 part sugar to 8 parts water. The reason for diluting the solution is that hummingbirds can sometimes suffer a fatal liver disorder if they get too much sugar. (For related text, see page 198.)

IRIS ENERGIZER TONIC

½ cup of beer
Vitamin B_1 Plant Starter (mixed at 25 percent of the recommended rate)
2 tbsp. of dishwashing liquid
1 gal. of warm water

Mix the ingredients together in a bucket and drench the soil around your newly planted irises to get them off on the right root! (For related text, see page 239.)

IRIS GET-UP-AND-GROW MIX

4 parts bonemeal
6 parts hydrated lime

Mix the ingredients together and sprinkle around established plants in spring. Work it into the ground when the soil is dry enough, and your irises will be off to a flying start! (For related text, see page 237.)

KNOCK 'EM DEAD TONIC

Get rid of whatever's bugging your bulbs by giving your garden a spray of this surefire insect killer:

6 cloves of garlic, chopped finely
1 small onion, chopped finely
1 tbsp. of dishwashing liquid
1 qt. of warm water

Mix all of the ingredients together and let the mixture sit overnight. Strain out the solids, pour the liquid into a handheld sprayer, and blast the bugs dead! (For related text, see page 311.)

NATURAL NUTRIENTS FOR NEGLECTED SOIL

6 parts greensand or wood ashes
3 parts cottonseed meal
3 parts bonemeal
Gypsum
Limestone

Mix the greensand or wood ashes, cottonseed meal, and bonemeal together. Add 2 cups of gypsum and 1 cup of limestone per gallon-size container of blend. Apply 5 pounds per 100 square feet a few weeks before planting perennials. (For related text, see page 258.)

OUT-TO-LUNCH

Give your fall-planted bulbs this organic lunch to snack on over the winter:

10 lbs. of dehydrated manure or compost
5 lbs. of bonemeal
1 lb. of Epsom salts

Mix and apply per 100 square feet of soil. For an extra treat, add up to 15 pounds of fireplace ashes to the soil. (For related text, see page 287.)

PERENNIAL PLANTING POTION

To get your perennials growing on the right foot, feed them this potion:

½ can of beer
¼ cup of ammonia
2 tbsp. of hydrogen peroxide
1 tbsp. of dishwashing liquid
2 gal. of warm water

Mix the ingredients together and pour into the planting holes. (For related text, see page 65.)

PERFECT POTTING MIX

If you've got a lot of perennials to pot, you'll need plenty of potting soil. So instead of constantly running out (and running to the store), mix up a batch of this simple blend and keep it handy:

1 part topsoil
1 part peat moss
1 part vermiculite
1 part compost

Mix all of the ingredients together and use for potting up all kinds of perennials and bulbs. (For related text, see page 105.)

PERFECT POTTING SOIL

Here's how to make the perfect blend of soil for all your container-grown perennials:

1 part sharp sand
1 part clay loam
1 part compost, peat moss, or potting soil

Per cubic foot of soil mixture, add:

1½ cups of Epsom salts
¾ cup of coffee grounds (rinsed)
12 eggshells (dried and crushed to
*   a powder)*

Blend all of the ingredients together in a large tub or wheelbarrow, and use the mixture to make your perennials feel comfy and cozy in their new home. (For related text, see page 207.)

POTTED PLANT PICNIC

Here's a meal your flower-filled containers are sure to appreciate:

2 tbsp. of brewed black coffee
2 tbsp. of whiskey
1 tsp. of fish emulsion
½ tsp. of unflavored gelatin
½ tsp. of baby shampoo
½ tsp. of ammonia
1 gal. of water

Mix all of the ingredients together and water your potted perennials and bulbs with it on a weekly basis. (For related text, see page 107.)

POWDERY MILDEW CONTROL

4 tbsp. of baking soda
2 tbsp. of Murphy® Oil Soap
1 gal. of warm water

Mix all of the ingredients together. Pour into a handheld mist sprayer, and apply liberally, as soon as you see the telltale white spots on your perennials. (For related text, see page 157.)

QUASSIA SLUG SPRAY

4 oz. of quassia chips (bark of the quassia tree; available at health food stores)
1 gal. of water

Crush, grind, or chop the chips, then add them to the water in a bucket. Let steep for 12 to 24 hours. Strain through cheesecloth, then spray the remaining liquid on slug-prone plants, such as hostas. This spray also helps control aphids. (For related text, see page 236.)

REPOTTING BOOSTER TONIC

Once you've repotted your rooted cuttings, give them a dose of this tonic to help them adjust to their new homes:

½ tsp. of all-purpose plant food
½ tsp. of Vitamin B₁ Plant Starter
½ cup of weak tea water*
1 gal. of warm water

Mix all of the ingredients together, and gently pour the tonic through the soil of your repotted plants. Allow it to drain through for 15 minutes or so, then pour off any excess tonic that's in the tray. (For related text, see page 118.)

*Soak a used tea bag in a mix of 1 gallon of warm water and 1 teaspoon of dishwashing liquid until the mix is light brown.

ROOT REVIVAL TONIC

¼ cup of brewed tea
1 tbsp. of dishwashing liquid
1 tbsp. of Epsom salts
1 gal. of water

Let bare-root plants sit in this tonic for up to 24 hours. This will revive the plants and get them up and rarin' to grow. (For related text, see page 56.)

ROOT-ROUSING TONIC

1 can of beer
1 can of regular cola (not diet)
1 cup of dishwashing liquid
1 cup of antiseptic mouthwash
¹⁄₄ tsp. of instant tea granules

Mix all of the ingredients in a large bucket, then pour into a 20 gallon hose-end sprayer and spray liberally over all of your flowerbeds. (For related text, see page 73.)

SCAT CAT SOLUTION

Cats can be great pets, but they can also be a real problem if they dig in your garden. Try this spicy solution to keep them away from your prized plantings:

5 tbsp. of flour
4 tbsp. of powdered mustard
3 tbsp. of cayenne pepper
2 tbsp. of chili powder
2 qts. of warm water

Mix all of the ingredients in a large watering can, and sprinkle the solution around the perimeter of the areas you want to protect. (For related text, see page 164.)

SEEDLING STARTER TONIC

Give your transplants a break on moving day by serving them a sip of my starter tonic. This will help them recover more quickly from the transplanting shock.

1 tbsp. of fish emulsion
1 tbsp. of ammonia
1 tbsp. of Murphy® Oil Soap
1 tsp. of instant tea granules
1 qt. of warm water

Mix all of the ingredients in the warm water. Pour into a handheld sprayer bottle, and mist the seedlings several times a day until they're back on their feet and growing again. (For related text, see page 116.)

SEEDLING STRENGTHENER

To get your seedlings off to a healthy, disease-free start, mist-spray them every few days with this elixir:

2 cups of manure
¹⁄₂ cup of instant tea granules
Warm water

Put the manure and tea in an old nylon stocking, and let it steep in 5 gallons of water for several days. Dilute the mixture with 4 parts of warm water (for example, 4 cups of water for every cup of mix) before spritzing your seedlings with a handheld sprayer. (For related text, see page 111.)

SIMPLE SOAP-AND-OIL SPRAY

For summertime perennial pest control, try this tonic.

1 tbsp. of dishwashing liquid
1 cup of vegetable oil
1 cup of water

Mix together the dishwashing liquid and vegetable oil. Add 1 to 2 teaspoons of the soap and oil mixture to the water in a handheld sprayer. Shake to mix, then spray on plants to control aphids, whiteflies, and spider mites. (For related text, see page 184.)

SUPER SLUG SPRAY

For slugs that are too small to handpick, try this super spray:

1¹/₂ cups of ammonia
1 tbsp. of Murphy® Oil Soap
1¹/₂ cups of water

Mix all of the ingredients in a handheld sprayer bottle, and spray any areas where you see signs of slug activity. (For related text, see page 146.)

SUPER SPIDER MITE MIX

Send spider mites to an early grave with this suffocating mix:

4 cups of wheat flour
¹/₂ cup of buttermilk
5 gal. of water

Mix all of the ingredients together, and apply to your plants with a handheld sprayer. Spray to the point of run-off. (For related text, see page 144.)

TEA TIME FOR APHIDS

Aphids start showing up near the end of spring, and they love lush bulb shoots. If these pests are bugging your bulbs, give them a sip of this tantalizing "tea":

¹/₂ cup of parsley flakes
2 tbsp. of minced garlic
3 cups of water

Mix all of the ingredients together, and boil down to 2 cups. Strain and cool. Put two cups of the tea in your 20 gallon hose-end sprayer and apply to your beds and borders. (For related text, see page 282.)

TRANSPLANT TONIC

¹/₂ can of beer
1 tbsp. of ammonia
1 tbsp. of instant tea granules
1 tbsp. of baby shampoo
1 gal. of water

Mix all of the ingredients together. Use 1 cup of the tonic for each perennial you are transplanting. (For related text, see page 54.)

ULTRALIGHT POTTING SOIL

To keep your really big pots and planters from being back-breakers, fill them with this ultra-light potting soil mix:

4 parts perlite, moistened
4 parts compost
1 part potting soil
½ part cow manure

Mix all of the ingredients together, then use the mixture to fill your planting containers. This mix dries out very quickly, particularly in the hot summer sun, so be sure to keep an eye on your containers and water them as needed. (For related text, see page 106.)

WEED WIPEOUT

Zap those hard-to-kill weeds with this lethal weapon:

1 tbsp. of gin
1 tbsp. of apple cider vinegar
1 tsp. of dishwashing liquid
1 qt. of very warm water

Mix all of the ingredients together in a bucket, then pour into a handheld sprayer to apply. Drench weeds to the point of run-off, taking care not to get any of this elixir on the surrounding plants or grass. (For related text, see page 91.)

YEAR-ROUND REFRESHER TONIC

Use this elixir every three weeks from spring through fall to keep your flower gardens gorgeous. (In warm climates, you can use it as a year-round tonic.)

1 cup of beer
1 cup of baby shampoo
1 cup of liquid lawn food
½ cup of molasses
2 tbsp. of fish emulsion
Ammonia

Mix the beer, shampoo, lawn food, molasses, and fish emulsion in a 20 gallon hose-end sprayer, and fill the balance of the jar with ammonia. Then spray away! (For related text, see page 86.)

INDEX